Perspectives on Pantomime

Advances in Interaction Studies (AIS)

ISSN 1879-873X

Advances in Interaction Studies (AIS) provides a forum for researchers to present excellent scholarly work in a variety of disciplines relevant to the advancement of knowledge in the field of interaction studies. The book series accompanies the journal *Interaction Studies: Social Behaviour and Communication in Biological and Artificial Systems*.

The book series allows the presentation of research in the forms of monographs or edited collections of peer-reviewed material in English.

For an overview of all books published in this series, please see
benjamins.com/catalog/ais

Editors

Kerstin Dautenhahn
University of Waterloo

Angelo Cangelosi
The University of Manchester

Editorial Board

Henrik Christensen
University of California, San Diego

Harold Gouzoules
Emory University

Takayuki Kanda
Kyoto University

Tetsuro Matsuzawa
California Institute of Technology

Giorgio Metta
IIT, Genoa

Adam Miklosi
Eötvös Loránd University

Robert W. Mitchell
Eastern Kentucky University

Chrystopher L. Nehaniv
University of Waterloo

Stefano Nolfi
CNR, Rome

Pierre-Yves Oudeyer
INRIA, Bordeaux

Irene M. Pepperberg
Harvard University & Brandeis University

Stefan Wermter
University of Hamburg

Volume 12

Perspectives on Pantomime
Edited by Przemysław Żywiczyński, Johan Blomberg
and Monika Boruta-Żywiczyńska

Perspectives on Pantomime

Edited by

Przemysław Żywiczyński
Nicolaus Copernicus University

Johan Blomberg
Lund University

Monika Boruta-Żywiczyńska
Nicolaus Copernicus University

John Benjamins Publishing Company
Amsterdam / Philadelphia

The paper used in this publication meets the minimum requirements of the American National Standard for Information Sciences – Permanence of Paper for Printed Library Materials, ANSI z39.48-1984.

DOI 10.1075/ais.12

Cataloging-in-Publication Data available from Library of Congress:
LCCN 2023053596 (PRINT) / 2023053597 (E-BOOK)

ISBN 978 90 272 1452 2 (HB)
ISBN 978 90 272 4724 7 (E-BOOK)

© 2024 – John Benjamins B.V.
No part of this book may be reproduced in any form, by print, photoprint, microfilm, or any other means, without written permission from the publisher.

John Benjamins Publishing Company · https://benjamins.com

Table of contents

INTRODUCTION Perspectives on pantomime: Evolution, development, interaction   **1**
*Przemysław Żywiczyński, Johan Blomberg
& Monika Boruta-Żywiczyńska*

CHAPTER 1. Pantomime within and beyond the evolution of language   **16**
Michael Arbib

CHAPTER 2. The relations of demonstration and pantomime to causal reasoning and event cognition   **58**
Peter Gärdenfors

CHAPTER 3. Narrative and pantomime at the origin of language   **78**
Francesco Ferretti

CHAPTER 4. Two types of bodily-mimetic communication   **100**
Sławomir Wacewicz & Przemysław Żywiczyński

CHAPTER 5. Can pantomime narrate?   **115**
*Jordan Zlatev, Marta Sibierska, Przemysław Żywiczyński,
Joost van de Weijer & Monika Boruta-Żywiczyńska*

CHAPTER 6. The pantomimic origins of the narrative arts   **139**
Steven Brown

CHAPTER 7. The pantomime roots of Sao Tome and Principe Sign Language   **159**
Ana Mineiro & Mara Moita

CHAPTER 8. Symbolic distancing in three-year-old children's object-use pantomime   **188**
Paula Marentette, Chelsea Inaba & Rebecca Petrie

CHAPTER 9. Gestural mimesis as "as-if" action   **217**
Cornelia Müller

Index   **243**

INTRODUCTION

Perspectives on pantomime

Evolution, development, interaction

Przemysław Żywiczyński[1] Johan Blomberg[2]
& Monika Boruta-Żywiczyńska[1]
[1] Nicolaus Copernicus University | [2] Lund University

1. Pantomime in human communication

Pantomime has not been a key topic in the study of human communication, which has focused primarily on language and – in the area of bodily-visual communication – cospeech gesture (e.g., McNeill, 1992; Kendon, 2004; Kita 2009). Pantomime is instead often seen as an emergency form of communication, which we resort to when we have to transfer information to people whose language we don't know; or when for the sake of entertainment, the possibility of using language is blocked, as in charades (Żywiczyński et al., 2021).

Particularly in gesture studies, there is a tendency to assume that pantomime is a vestige that is replaced by other and more efficient forms of communication:

- *developmentally*, as argued by e.g., Levy & McNeill (2015), who claim that around the age of three children start to consciously use speech and corresponding gesture more often than pantomime (see Marentette et al., this volume); and
- *evolutionarily*, as argued by McNeill (2012: 51), who considers pantomime a blind alley in the evolution of language because, in McNeill's way of thinking, pantomime repels combing gesture with vocalisation. This would imply that pantomime as a purely (or at least primarily, see Zlatev et al. this volume; Zlatev et al., 2020) gestural form of communication cannot be a precursor to language, which is thought to have begun with the integration of vocalisation and gesture (cf. the postulate of the equiprimordiality of gesture and speech, McNeill, 2012).

Despite the fact that pantomime has not been at the centre of attention in many lines of research on communication, there has nevertheless been a continued interest in it across various disciplines. This can in part be attributed to precisely the characteristics of pantomime that make it a peripheral form of expression in

https://doi.org/10.1075/ais.12.00zyw
© 2024 John Benjamins Publishing Company

modern humans: its independence of speech (cf. "dumb show"; McNeill, 2012:15) and lack of communicative conventions (McNeill, 2005:2). Importantly, this understanding of pantomime is radically different from the notion of pantomime in the theatrical tradition which goes back to Ancient Greece, where it designates a highly conventionalised form of action based on "corporal impression" (Lecoq in Peacock, 2007:217; see also Arbib this volume; Brown this volume; and Müller this volume). The qualities of pantomime spelt out above have made it a strong contender in language evolution scenarios, where it can be recruited to explain an early bootstrapping stage in the development of human-specific communication (Zlatev et al., 2020; Żywiczyński et al., 2021; this volume: Arbib; Gärdenfors; Ferretti; Wacewicz & Żywiczyński; & Zlatev et al.).

For a somewhat comparable reason, pantomime is studied by developmental psychologists to evaluate the extent to which it can provide scaffolding for the development of children's representational abilities (Mitchell & Clark, 2015; Levy & McNeill, 2015; Marentette et al., this volume). The role that pantomime plays in the development of linguistic communication systems is also investigated in the study of emerging sign languages, where new signs develop from interactions between communicating individuals (Sandler, 2012; Mineiro et al., 2017; Mineiro & Moita, this volume). There is also interest in the narrative capacities of pantomime (Ferretti et al., 2022; this volume: Brown; Ferretti), either occurring naturally (Peacock et al., 2007; Müller, this volume) or experimentally (Motamedi et al., 2019; Zlatev et al., this volume). Demonstrative uses of pantomime have come under the attention of research into various aspects of teaching, for example in parents' interactions with children (cf. Motionese, Brand et al., 2007) or tool-making (Gärdenfors, 2021, & this volume). Another problem that has been investigated is the neural infrastructure of pantomime (Arbib, 2012, & this volume), often in the context of its separability from the cortical structures for language (Arbib, 2006), which is of great importance for the understanding of neurally induced deficits in language (e.g., aphasia, Berthier, 2005) and gesture (e.g., ideomotor apraxia, Buxbaum, 2003) as well as for developing their therapy (Fex et al., 1998). Finally, comparative primatology has explored the incidence of pantomime, or more generally iconic gesture, in great apes (Russon, 2018; Arbib, this volume).

Although the main focus of the present volume is pantomime in language evolution, its ambition is to bring all these approaches to pantomime together, to see how they communicate with each other, or sometimes talk past each other. Doing this will reflect on the state of the art, but also demonstrate avenues for further research across traditional disciplinary boundaries.

1.1 Pantomime and the Origin of Language

Although motivated by contemporary research (e.g., neuroscience, Arbib, this volume; cognitive studies, Gärdenfors, this volume; developmental psychology, Marentette et al., this volume; or sign language linguistics, Mineiro & Moita, this volume), the problem of pantomime resonates with one of the key ideas in traditional glossogeny: the emergence of language was preceded by a stage of bodily-visual communication, during which our ancestors communicated with their hands, arms, and the entire body, as argued by e.g., Mandeville, Condillac & Laromiguiére (for a discussion, see Żywiczyński, 2018; Żywiczyński & Wacewicz, 2021). For the past and modern thinkers alike, the attractiveness of such a scenario lies in the intuition derived from our everyday experience that in the absence of a shared spoken language, modern humans (taken as a proxy for our prelinguistic ancestors) typically resort to bodily-visual communication (for a discussion, see Żywiczyński et al., 2021). This intuition is accompanied by the assumption about the transparency of bodily-visual communication, whereby a relation between a bodily-visual form and its meaning is relatively transparent and hence does not require extensive learning – the view that has some support in modern research on e.g., language impairments (Fex et al., 1998; Klippi, 1915), home-signing children (Goldin-Meadow & Mylander, 1998) and silent gesture (e.g., Schouwstra et al., 2019; Ortega & Özyürek, 2019a; for a more nuanced view, see Perniss et al., 2010; & Marentette et al., this volume).

The "transparency" of the form-meaning relation is crucially important for research on language origins, which has to explain how the first signs could have emerged in the absence of any pre-establishing communicative conventions. In the case of pantomime, this is brought about by iconicity. While it is difficult to define iconicity in a theory-neutral manner (cf. Dingemanse et al., 2020), as much as it is possible to define anything in such a way, one proposal for capturing its general features is inspired by Peirce's understanding of iconicity as a sign that depends on an inherent resemblance between form and referent (Sonesson 2007, Sonesson, 2010). On such an account, the iconicity of pantomime consists in that body movements schematically illustrate the features of the represented object or action (e.g., flapping one's hands to represent a bird, Müller, 2016; see also Żywiczyński et al., 2018).

1.2 Defining pantomime

There are various definitions of pantomime in different strands of the research on the evolution of language and in the other areas of knowledge that are interested in the phenomenon (see 1.2). However, most of them seem to accept McNeill's basic formulation that pantomime is an improvised iconic (see above) gesture produced without accompanying speech and not integrated within an utterance (McNeill, 2005), at least when a broad notion of gesture is accepted as visual-bodily communication that not necessarily makes use of hands alone (cf. manual vs. whole-body gesture, Żywiczyński et al., 2018). Such an account is close to the intuitive sense of pantomime (or mime; see Müller, this volume)[1] and makes it distinct from the following types of bodily-visual communication (cf. McNeill's idea of "gesture continuum," 2005):

- co-speech iconic gestures, which are, by definition, accompanied by speech and integrated within the structure of an utterance (e.g., the gesture of moulding the space co-occurring with the lexical item "ball," Müller, 2014);
- language-slotted gestures, which, although themselves unaccompanied by speech, fill in a slot in an utterance; to give McNeill's example: in the utterance "the parents were all right, but the kids were [GESTURE]," where the gesture fills in the slot of an adjective (1992: 37);
- emblematic gestures, which have conventional meaning (shared by a community of communicators) and standards for production (e.g., the OK gesture, which is performed by touching the thumb and the index finger and forming a circle; to exemplify the conventional nature of emblems, a very similar gesture in Japan stands for money; Parhizgar, 2002: 382);
- signs of sign languages, as they are lexemes of fully fledged languages (Stokoe, 2001);
- baton gestures, i.e., rhythmic movements of hands, which work together with accompanying speech to accentuate the most important elements of the communicated message (cf. focus prosody; Efron, 1941);
- both co-speech and non-co-speech indexical gestures, which are contiguity-based (e.g., the direction of a pointing finger is associated with the location of a referent, Nöth, 2001);
- adaptors, which involve touching one's body or an external object, and do not serve any instrumental or intentionally communicative goals (Ekman & Friesen, 1969);
- orofacial gestures, i.e., movements of facial muscles and the tongue for speech production or non-articulatory purposes (e..g the tongue and mouth imitating limb movements, Orzechowski et al., 2016).

---

1. Outside communication studies, pantomime denotes a particular form of the theoretical art which "suggest[s] action, character, or emotion without words, using only gesture, expression, and movement" (https://www.trinitycollege.com/resource/?id=7919; cf. Brown this volume).

Apart from the general formulation given above, the definitions of pantomime differ, both in content and amount of detail, which, to a larger extent, reflects the area of research that these definitions come from. There are, however, certain underlying themes in these definitions, which, at least in our view, warrants that they relate to essentially the same form of communication.

Some researchers who emphasise the role of pantomime in the evolution of language put forward lean definitions, which in terms of its structural or semiotic characteristics align with McNeill's understanding of pantomime. For Arbib, the author of probably the most influential pantomimic scenario of language origin, it is a silent, ad-hoc, non-conventionalised (although may involve ritualisation aka simplification, see also Gärdenfors, below), iconic (at least for most part) gesture that stands for "a situation, object, action, character, or emotion," e.g., flapping one's wings to signify a bird or flying (Arbib, 2012, 2017; cf. the idea of "ur-pantomime" in Arbib, this volume). Tomasello understands "pantomiming" (the term he uses preferentially to "pantomime") as a gesture that is unaccompanied by speech. On his view, pantomiming enacts (i.e., the communicator maps her body onto the "body" of the referent, cf. Zlatev et al., 2020, & this volume; Müller, 2016, & this volume) "to induce the recipient to imagine some corresponding referent" (Tomasello, 2008: 66).

Researchers affiliated with mimesis theory (Donald, 1991; 2001), who seek to explain how human-specific cognition and communication emerged from bodily experience, offer more detailed definitions. Gärdenfors underlines the structural differences between praxic action and pantomime, whereby the latter is not a literal re-enactment of the former but involves movement exaggeration and deceleration, so that the learner, in the case of pantomime for teaching, or the recipient, in the case of pantomime for communication, is able to perceive important features of the referent (Gärdenfors, 2017, & this volume). A somewhat different intuition, though not incompatible, is found in Zlatev and colleagues' definition of pantomime (Zlatev et al., 2020). For them, pantomime is a polysemiotic communicative system that includes vocalizations but is dominated by highly iconic gestures or "pantomimic gesture," as they call it, which must maximally resemble the represented object (cf. the notion of primary iconicity, Sonneson, 2007). They enumerate a set of gestural characteristics that help meet this requirement. These include:

- the enacting mode of representation, e.g., representing how the body interacts with an object rather than representing its salient features (e.g., pretending to kick the football vs. moulding one's hands to represent its shape, cf. Müller, 2016; & this volume);
- first-person perspective, in the sense of "explicit or implicit mapping of the whole body onto the signified, even if only a part of the body is foregrounded" (e.g., in the football example, the communicator's body is mapped on the

body of a football player and the leg action of kicking the ball is thematised, Zlatev & Andrén, 2009)
– use of gestures standing for objects and actions in peripersonal space, i.e., the space immediately surrounding one's own body (in the football example, the pantomime must be about a ball within one's reach rather than a ball that it is away on the field, Brown et al., 2019, & this volume).

An important issue in defining pantomime is whether it involves only whole-body gestures or whether it subsumes manual gestures, too. Accounts that appeal to mimesis theory often stress that pantomime is a whole-body gesture (e.g., Donald, 1991; Żywiczyński et al., 2018; Gärdenfors, 2021; Zlatev et al., 2020; Ferretti, this volume; but also Tomasello, 2008, see above). This claim is derived from the requirement that pantomime has to fulfil: "since many everyday actions (e.g., walking, pushing, jumping) involve coordinated muscular activity across the entire body, to represent these as iconically as possible would require a similar use of the whole body" (Żywiczyński, 2021: 4). However, due to the same requirement actions performed by specific body parts will be pantomimed accordingly. For instance the activity of eating will be pantomimed by movements of the orofacial area and perhaps hands, rather than movements of the whole body (cf. Arbib, this volume).

There is a similarity between mimesis theory and the understanding of pantomime in the research on emerging sign languages, on the one hand, and a marked difference with gesture studies, on the other. Salient features of early signs in developing sign languages commonly make use of enactment and first-person perspective, refer to objects in the peripersonal space and involve whole body movement. One example of such an early sign is AIRPLANE in Sao Tome and Principe Sign Language, which is produced with open arms standing for the wings of the airplane and the rest of the body for the fuselage (Mineiro et al., 2017; Mineiro & Moita, this volume), which exemplifies personification, a special type of pantomimic enactment[2] (Ortega & Özyürek, 2019b).

In gesture studies, pantomime is understood differently. Here, most of the researchers follow McNeill's definition discussed above: silent, improvised and iconic gesture not integrated within the utterance. A different approach is taken by Müller, whose concept of "miming as if action" describes how gestures, understood as movement images, ground linguistically communicated meanings in corporeal experience (Müller, 2016; & this volume). Although it is not definitionally required by these approaches, pantomiming (or miming) is typically exemplified

---

2. Personification is an enacting gesture, which maps 'the body of a non-human entity onto the human body, using the human head to represent parallel locations on a nonhuman head, the human body to represent a non-human body, and human appendages to represent non-human appendages' (Hwang et al., 2017: 4; cf. Ortega & Özyürek, 2019b)

by manual gestures (e.g., Ortega & Özyürek, 2019b). This tendency is particularly visible in experimental studies that employ the paradigm of "elicited pantomime" (or "silent gesture"), where participants are expressly asked to use their hands only (e.g., Goldin-Meadow et al., 2008) or forced to do so by experimental logistics (e.g., when participants are seated, Fay et al., 2013). A version of this paradigm, with its underlying definition of pantomime, is often used in neurocognitive studies (Emmorey et al., 2011), including studies on communicative deficits (most importantly, apraxia, Buxbaum, 2001; Goldenberg, 2009), where participants are asked to produce or observe meaningful vs. meaningless gestures. However, it is interesting to note that some diagnostic tools for apraxia consist in subjects imitating a simple action that has an instrumental goal (e.g., tool use), and hence requires the production of pantomime sensu Zlatev and colleagues (i.e., the use of enacting mode, first-person perspective, peripersonal space; Dumont et al., 1999; Rothi et al., 1985).

Neuro-developmental research is not focused on whether pantomime is accompanied by language or on the problem of bodiness, i.e., which articulators are involved in the execution of pantomime (Marentette et al., this volume). Similarly to the approach to pantomime in mimesis theory, this line of research is interested in representational strategies characteristic of pantomimic communication, and more specifically in the "symbolic distance" (in a metaphorical sense of the term) between the pantomimic form and its meaning. However, in doing so, it uses a different logic. From the perspective of mimesis theory, the greater the iconicity of a pantomime is, the smaller this "symbolic distance" is supposed to be. In the neuro-developmental literature, which goes back to the seminal work of Werner and Kaplan (1963), the crucial element responsible for the "symbolic distance" is whether pantomime represents the referent (body-part-as-object gesture, or BPO), or the action directed at or involving the referent (imaginary object, or IO). It is argued that the BPO covers a short symbolic distance because the communicator requires a perceptually conspicuous manifestation of the referent in the form of body movements that stand for it. In the case of the IO, the symbolic distance is increased as the communicator's body movements operate on an imagined object (for details see Marentette et al., this volume). The view about the "symbolic distance" attributed to BPOs and IOs is supported by the evidence that BPOs are more often used by younger children than older children as well as adults, and more often by aphasiacs than non-aphasiacs (see Marentette et al., this volume).

In terms of Müller's modes of representation (2013, & this volume), BPO includes:

– moulding gestures, where the hands show a three-dimensional object in space (see above);

–   drawing gestures, where the hands show the contour of an object as a reduced two-dimensional shape; and
–   embodying, where the hands stand in for an object as a whole (cf. Brown et al., 2019; Brown, this volume; Zlatev et al., 2020; Sibierska et al., 2022).

IO gestures, on the other hand, make use of the enacting mode, where, as already explained, the body of the gesturer maps onto the body of the represented object, and from this perspective should in fact have a smaller "symbolic distance" than BPO gestures. It should be noted that the modes characteristic of BPO favour, if not require, manual gestures, while Ios may involve whole body movements. Brown (Brown et al., 2019; & Brown, this volume), who incorporates the BPO-IO distinction into his typology of pantomime, argues that Ios necessarily involve peripersonal space, whereas BPOs may either represent objects or actions in one's peripersonal space (e.g., the gesture of cutting one's hair, where one's index and middle finger embody the scissors) or extrapersonal space, i.e., the space away from one's body (e.g., the gesture where the fists coming together embody the collision of two cars).

2.   Summary of the papers collected for the volume

The papers in the volume explore pantomime from different standpoints, but, as already noted, the dominant theme is the evolution of language. The role of pantomime in the evolution of language, and more generally human-specific communication, is the main topic of the contributions by Arbib, Gärdenfors, Ferretti, and Wacewicz and Żywiczyński. Although the first three authors are primarily concerned with the cognitive adaptations that allowed our ancestors to develop the system of pantomime and how later this system – mainly due to cultural evolution – developed into fully fledged language, their papers have different points of emphasis. Arbib stresses the role of the brain evolution in this process, Gärdenfors shows how the development of communication is implicated in the evolution of teaching, and Ferretti argues that pantomimic scenarios of language emergence should be constrained by the consideration of hominin representational capacities. In this context, Wacewicz and Żywiczyński take a distinct position, by bringing in a socio-ecological perspective to explain trajectories of the evolution of pantomime in terms of signalling theory.

Reflection on the evolution of language also runs through the remaining papers. It is key to Zlatev and colleagues' contribution, which focuses on the constraints of pantomime to "tell" stories. Brown discusses it in the context of the main theme of his paper – the pantomimic origins of narrative arts. Mineiro and

Moita use their research on the Sao Tome and Príncipe Sign Language as a source of insight into the early, bootstrapping phase of language emergence and its subsequent development. Marentette and colleagues critically examine how evidence coming from developmental studies can inform language evolution. Müller develops the idea of "miming as-if action" – movement images that having their basis in practical actions have been recruited for communicative purposes,

In "Pantomime within and beyond the evolution of language," Michael Arbib reflects both scientifically and personally on the phenomenon and concept(s) of pantomime. Just as this volume in its entirety, the paper places pantomime within a broad interdisciplinary context, including such key issues as language origins, teaching and narrative. These considerations are informed by Arbib's extensive work on the Mirror System Hypothesis, which, in his own words, posits that "manual skill could provide a scaffolding for the evolution of language with the parity property: that the meaning of utterances produced by a 'speaker' (or signer) could be (more or less) recognized by other members of the same language community." Whereas any discussion of mirror neurons is absent from his paper, Arbib instead develops the thesis that a "language-ready brain" emerged through biocultural evolution which crucially involved an increased ability for "action recognition, imitation and pantomime." In this process that eventually led to the emergence of language, pantomime and its conventionalisation into proto-signs served as an important stepping stone.

Peter Gärdenfors' contribution connects the evolution of pantomimic communication to event cognition and causal reasoning. Pantomimes function as a way to demonstrate actions and are hence useful for the pedagogical purpose of showing how to perform an action. Gärdenfors argues that this ability is dependent on a complex form of event cognition, including distinguishing event participants. This so-called "pantomime-for-showing" is distinguished from "pantomime-for-telling" on the basis of their communicative function: the former is connected to the pedagogical aim of teaching how to perform an action; the latter, to conveying or communicating an intention. By virtue of its connection to event cognition and causal reasoning, "pantomime-for-showing" is argued to be evolutionarily more primary with "pantomime-for-telling" being its further "extension for communicative purposes."

A recurrent topic for many contributions is that of narrative, and to what extent pantomimes can narrate. This issue is explored in Francesco Ferretti's "Narrative and Pantomime at the Origin of Language." Ferretti argues that human thoughts have a narrative structure, which then is also reflected in communication. It is thus proposed that explicit storytelling was invented to share the narrative form of thoughts, rather than something that followed the evolution of language.

In terms of implications for language evolution, Ferretti argues that pantomimes were used to express the narrative form of thoughts long before language.

Sławomir Wacewicz and Przemysław Żywiczyński initiate a dialogue between language evolution and its pantomimic origins with signalling theory. They do so by claiming that the gradualist models adopted by many pantomimic scenarios of language origin involve a progressive increase in complexity and expressive power. Signalling theory, on the other hand, differentiates two distinct forms for the evolution of communication: costly and loud displays ("expensive hype") vs. inexpensive and efficient signals or signs ("conspiratorial whispers") (Krebs & Dawkins, 1984). The latter form is clearly connected to language and other forms of sign-based communication, but the emergence of conspiratorial whispers is quite rare in nature and requires "very specific socio-ecological conditions, such as very close alignment of interests." For that reason, Wacewicz and Żywiczyński argue that taking such insights from signalling theory into account would fruitfully inform the contemporary discussion on language origins.

The title of Jordan Zlatev, Marta Sibierska, Przemysław Żywiczyński, Joost van de Weijer and Monika Boruta-Żywiczyńska's paper asks the question "Can pantomime narrate?" To answer this question, they argue that the notion of "narrative" requires theoretical clarification. Given that narratives consist of signs, they propose narrative to have the tripartite semiotic structure of expression, content and object that is definitional for signs. Applied to narrative, this leads to the three layers: Narration, Story, Event sequence (with capitals to mark the technical nature of the terms). On this basis, they distinguish between primary narrativity (understanding the Story on the basis of the Narration) and secondary narrativity (understanding the Narration on the basis of the Story), and make it clear that what is of issue concerning the capacity of pantomime is the former. To answer this, the authors review and elaborate on a study described in Sibierska et al. (2023). In it, participants in a communicative game were asked to pantomimically narrate both chronological and achronological stories. The authors of the paper established that participants had a much harder time to convey the latter, but that dyads found ways to express the fact that narration was not isomorphic to the event sequence by more or less conventional markers of event order, which implies transitioning from pantomime to protolanguage. Zlatev and colleagues thus conclude with a positive answer to their initial question – patnomime can narrate as long as "stories to be communicated are of 'moderate' complexity."

Steven Brown's chapter "The pantomimic origins of the narrative arts" argues that pantomime may not just have been an evolutionary precursor to modern language but also served as a basis for the narrative arts, which are typically used to tell stories (e.g., theatre). Appealing to the classical distinction between diegetis and mimetis in Plato's "The Republic," Brown argues that these two art forms are evolutionarily connected to two different forms of pantomimes: egocentric and allocentric pantomimes. The former are instances where "the parts of the body that are used in pantomime production preserve their identity," whereas the latter are those cases where "parts of the body ... used for the pantomiming change their identity and come to symbolically represent an object other than the body part itself." With the help of this distinction, Brown argues that egocentric pantomimes served as the basis for diegetic arts whereas allocentric pantomime had a similar evolutionary function for mimetic arts.

Ana Mineiro and Mara Moita's paper "The pantomime roots of Sao Tome and Principe Sign Language" (LGSTP) summarises findings from extensive research on Sao Tome and Principe Sign Language, an emerging language used on two islands by the Northwest coast of Gabon. The development of this language is a recent initiative where Mineiro and colleagues have been able to document its emergence. The present paper synthesises findings from five of their previous papers in the context of language evolution – specifically, showing how signs in LGSTP have become less iconic over time. With the decrease in transparency came an increase in systematicity and grammatical complexity, which the authors interpret as a support for a common gestural and vocal origin of language.

A key idea in Werner and Kaplan's (1963) seminal work on language development is that of "symbolic distancing" where a child's cognitive development involves increasing awareness of the separation between the sign and its referent. Paula Marentette, Chelsea Inaba and Rebecca Petrie's study investigates whether children's pantomime exhibits symbolic distancing, which would be manifested in an increasing form of pantomimic representations without representing the object (so-called "imagined object," as opposed to those pantomimes where a body represents a particular object). Their study found that pantomimic production may not reflect an increasing degree of symbolic distancing as much as a functional and social knowledge of objects and the communicative conventions they are associated with.

Cornelia Müller's paper "Gestural mimesis as as-if action" presents a cohesive approach to gestures including conceptual, empirical and methodological considerations. Müller contrasts "pantomime," which she primarily restricts to "artistic practice," with "miming as-if action" – movement images that having their basis in practical actions have been recruited for communicative purposes. Following the idea of a transition from action to gesture, the latter are then claimed to be exist on a continuum from spontaneously created singular gestures through recurrent gestures to fully stabilised, conventionalised gestures. The chapter provides theoretical, empirical and methodological arguments for thinking of gestural mimesis as as-if action and for a continuum from practical actions to as-if actions. It suggests that thinking and acting by hand is anchored in the embodied practice of miming as an as-if action and advances an understanding of gestures as mimetic expressive movements. The concept of mimetic expressive movements not only captures the transition from action to communication, but also explains that their coherence emerges in the process of embodied understanding of movement as images. An important source of insight for the "miming as-if action" approach is the conception of mimesis derived from Aristotle, who identified three conditions of mimesis: means, i.e., bodily articulators; objects, i.e., referents of mimetic acts; and modes, which describe how actions of bodily articulators perform referential function. Müller argues that gestural mimesis dynamically organises face-to-face communication, and demonstrates how this concept can be applied analytically to the study of conversational interaction.

Funding

The preparation and publication of this volume was supported by the Polish National Science Centre (NCN) under grant agreement UMO-2017/27/B/HS2/00642 awarded to Przemysław Żywiczyński.

References

Arbib, M. (2006). Aphasia, apraxia and the evolution of the language-ready brain. *Aphasiology*, 20(9), 1125–1155.

Arbib, M.A., (2012). *How the brain got language: The mirror system hypothesis* 16. Oxford University Press.

Arbib, M.A. (2017). Toward the language-ready brain: biological evolution and primate comparisons. *Psychonomic Bulletin & Review*, 24(1), 142–150.

Berthier, M.L. (2005). Poststroke aphasia. *Drugs & Aging*, 22(2), 163–182.

Brand, R.J., Shallcross, W.L., Sabatos, M.G., & Massie, K.P. (2007). Fine-grained analysis of motionese: Eye gaze, object exchanges, and action units in infant-versus adult-directed action. *Infancy*, 11(2), 203–214.

Brown, S., Mittermaier, E., Kher, T., & Arnold, P. (2019). *How pantomime works: Implications for theories of language origin, Frontiers in Communication*, 4, 9.

Buxbaum, L.J. (2001). Ideomotor apraxia: a call to action. *Neurocase*, 7(6), 445–458.

Buxbaum, L.J., Sirigu, A., Schwartz, M.F., & Klatzky, R. (2003). Cognitive representations of hand posture in ideomotor apraxia. *Neuropsychologia*, 41(8), 1091–1113.

Dingemanse, M., Perlman, M., & Perniss, P. (2020). Construals of iconicity: experimental approaches to form–meaning resemblances in language. *Language and Cognition*, 12(1), 1–14.

Donald, M., (1991). *Origins of the modern mind: Three stages in the evolution of culture and cognition*. Harvard University Press.

Donald, M., (2001). *A mind so rare. The evolution of human consciousness*. Emery.

Dumont, C., Ska, B., & Schiavetto, A. (1999). Selective impairment of transitive gestures: An unusual case of apraxia. *Neurocase*, 5(5), 447–458.

Efron, D., (1941). *Gesture and environment*. King's Crown Press.

Ekman, P., & Friesen, W.V. (1969). The repertoire of nonverbal behavior: Categories, origins, usage, and coding. *Semiotica*, 1(1), 49–98.

Emmorey, K., McCullough, S., Mehta, S., Ponto, L.L., & Grabowski, T.J. (2011). Sign language and pantomime production differentially engage frontal and parietal cortices. *Language and Cognitive Processes*, 26(7), 878–901.

Fay, N., Arbib, M., & Garrod, S. (2013). How to bootstrap a human communication system. *Cognitive Science*, 37(7), 1356–1367.

Ferretti, F., Adornetti, I., & Chiera, A. (2022). Narrative pantomime: A protolanguage for persuasive communication. *Lingua*, 271, 103247.

Fex, B., & Månsson, A.C. (1998). The use of gestures as a compensatory strategy in adults with acquired aphasia compared to children with specific language impairment (SLI). *Journal of Neurolinguistics*, 11(1–2), 191–206.

Gärdenfors, P. (2017). Demonstration and pantomime in the evolution of teaching. *Frontiers in Psychology*, 8, 415.

Gärdenfors, P. (2021). Demonstration and pantomime in the evolution of teaching and communication. *Language & Communication*, 80, 71–79.

Goldenberg, G. (2009). Apraxia and the parietal lobes. *Neuropsychologia*, 47(6), 1449–1459.

Goldin-Meadow, S., & Mylander, C. (1998). Spontaneous sign systems created by deaf children in two cultures. *Nature*, 391(6664), 279–281.

Goldin-Meadow, S., So, W.C., Özyürek, A., & Mylander, C. (2008). The natural order of events: How speakers of different languages represent events nonverbally. *Proceedings of the National Academy of Sciences*, 105(27), 9163–9168.

Hwang, S.O., Tomita, N., Morgan, H., Ergin, R., Ilkbasara, D., Seegers, S., Lepic, R., & Padde, C. (2017). Of the body and the hands: patterned iconicity for semantic categories. *Lang. Cognit.* 9, 573–602. .

Kendon, A., (2004). *Gesture: Visible action as utterance*. Cambridge University Press.

Kita, S. (2009). Cross-cultural variation of speech-accompanying gesture: A review. *Language and cognitive processes*, 24(2), 145–167.

Klippi, A. (2015). Pointing as an embodied practice in aphasic interaction. *Aphasiology*, 29(3), 337–354.

Krebs, J.R., & Dawkins, R. (1984). Animal Signals: Mind-Reading and Manipulation. In *Behavioral Ecology*. Blackwell, 380–402.

Levy, E.T., & McNeill, D., (2015). *Narrative development in young children: Gesture, imagery, and cohesion*. Cambridge University Press.

McNeill, D., (1992). *Hand and mind: What gestures reveal about thought*. University of Chicago Press.

McNeill, D., (2005). *Gesture and thought*. The University of Chicago Press.

McNeill, D., (2012). *How language began: Gesture and speech in human evolution*. Cambridge University Press.

Mineiro, A., Carmo, P., Caroça, C., Moita, M., Carvalho, S., Paço, J., & Zaky, A. (2017). Emerging linguistic features of Sao Tome and Principe Sign Language. *Sign Language & Linguistics*, 20(1), 109–128.

Mitchell, R.W., & Clark, H. (2015). Experimenter's pantomimes influence children's use of body part as object and imaginary object pantomimes: a replication. *Journal of Cognition and Development*, 16(5), 703–718.

Motamedi, Y., Schouwstra, M., Smith, K., Culbertson, J., & Kirby, S. (2019). Evolving artificial sign languages in the lab: From improvised gesture to systematic sign. *Cognition*, 192, 103964.

Müller, C. (2014). 128. Gestural modes of representation as techniques of depiction. In *Body – Language – Communication Volume 2* (pp. 1687–1702). De Gruyter Mouton.

Müller, C. (2016). From mimesis to meaning: A systematics of gestural mimesis for concrete and abstract referential gestures. In J. Zlatev, G. Sonesson, & P. Konderak (Eds.), *Meaning, mind and communication: Explorations in cognitive semiotics* (pp. 211–226). Frankfurt am Main, Germany: Peter Lang.

Nöth, W. (2001) The growth of signs. *Sign Systems Studies*, 42(2/3), 172–192.

Ortega, G., & Özyürek, A. (2019a). Systematic mappings between semantic categories and types of iconic representations in the manual modality: A normed database of silent gesture. *Behavior Research Methods*, 52(1), 51–67.

Ortega, G., & Özyürek, A. (2019b). Types of iconicity and combinatorial strategies distinguish semantic categories in silent gesture across cultures. *Language and Cognition*, 12(1), 84–113.

Orzechowski, S., Wacewicz, S., & Żywiczyński, P. (2016). The problem of "modality transition" in gestural primacy hypothesis in language evolution: Towards multimodal hypotheses. *Studia Semiotyczne – English Supplement Volume XXVIII*, 112.

Parhizgar, K.D., (2002). *Multicultural behavior and global business environments*. Routledge.

Peacock, D.K. (2007). *Changing performance culture and performance in the British Theatre since 1945*. Peter Lang.

Perniss, P., Thompson, R.L., & Vigliocco, G. (2010). Iconicity as a general property of language: Evidence from spoken and signed languages. *Frontiers in Psychology*, 1, 227.

Rothi, L.J., Heilman, K.M., & Watson, R.T. (1985). Pantomime comprehension and ideomotor apraxia. *Journal of Neurology, Neurosurgery & Psychiatry*, 48(3), 207–210.

Russon, A.E. (2018). Pantomime and imitation in great apes: Implications for reconstructing the evolution of language. *Interaction Studies*, 19(1–2), 200–215.

Sandler, W. (2012). Dedicated gestures and the emergence of sign language. *Gesture*, 12(3), 265–307.

Schouwstra, M., de Swart, H., & Thompson, B. (2019). Interpreting silent gesture: Cognitive biases and rational inference in emerging language systems. *Cognitive Science*, 43(7), e12732.

Sibierska, M., Żywiczyński, P, Zlatev, J., van de Weijer, J, Boruta-Żywiczyńska, M. (2023). Contraints on communicating the order of events in stories. *Journal of Language Evolution*, XX: 1–15.

Sonesson, G. (2007). From the meaning of embodiment to the embodiment of meaning: a study in phenomenological semiotics. In *Body, language and mind*. Vol 1: embodiment, Mouton de Gruyter.

Sonesson, G. (2010). From mimicry to mime by way of mimesis: Reflections on a general theory of iconicity. *Sign System Studies*, 38 (1): 18–66.

Sibierska, M., Boruta-Żywiczyńska, M., Żywiczyński, P., & Wacewicz, S. (2022). What's in a mime? An exploratory analysis of predictors of communicative success of pantomime. *Interaction Studies*, 23(2), 289-321.

Stokoe, W.C., (2001). *Language in hand: Why sign came before speech*. Gallaudet University Press.

Tomasello, M., (2008). *The origins of human communication*. MIT Press.

Werner, H., & Kaplan, B. (1963). *Symbol formation: An organismic-developmental approach to language and the expression of thought*. Wiley.

Zlatev, J., & Andrén, M. (2009). Stages and transitions in children's semiotic development. *Studies in language and cognition*, 380–401.

Zlatev, J., Sibierska, M., Żywiczyński, P., van de Weijer, J., & Boruta-Żywiczyńska, M. Can pantomime narrate? A cognitive semiotic approach. In *Perspectives on Pantomime*. John Benjamins.

Zlatev, J., Żywiczyński, P., & Wacewicz, S. (2020). Pantomime as the original human-specific communicative system. *Journal of Language Evolution*, 5(2), 156–174.

Żywiczyński, P., (2018). *Language origins: From mythology to science*. Peter Lang.

Żywiczyński, P., Wacewicz, S., & Sibierska, M. (2018). Defining pantomime for language evolution research. *Topoi*, 37, 307-318.

Żywiczyński, P., Wacewicz, S., & Lister, C. (2021). Pantomimic fossils in modern human communication. *Philosophical Transactions of the Royal Society B*, 376(1824), 20200204.

Żywiczyński, P., Sibierska, M., Wacewicz, S., van de Weijer, J., Ferretti, F., Adornetti, I., ... & Deriu, V. (2021). Evolution of conventional communication. A cross-cultural study of pantomimic re-enactments of transitive events. *Language & Communication*, 80, 191–203.

CHAPTER 1

Pantomime within and beyond the evolution of language

Michael Arbib
University of California San Diego

The core of the paper is a critique of the role of pantomime in the author's theory (the Mirror System Hypothesis, MSH, itself evolving) of the biocultural evolution that led to human brains that were "language ready" long before humans developed languages. We argue that the notion of "ad hoc" pantomime posited there should be modified to a notion of "ur-pantomime" in which pantomimes are somewhat ritualized by individual users but not yet conventionalized by the group. We extend this to offer a taxonomy of pantomime, with the above forms distinguished from both pantomime exhibited by apes and theatrical pantomime.

Complex action recognition and imitation play a crucial role in MSH, as well as conventionalization of pantomime to "protosigns" as possible stepping stones to protolanguage. Pantomimes can also emphasize flexible trajectories to indicate the ways in which an action might vary depending on the current affordances of objects. Both features are shown to be helpful in pedagogy, but are not restricted to this domain. Trajectory variation may be the underpinning of present-day cospeech gestures.

We then turn to a hypothesis on the cultural evolution whereby protolanguages became languages through the emergence of a broader lexicon and a grammar comprised of diverse constructions supporting a compositional syntax.

Noting that MSH has focused on the emerging structure of single utterances, we assess how MSH may be modified to incorporate an account of the emergence of narrative.

Finally, we assess to what extent mindreading, navigation in space, and navigation in time are to be added to the capabilities of the language-ready brain, while insisting that their form in modern humans results from an expanding spiral linked with capacities for language and narrative through cultural evolution.

Keywords: affordances, cospeech gestures, imitation, language-ready brain, Mirror System Hypothesis, narrative, pantomime, pedagogy, protolanguage, protosign

https://doi.org/10.1075/ais.12.01arb
© 2024 John Benjamins Publishing Company

MSH: The early stages

My work on pantomime has been primarily in the context of developing a theory of language origins that privileges manual over vocal skills for the initial scaffolding (Arbib, Liebal, & Pika, 2008; see the section "The Vocal-Manual Debate" below for further analysis). The inspiration for positing a role for pantomime emerged from research on the brain mechanisms that link eye and hand in reaching and grasping, and an interest in work on sign language as showing that language could be fully acquired by modern humans in the visuo-manual domain, and not just the audio-vocal domain. The Mirror System Hypothesis (MSH)[1] is so named because of two observations (Arbib & Rizzolatti, 1997; Rizzolatti & Arbib, 1998):

i. The mirror neurons discovered in macaque that fire both during execution of certain manual actions and observation of similar actions were in a brain region homologous to human Broca's area; and

ii. Although Broca's area was traditionally linked to speech production, damage there could also yields aphasias of sign language production (Poizner, Klima, & Bellugi, 1987).

Mirror neurons play no overt role in *this* paper, though they do offer a possible neural underpinning for the emergence of parity in language, in that even a novel utterance can be produced and understood by all (many) members of a language community. However, we shall see that much "beyond the mirror" has to be added to get from recognizing the visual or auditory form of words to making sense of utterances formed by combining the words of a language according to the rules of its grammar.

Here, we start with the MSH hypothesis that the capacity of modern apes for *ontogenetic ritualization* (OR) – discussed below – was shared by our last common ancestor with the great apes (LCA-ga, aka LCA-c with c for chimpanzee), but that biocultural evolution on the path from LCA-ga yielded increasing capacity for action recognition, imitation and pantomime, and that these yielded a language-*ready* brain as distinct from a language-*using* brain.

---

1. Arbib (2012) offers a book-length exposition, but MSH has been critiqued and updated over the years. It benefited from three major rounds of commentary: (Arbib, 2005a); a special issue (Volume 5, Issues 2–3) of *Language and Cognition* edited by David Kemmerer; and the commentaries following (Arbib, 2016b). An edited volume based on an ABLE (Action, Brain, Language, Evolution) workshop held in 2017 offers a range of contributions to developing a new road map for how the brain got language (Arbib, 2020b).

A key notion is that of a *protolanguage* as an open system of communication used by a particular hominin grouping which was distinct from an animal communication system and was a *potential* precursor of "true" language – *potential* because many protolanguages would have died out without being succeeded by full languages and yet shared all relevant properties with those that did serve as precursors. Specifically, a protolanguage is a system of protowords with little or no grammar – with the debate (spelled out in the section "MSH: the emergence of grammar") between those who consider protowords as being akin to the words of present-day languages, and those who do not.

Part of MSH asserts that the language-ready brain was enough to support simple protolanguages, but the transition to modern languages (Figure 1) that involved enrichment of the lexicon in tandem with the invention of increasingly powerful grammars (more, and more powerful, constructions) required only cultural evolution without necessary changes in the genome. In other words, we hypothesize that early humans had the developmentally malleable neural capacity that we now exploit in using language, but that it took tens of millennia of subsequent cultural evolution to develop languages and their extended role in social interaction.

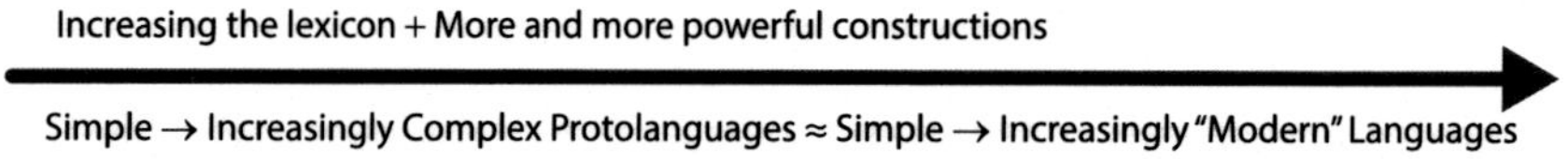

Increasing the lexicon + More and more powerful constructions

Simple → Increasingly Complex Protolanguages ≈ Simple → Increasingly "Modern" Languages

Figure 1. The protolanguage-language continuum

Tomasello and Call (1997) note that some apes exhibit ontogenetic ritualization (OR), wherein the performance of a sequence of transitive actions by A elicits a desired response from B that over time becomes ritualized into an intransitive gesture that A can use to elicit the desired response from B (see also Halina, Rossano, & Tomasello, 2013).[2] For example, a child's reaching out to grasp the mother's arm and trying to pull her closer to get a hug might be ritualized into a form of beckoning gesture that the mother will respond to. Here, the new gesture may be unique to A and B, and be used only by one partner, A, of the dyad (see Arbib, Ganesh, & Gasser, 2014, for a computational model). This does not require that B can produce the gesture, or that A would understand it if B did so. Moreover, since it emerges as a means for A to elicit a response from B there is no need for imitation by others to master use of the novel gesture – whereas imitation plays a pivotal role in propagation of production and recognition of a (manual or vocal) gesture through a community.

---

2. OR offers evidence that intentional communication is already present in, at least, the novel gestures of present-day apes, so MSH suggests that LCA-ga also had it at least in simple form (Abramova, 2018; Arbib, 2018).

What is perceived is greatly dependent on the attention, motivation, and *prior experience* of the observer. In looking at an object, we may recognize *what it is*, but also *what actions it makes possible*. The *affordances* (Gibson, 1979), the relevant perceptual cues for actions, depend on the *effectivities*, the actions of which the agent is capable – a rock face might afford climbing for some, but not for most of us. Pantomime involves a crucial change from *transitive* actions (actions upon objects, guided by the object's affordances) to *intransitive* actions (actions conducted in the absence of objects, possibly guided by proprioceptive patterns abstracted from "images" of specific object affordances).[3] This transition is important in pedagogy (see Gärdenfors, 2023, & the section "Pedagogy and other forms of social coordination" below): When *demonstrating* some skill, the teacher may make transitive movements on the relevant objects, but once the student is attempting the skill and acting upon the object, then the teacher will, possibly among others hints, be making intransitive movements that suggest the form of the transitive movements the student is to perform next.

MSH posits that, like today's great apes, LCA-ga had OR as well as a capacity for "simple" imitation in recognizing subgoals (including the availability of affordances) but – if the action is not recognized as one already in its repertoire – the animal uses trial-and-error to develop actions to pass from one subgoal to the next rather than paying attention to trajectories whereby those subgoals were reached (Byrne, 1999, 2003; Byrne & Russon, 1998). The transition from LCA-ga to *Homo sapiens* (and possibly Neanderthals, but that is a topic to explore elsewhere) involved biocultural evolution (changes in genome for brain and body as well as changes in social practice to exploit the new potentialities) that yielded capacities for complex action recognition and imitation and for pantomime that in turn support the emergence of an expanding spiral of protolanguages:

Complex action recognition and imitation combines
- *complex action recognition* – the capacity to "parse" another's behavior into constituent actions, recognizing familiar actions, but adding attention to the motion as well as the goals of subactions; with
- *complex imitation*, which exploits this ability to, possibly, achieve a first approximation to that motion *without* trial and error.

---

3. Brown (this volume) observes that "[d]rawing, as a motoric activity, shows a strong resemblance to tracing pantomimes. The main difference is that drawing generates an enduring image on a surface, whereas pantomime is 'drawing in the air.'" Arbib (2021a, 2021b) makes a similar point, arguing that the language-ready brain is also "drawing-ready" – but adding that drawing enduring images required the cultural evolution of a suitable technology such as that found in cave paintings whose dating suggests they were developed long after protolanguages. See Donald (1991) for discussion of the importance of pictorial representation in providing external forms of long-term memory that could accelerate cultural evolution.

Such complexity is a graded variable – the range of behaviors that can be mastered at the event-level will depend on the depth of hierarchical structure and the range of sub-behaviors that can be captured in working memory. A further posited benefit of complex action recognition and imitation, as it evolved in subtlety, was the ability not only to recognize that the observed action was "somewhat like" an action already in the observer's repertoire but also to recognize that the observed action differed from that familiar action in part by one or more familiar *tweaks* (small movements that are frequent components of many actions) that could be used to adjust a known action to better match an observed novel action (Arbib, 2012: 201–208). The availability of tweaks accelerates the mastery of novel skills.

A **pantomime system** provides the ability to freely pantomime performances (i.e., perform intransitively) with the expectation that the observer will interpret this correctly as a request or instruction. The latter may be part of pantomime-for-teaching in the sense of Gärdenfors (this volume), who understands demonstration as a form of request to copy the teacher, but may also be instructing someone to perform a behavior they have already mastered.

MSH posits that this capability emerged as part of the long path of biocultural evolution in the 5 to 7 million years that separate us from LCA-ga. Nonetheless, Russon (2016, 2018; Russon & Andrews, 2010, 2011) has convincingly demonstrated that some great apes exhibit "pantomime-like" behavior. We address this apparent contretemps in the section "A taxonomy of pantomime" where we also distinguish ad hoc pantomime from Ur-pantomime.

MSH then posits that protolanguages of increasing complexity emerged through an **expanding spiral** of protosign and protospeech:

–   **protosign**: a manual-based communication system whose conventionalized form may support parity, while breaking through the fixed repertoire of primate vocalizations to yield an open repertoire. It is based in part – *but only in part* – on the conventionalization of pantomimes. As OR demonstrates, the signs may but need not be iconic. Moreover, attempts to "distinguish" protosigns that may have distinct meanings despite shared "etymology" conspires to establish that protosigns may not reveal their pantomimic or other roots. Further, novel protosigns may be needed to clarify pantomimic sequences or to represent concepts like "blue" for which iconic gestures are not available.[4]
–   **protospeech**: resting on the "invasion" of the vocal apparatus by collaterals from the communication system based on F5/Broca's area.[5]

---

4. As elsewhere in this paper, the statement offered in such paragraphs is a *refinement* of that offered in Arbib (2012)

Here we use the form "Proto-X" to indicate something with some, but by no means all, of the attributes of X that nonetheless provided an evolutionary precursor of what X provides for modern humans. In MSH we endow the term "protosign" with a specific meaning in relation to a specific account of protolanguage. Note here the twofold use of the term for the unit and the system itself. The motivation here is not any general notion of "sign," but rather the way the term "sign" is employed both for "a signed language" and the use of a unit of such a language. It is the embedding of the unit in an understood system of communication that makes it a sign.

The key issue here is the distinction between the emergence of dyadic gestures and the emergence of a communally shared strategy for generating new gestures that extends beyond dyads. It is important to be clear about the distinction made in this paper between the ritualization exemplified in OR and the conventionalization of pantomime (but, we stress, not only pantomime) that yields protosign:[6]

- **Ritualization**: an individual simplifies the form of a performance with another who recognizes the communicative goal. Note that the other may have had to participate as a witness to the transitions involved to recognize the cumulative result.
- **Conventionalization** occurs where *novel* gestures with similar communicative goals become shaped and shared by that community to yield a protosign whose performance and interpretation is more or less shared by a community (the emergence of parity). Whereas OR did not involve imitation, this key transition to conventionalization must involve the use of imitation.

Note that conventionalization here exploits the capacity required for the success of pantomime in a community: Members of that community have learned when observing an action to seek to understand not only what practical goal the actor is trying to achieve but, when this fails, to seek instead to understand what *communicative* goal the actor is trying to achieve. In either case, understanding may only succeed in relation to aspects of the current context in which the action takes place. An ad hoc pantomime is structured so that the intention of its use within a context can be recognized with some likelihood of success even by (proto)humans from other communities so long as the things, actions or events involved in the

---

5. Such a notion as "invasion" is an informal placeholder pending more specific accounts. Various papers (Bergman, Beehner, Cheney, & Seyfarth, 2003; Bergman, Beehner, Painter, & Gustison, 2019; Ghazanfar & Eliades, 2014; Ghazanfar, Liao, & Takahashi, 2019) offer some pointers, but crucial data and detailed hypotheses remain lacking.

6. These definitions are implicit in earlier statements of MSH but have not been stated so explicitly – and further clarification may be apropos.

communicative act are familiar to them. A protosign may resemble a pantomime from which it is derived, or may have a history that obscures the relation between sign and meaning – in the latter case having little meaning to those outside communities in which its use has been adopted (where use implies the ability both to perform the protosign and to understand something of its context-dependent meaning – the parity principle again). The challenge in "MSH: the emergence of grammar" below will be to understand how this discussion holds up when we turn from "basic" pantomimes (as defined in the Taxonomy of the next section) to more complex communicative situations.

Pantomime opened up the semantic space for communication, expanding and exploiting the primates' open-ended manual dexterity. It establishes what Zlatev, Persson, and Gärdenfors (2005) call the *communicative sign function*: "The agent intends for the act to stand for some action, object or event for an addressee, and for the addressee to realize that the act is a representation." Ambiguity in pantomime may have provided an "incentive" for coming up with "protosigns" as conventionalized forms with restricted ranges of meaning in certain contexts. In one example from ASL, a pantomime of an airplane flying (hand shaped like a plane and "flown through the air") became conventionalized in two different ways: with the handshape moved back and forth on a short trajectory, it means AIRPLANE, whereas with conventionalized form of a single traverse of the long trajectory it means FLY. While no airplanes flew when protohumans first developed protosigns, the principle exemplified here already applied: As a pantomime becomes familiar to a group, it becomes conventionalized – which may involve simplification, but may also involve arbitrary changes to distinguish different aspects of the original cloud of meanings – and thence may become a symbol recognized only by members of the group. Once a group has acquired the understanding that new symbols can provide non-iconic messages, the difficulty of separating certain meanings by pantomime encourages creation of further new signs.

We take up the debate concerning the relation of protosign (manual) and protospeech (vocal) in the next section. Whatever the outcome of that debate, *the doctrine of expanding spirals* is a crucial one, reminding us that when we consider two capabilities of modern humans, it will often be a mistake to consider that one of them necessarily achieved modern form before the other began to emerge. Rather, the development of each one may have assisted in the emergence of the other as in the co-evolution of protosign and protospeech, or (below) protolanguage and pedagogy. The claim is that the above "stages" together yield early humans with language-ready brains, and the ability to employ simple protolanguages with parity. The cultural evolution that MSH posits to lead from protolanguages to language will be our focus in the section "MSH: the emergence of syntax."

The vocal-manual debate

Since other present-day nonhuman primates exhibit limited learning and flexibility in vocal control, MSH posits that even a limited set of protosigns could have provided the basis for open-ended semantics based on "abstracted" gestures (i.e., as in the OR example, not necessarily iconic) and that this in turn provided essential scaffolding for the emergence of "protospeech," with evolutionary and cultural changes along the hominin line seeing advances in both protosign and protospeech feeding off each other in an expanding spiral. It does not require that an extensive protosign system be in place before protospeech begins to emerge (Arbib, 2005b).

The crux is this: Present-day nonhuman primates lack the vocal control necessary to support speech. Thus, to support a protospeech-first hypothesis, or put protosign and protospeech on an equal footing, one must postulate a successor to LCA-ga that has flexible vocal control and learning, not just the flexible manual control and learning shared by present-day monkeys and apes. MSH posits that protosign provided an adaptive opportunity for the emergence of brain mechanisms for flexible vocal control; not everyone agrees. This subhypothesis has been subject to a number of critiques – see, e.g., (Fitch, 2010; MacNeilage & Davis, 2005), and the trio (Aboitiz, 2013; Fogassi, Coudé, & Ferrari, 2013; Sandler, 2013) with my response (Arbib, 2013). Other authors – whether or not they subscribe to the MSH subhypothesis – have supported the importance of manual gesture (Armstrong, Stokoe, & Wilcox, 1995; Corballis, 2002; Hewes, 1973; Stokoe, 2001; Tomasello, 2008), and many have advocated that the voice may have played an equal role – the multimodal view (Kendon, 1980; McNeill, 1998; Slocombe, Waller, & Liebal, 2011; Zlatev, Żywiczyński, & Wacewicz, 2020). In their analysis of language emergence in Sao Tome and Principe Sign Language, Mineiro and Moita (this volume) assess Sandler's critique, and argue that "both modality systems (manual and vocal) co-evolved together and seem to be coordinated in our specie[s]."

Let me insert an apparent non sequitur: The Riemann Hypothesis is one of the great unproved theorems of mathematics. Many decades ago, my Ph.D. supervisor told me of an amazing proof of a theorem, call it T. The proof had two parts: the first showed that if the Riemann Hypothesis is correct, then T was true; the second showed that if the Riemann Hypothesis is false, then T is still true – and since the Riemann Hypothesis is either true or false, T must be true. The study of language origins is similar. In this case we already know that T is true when T is "modern humans have diverse spoken and signed languages," but we seek a "proof" in terms of a biocultural evolutionary pathway that led to the current situation. In this case, an equivalent for the above role of the Riemann hypothesis is the unproved claim that "protohumans had flexible vocal control and learning before they had early protolanguages." Perhaps the majority of researchers support this claim, whereas MSH offers a "proof" (evolutionary account) based on its rejection – exploring how even a small collection of protosigns may have opened up the social niche in which expanded vocal control could prove adaptive. Arbib (2012, Chapter 9) assessed the claims and counterclaims, but the assessment needs revisiting (though not here) after a decade. Indeed, even as this paper was being written, Girard-Buttoz et al. (2022) published their analysis of 4826 recordings of 46 wild adult chimpanzees from Taï National Park. They observed 390 unique vocal sequences, with most vocal units that were emitted singly being also emitted in two-unit sequences (bigrams), which in turn were embedded into three-unit sequences (trigrams). Charting this capacity to organize a limited set of single units into a range of structured sequences is a valuable contribution, but – as one gathers from hearing the limited vocal control apparent in recordings of such vocalizations – it is a far cry [sic] from establishing the type of vocal control need to support the learning and meaningful use of the diverse phonologies of human spoken languages.

Why then the invocation of the Riemann hypothesis story? The point is that, whatever the state of protohuman vocal control, we know that we share manual dexterity with great apes and monkeys, and thus – whether aided by vocal flexibility or not – the hands may plausibly be included in the range of effectors brought into play in the emergence of protolanguage. The relevance of pantomime is then that far more meanings can be conveyed by pantomime than by imitating sounds of ongoing events (Fay, Arbib, & Garrod, 2013; Fay, Lister, Ellison, & Goldin-Meadow, 2014) and thus understanding how pantomime contributed to the emergence of language remains important even if one posits a crucial role for vocal signals.

A taxonomy of pantomime

It will be useful to calibrate the role attributed to pantomime in MSH against other approaches to pantomime exemplified in this volume. The key issue is that when we use theoretical terms, we may need to "add adjectives" to distinguish between different "subcategories," even if there are no strict boundaries between them, such as exemplified in the distinction between simple and complex imitation.

For Ferretti (2021), "pantomimic movements refer to whole events or sequences of events, which are not divisible into individual parts. Pantomime is a means of expression capable of representing the narrative character of mental representations of which humans are capable. As such, it constitutes a transition point for the advent of language." We will see in the next section that MSH, in considering how fractionation may offer one path to the emergence of words and constructions, certainly embraces the notion that there are pantomimes that are not divisible into individual parts that correspond to the words in how we might paraphrase the pantomimed event in a modern language. However, to proceed, it will be useful to recall the somewhat slippery notion of a **"basic" pantomime** as corresponding to one action within what may be a larger performance of pantomime as might occur in teaching the various stages of a skill, in developing a narrative, or in social coordination of multifaceted behaviors. Note that in conveying even a minimal subscene (Itti & Arbib, 2006) of a larger scene, such as "A does X to B," *at least* three basic pantomimes will be required to convey A, X and B, *unless* the context already makes clear the nature of A and/or B.

Next, note that in the 2012 version of MSH, the form of pantomime posited to precede protosign in human evolution is what may be called ad hoc pantomime:

Ad hoc pantomime: This embraces the case where any pattern of movement is mapped "for the first time" onto movements of arms and hands (especially) and other effectors, without necessary dependence on the objects that constrain "real-life" performance of these movements during praxic actions in, e.g., manipulation, locomotion, hunting or child-care.[7] This includes both *direct mimesis* (employing the same effectors as another human would in performing the pantomimed behavior) and *indirect mimesis* where this condition is relaxed – e.g., to use arms or the two hands to indicate the flapping wings of a bird or butterfly; to use two fingers to represent legs walking; to move the hand through a trajectory to represent the path taken by a person walking or a bird flying; or to move the hands as if tracing the contours of an object to represent the object. Moreover, this notion includes the stipulation of *partial* parity: that others will be able to understand the intended message within its current context, though perhaps with low success rates.

As noted earlier, Anne Russon has demonstrated that some "pantomime-like" behavior is exhibited by great apes. Rather than debate whether or not great apes "really" have pantomime, I suggest we view their behavior as pantomime of a distinctive kind:

Great-ape pantomime: This is exhibited by great apes, and is a form of ad hoc pantomime based on direct mimesis. My impression is that this is produced more

---

7. Other authors at the Workshop "Perspectives on Pantomime" (https://cles.umk.pl/conferences-events/perspectives-on-pantomime-evolution-development-interaction/) noted distinctions that will not be pursued here. For Zlatev et al. (this volume; 2020), the first and the second example represent a more and a less pantomimic gesture; the former primarily uses the mode of *enacting* and the other, the mode of *representing* (Müller, 2014, 2016). Marentette, Inaba, & Petrie (this volume) writes about modes of representation where flapping wings are BPO (body part as object) and two fingers, IO (imaginary object).

for humans, rather than assuming other apes will recognize it. Neither ritualization nor conventionalization (and thus no parity) is involved.

It would be useful to relate this form of pantomime to research on ape pointing, which is rare unless human-directed. I have argued (Arbib, 2012: 82) for a notion of *human-assisted ritualization* suggesting that an attempt to reach an object becomes ritualized as a gesture asking a human to hand over the object (other apes would take the object for themselves).

> This hypothesis finds support in the observation that pointing in human babies occurs primarily towards targets which are clearly out of reach (Butterworth, 2003). The particularly immature state of the locomotion system of humans at birth may have driven the species to develop a deictic pointing behavior. The ability of apes (but not monkeys) in captivity to produce a similar behavior reveals some form of brain-readiness for a set of communicative gestures beyond those exhibited in the wild. This relates to the general view ... that biological substrate and "cultural opportunity" are intertwined in supporting the human readiness for language. Arbib (2012: 82)

As noted above, Arbib (2012) argued for *ad hoc* pantomime as the precursor of protosign. However, Sibierska, Boruta-Żywiczyńska, Żywiczyński, and Wacewicz (2023) study modern human actors performing pantomimes, and observe that these rapidly become somewhat ritualized (but, given the nature of the task, not conventionalized). One must always be aware of radical differences between the signing of contemporary pantomime performed by actors and the processes that took place in the evolution of language. Nonetheless, I now argue that this observation in modern humans licenses replacing the posited role for ad hoc pantomime in MSH by ur-pantomime, in the following sense:

Ur-pantomime has two components. First, that agents are able to produce novel ad hoc pantomimes using both direct and indirect mimesis, but ur-pantomime further involves *limited* ritualization, with conventionalization considered a separate "stage." Second, biocultural evolution has endowed the group with an understanding that ad hoc pantomime can be used to communicate and thus that certain performances by others may be seen as pantomimes and thus one is to seek to understand the communicative goal.

Ritualization must be limited here so that new observers may understand something of what is intended by the pantomime. However, there is no need to suppose that ur-pantomime comes to an end as further conventionalization takes place – communication can (and does) combine pantomime and protosign. Crucially, someone who uses a (possibly ritualized) pantomime and is not understood has the option of creating another (possibly ad hoc) pantomime to help convey the intended meaning. The notion of "understanding" at this stage of protolan-

Chapter 1. Pantomime within and beyond the evolution of language **27**

guage communication would be far simpler than any philosophy of modern language would countenance. At this stage, most utterances would be intended to elicit some immediate change in behavior of the other, and failures of the other to behave in the suggested way would provide the error signal that indicates that the utterance was not "understood."

Wacewicz and Żywiczyński (2018, this volume) emphasize the establishment of a *platform of trust* as a necessary prerequisite for the development of a conventionalized communication system, in which all members of a community can "trust" what they understand others to be communicating. Sławomir Wacewicz (personal communication) suggests that ritualization is possible "before a platform of trust," i.e., when the communicative behavior is (more or less) directly governed by the calculation of its (more or less) immediate costs and benefits, but that ad-hoc pantomime already depends on a platform of trust which allows such calculations of immediate cost/benefit to be bracketed so that the "receiver" can (more or less) safely assume that the "sender" provide honest and useful information. They thus suggest expanding the second component of the definition of ur-pantomime to emphasize that the communicative interests of group members are sufficiently aligned to achieve a level of trust between them, so that the recipient may assume the communicative goal of the sender is worth seeking.

I am no expert on the platform of trust, but the above prompts several observations and a speculation: As modern humans, we often assume that the information people give us is correct, but we also continually assess whether their interests differ from ours. We tend not to evaluate message-by-message but rather by category (the checkout clerk at the market is probably truthful about merchandise issues; salesmen who phone one should be treated with care) and by person but with caveats (Uncle Harry is trustworthy except on politics); and when you meet a stranger and stray beyond topics-of-trust, you may evaluate messages carefully before deciding whether to act upon them. My speculation, then, is that rather than looking at evolution of communication as building on an established platform of trust, we should factor evaluation of (dis)alignment of interests into the evolution right from the start. In the same spirit, Heintz, Karabegovic, and Molnar (2016) suggest the co-evolution of honesty and strategic vigilance. Ontogeny does not recapitulate phylogeny, but the child does (usually) start with a family that the child can trust, and part of growing up is extending lexicon and grammar ... and how to adjust one's assessment of others to assess trustworthiness of the utterances one receives as one's contacts expand.

Brown (this volume) presents pantomime as a theatrical form in ancient Greece and Rome. This occurs at a very different stage of cultural evolution from that which provided a foundation for the emergence of protolanguages, and so I add another form of pantomime to the taxonomy, but will not discuss it further in this paper:

Theatrical pantomime: This is a form of pantomime in which skilled actors (Greek and Roman drama, Marcel Marceau, etc.) have ritualized a set of pantomimes to maximize recognition of communicative intent by a large (but perhaps well-prepared) audience of non-performers. Unlike ur-pantomime that precedes protolanguages and languages in human biocultural evolution, theatrical pantomime is performed by and for people with fully-fledged languages and narrative traditions.

Finally, Sibierska et al. (2023) and Zlatev et al. (this volume) report experiments with actors and subjects who have mastered both a language and some form of pictorial representation (e.g., drawings and comic strips), and so I add one more variation on the theme:

Modern ad hoc pantomime: I am not happy with the label, but the notion is that it is a form of ad hoc pantomime, perhaps slightly ritualized, that is performed by and for people with fully-fledged languages and pictorial representations as well as narrative traditions.

To close this section, let's calibrate the above against the way pantomime was defined for language evolution research by Żywiczyński, Wacewicz, and Sibierska (2018)

> Pantomime is, "a non-verbal, mimetic and non-conventionalised means of communication, which is executed primarily in the visual channel by coordinated movements of the whole body, but which may incorporate other semiotic resources, most importantly non-linguistic vocalisations. Pantomimes are acts of improvised communication that holistically refer to a potentially unlimited repertoire of events, or sequences of events, displaced from the here and now."

This was the primary definition employed at the Workshop "Perspectives on Pantomime" (Toruń, 18–19.11.2021). The term "non-conventionalized" is consistent with the notion of "mild" ritualization in the definition of ur-pantomime offered above, and their definition is also consistent with pantomime based on both direct and indirect mimesis. However, I suggest this definition has three shortcomings:

i.   It requires movements of the whole body, whereas movements of arms or hands may suffice for pantomime.

ii. While pantomime may support expression of "a potentially unlimited repertoire," this represents only a small fraction of what can be expressed in language. Note the difficulty of charades. Later, we will consider getting from an immediate sequence of a few pantomimes related to the here and now (as in pedagogy, even when the hands are displaced from the object – versus "get another stone from the quarry") to "a potentially unlimited repertoire of events, or sequences of events, displaced from the here and now" in ways that require cultural evolution that went hand-in-hand (another expanding spiral) with the emergence of protosign and protospeech.

iii. It includes non-linguistic vocalizations, whereas MSH considers vocalization separately from pantomime (and protosign), with interaction between the two an important topic for investigation.

Zlatev, personal communication and citing Zlatev et al. (2020), comments that the above definition is not "cast in stone," and accepts that (i) is appropriate but is adamant about the inclusion of non-linguistic vocalizations. However, he stresses, in the spirit of this taxonomy, that the key issue is to be clear about the interpretation of pantomime used in any particular investigation. Żywiczyński, personal communication, adds that the important property of such pantomime is *displacement*, a property we address explicitly in the following sections.

In any case, it is an important challenge to assess how facial expression of emotion may both enrich pantomime and provide a pathway to recruitment of orofacial gestures and in turn the voice "beyond pantomime." Ferrari and colleagues (Coudé & Ferrari, 2018; Ferrari, Gerbella, Coudé, & Rozzi, 2017) have distinguished two different mirror neuron networks in the macaque, a sensorimotor (hand) network linked more to praxic action and a limbic (oro-facial) pathway linked more to emotion-supporting circuitry. Sandler (2013), in her critique of MSH, notes how sign language exploits not only arms and hands but related movements of eyeballs, head, face and torso. Clearly, an investigation of the evolution of coordinated expressiveness of these effectors might also yield insights into the evolution of increased control of the voice in tandem with them.

Pedagogy and other forms of social coordination

Whereas MSH focuses on conventionalization of pantomime to yield "protosigns" as possible stepping stones to protolanguages, pantomimes can also emphasize flexible trajectories to indicate the ways in which an action might vary depending on the current affordances of objects. Both may be helpful in pedagogy, but are not restricted to this domain. The latter can retain its relation to objects that are present but need not do so – it can be used in cospeech gestures, such as separating the hands to indicate how big something is.

Conventionalization versus trajectories

Peter Gärdenfors (2021; this volume)[8] distinguishes pantomime-for-teaching from pantomime-for-communication, while making an important case that pedagogical demonstration and pantomime played a key role in language evolution.[9] He distinguished *pantomime* as illustrating action by depicting the movements in a task from *object gestures* showing the shape, size, length, height, etc of an object – but both fall under the general notion of pantomime offered in this paper, with his pantomime corresponding to *direct mimesis* (miming human actions using the corresponding effectors), while object gestures are one of diverse forms of *indirect mimesis. Pointing* to indicate location provides the third element of his account of pantomime-for-teaching.

Much pedagogy will start with *demonstration* of a skill in which the teacher acts upon the affordances of the actual tools and objects. The importance of complex rather than simple imitation is two-fold:

- the student can learn from observing the trajectory and not just the subgoals, and
- the effective teacher can modify the demonstration by slowing it down where necessary to make the trajectory more obvious and by placing larger gaps to emphasize the breakpoints. This enables the student to break a performance into components even when these components are themselves still unfamiliar.[10]

As the student's skill increases, it is the student who operates with tools and objects, while the teacher employs *pantomime* to further guide the student. Such pantomime becomes displaced from *transitive* actions (actions upon tools and objects) to the *intransitive* version of the same trajectories (See Gärdenfors, 2023, for more on the relation between demonstration and pantomime). Here I emphasize the *two-fold nature of pantomime*:

---

8. See also Gärdenfors & Högberg (2017) for their account of the archaeology of teaching and the evolution of *Homo docens*, and Michelle Kline (2015) for a differentiation between teaching types according to the specific adaptive problems that each type solves and application of this framework to explain why some types of teaching are uniquely human.

9. For related discussion suggesting how the needs of pedagogy to support increasingly complex technology, such as the manufacture of stone tools, may have been a key to the evolution of language, see papers on the Technological Pedagogy Hypothesis of Dietrich Stout and colleagues (Arbib, Fragaszy, Healy, & Stout, 2023; Stout, 2010, 2011, 2018; Stout, Toth, Schick, & Chaminade, 2008).

10. Patricia Zukow-Goldring (2012; Zukow-Goldring & Arbib, 2007) examines the teaching skills of modern humans – showing the sophistication of the work of the caregiver in helping a child gain the affordances and effectivities, and not just the sequencing, of actions to master a new skill. She speaks of *assisted* imitation. See also (Arbib, 2012: 198–201).

Chapter 1. Pantomime within and beyond the evolution of language 31

- The *overt presentation of trajectories* of movement: In teaching a skill, each "basic" pantomime (i.e., corresponding to one action within the overall performance) often serves to indicate trajectory (including speed and some indication of force) of the action as well (perhaps implicitly, perhaps with explicit pointing in addition) as the affordance to which that action is to be applied.
- *Ritualization*, as emphasized in MSH, gains symbolic efficiency and flexibility at the cost of overriding the semantic weight given to variations in trajectory in overt demonstration. As the apprentice becomes more skilled, one might see an increasing use of pre-protosigns conventionalizing the actions within chunks of the overall behavior to remind the apprentice of "what" to do next with decreased use of the trajectory details that indicate "how to do it."

Here I must explain this ugly coinage: *pre-protosign*. In an earlier draft of the paper, I labelled the previous paragraph *Conventionalization* but have relabeled it *Ritualization* to stress that here, as in ontogenetic ritualization, what is created is private to a dyad, with one member A providing a gesture that need only be understood by the other member B. It is only when the (modified) gesture becomes shared in a community – perhaps grounded in teachers of a given craft and their apprentices – that the result can properly be called a protosign – with the term pre-protosign used for whatever emerges just within the dyad. Thus we come to a *new* bullet on conventionalization that better coheres with the framework established earlier in this paper.

- *Conventionalization* arises when, for example, different teachers of the same skill converge on a single protosign for some aspect of the skill for which each had earlier used diverse pre-protosigns.

The mechanisms that support this process would seem to be those which in the present day support the emergence of signs of a signed language based on the diverse home signs of children joining a Deaf community (see Polich, 2005, on the emergence of Nicaraguan Sign Language, NSL). In their study of the recent emergence of Sao Tome and Principe Sign Language (STPSL), Mineiro and Moita (this volume) report five studies of the transition from pantomime to proto and early signs, where by proto signs, they mean the first gestures that exhibit preferences for manual configurations, movements, locations as well as non-manual elements to represent specific semantic features of the referent.[11]

A crucial transition that MSH makes and that applies here distinguishes the use of gestures resulting from ontogenetic ritualization from protosigns (and the

---

11. The section on NSL in Arbib (2012) answers the question "If NSL [or STPSL] can emerge in a few years or decades, why wouldn't the transition for protohumans from pantomime to full languages have only required decades rather than, probably, tens of millennia?"

protolanguage and languages that emerge from it), and great-ape pantomime from ad hoc pantomime. In each case we move from the use of a single communicative gesture to the use of that gesture that rests on a shared understanding that there is a process in the community to open up the range of communicative strategies of this type – an opening-up of semantics from the (almost) closed communication systems of nonhuman animals.

- *A community of teachers:* The emergence of such protosigns changes the teaching process. Rather than a pre-protosign emerging through a possibly extended process of ritualization between teacher and apprentice, the teacher may explicitly teach the student the appropriate use of the pre-established protosign. We see here a mechanism whereby pantomime-for-teaching may provide one basis (among many, I suggest) for the emergence of protolanguage.

To summarize: At the early stage of teaching a new skill, the teacher will employ pantomimes that can remind the apprentice of the motion paths required to successfully complete the next action, with affordances visible, of the skill that is being taught. But this form of pedagogical pantomime involves little if any ritualization. Indeed, this would destroy the crucial trajectory information. Instead, it uses the presence of the tools and objects and the memory of overt demonstration to enable the student to relate each pantomimed trajectory to the appropriate affordances of the appropriate objects. A pantomime can thus remind students about the general motion to perform next and may be augmented by interleaving pointing to specific affordances, but may often count on prior demonstration having instilled in the student an understanding of which affordances each action must align with in practice.

For pantomime-as-teaching to be effective, all that is required is that the pantomime by the teacher be understood by the student within the current context; the student need not have mastered that pantomime while learning the corresponding skill. During training in a novel action, pantomime that demonstrates features of the action to the student will be crucial, but once a particular action has been mastered, then the teacher can substitute a pre-protosign or protosign, speeding up the process of instruction and application, with emphasis now placed on affordances and actions that still confuse the student. Even for a novel skill, the teacher can provide the novice with a readily learnable vocabulary that can then be used to supplement, focus, or replace overt demonstration. Meanwhile, facial expression can communicate the teacher's emotions concerning the apprentice's progress, and this may favor (cultural) evolution of "theory of mind" to better adjust these expressions to those that will aid learning.

The complementary abilities of student and teacher charted above, rooted not only in a capacity for pantomime but also for complex action recognition and imitation, can dramatically increase the diversity of skills that an individual can master, and thus lie at the heart of cultural evolution; supporting a form of ratcheting in which the chunks that can provide units with a particular process of complex imitation can become more and more complex.

The above account suggests further requirements for the path to protolanguage:

1. The first is that the need may emerge to go beyond demonstrating actions to communicating about the affordances and objects involved. When they are directly present they can be identified either on the basis of the stage of performance of the skill or by pointing. But a natural extension would be the ability to refer to objects in other situations, and we see the importance of this for supporting *displacement*. For example, the teacher might tell the apprentice to gather a new stone of a certain size and shape, and this might involve a pantomime that is no longer focused solely on the actions of the skilled behavior but, for example, (i) traces the shape of the desired object by making outlining contours with the hands in the air and (ii) complements this with a spacing of the hands to indicate object size. The former could exemplify a path to a ritualization and then conventionalization of pantomimes that distinguish one type of object from another, whereas with the latter we begin the separate path to the cospeech gestures that augment our everyday use of spoken language.

2. But the utility of pantomime for social coordination goes far beyond pedagogy. It need not be restricted to direct mimesis of human actions. In hunting, the person who has identified the prey might perform pantomimes that distinguish the flapping wings of a bird, the slithering of a snake, or the stealthy stalking of a leopard. Another development would be moving the hand through the air to illustrate the trajectory of someone walking or moving in a coordinated fashion required for hunting the prey. As above, other pantomimes could mime tracing the contours of an object to refer to the object, or showing how a tool is used with body part as object, or as if moving the hand while grasping an imagined object. Note, too, the distinction between conventionalized tracing of an object to suggest its general category and the relevance of trajectories to the emergence of drawing, as was discussed earlier.

In summary, we see two *partially parting paths for pantomime* providing the basis for two complementary processes: via conventionalization towards protosign and the emergence of language, and towards the continuous modulation of trajectories that continues to support complex imitation, and provides the continuing utility of cospeech or cosign gestures – and drawing – as a complement to language use.

From pantomime to (micro-)protolanguages

As mentioned above, Gärdenfors distinguishes between pantomime-for teaching and pantomime-for-communication. This is a useful distinction, but we have seen that there is great overlap – the same strategy might be used in telling a student what to do in mastering a new skill, and telling another (non-student) what to do in (already-mastered) coordinated behavior to achieve some joint goal (as in hunting or child-care). I thus reject the argument (Gärdenfors, 2021; this volume) that a principle of cognitive parsimony suggests that pantomime for teaching is evolutionarily older. Humans exhibit a variety of behaviors in which social coordination is important. In complex tasks, the work might extend over hours or even days, and involve more than one person.

As already suggested, a tool maker might request an assistant to go and find a new core. Here, the request cannot refer to actions or affordances for objects that are present; their very nature requires that pantomime or protolanguage or some combination be used specify the object as well as the action. We see the beginnings of *displacement* – communication beyond the here-and-now and here-and-next. Diverse behaviors such as building fires, preparing food, keeping the campsite tidy and habitable, finding water, caring for the young, disposing of the dead, big game scavenging (Bickerton, 2009) or big game hunting (Dediu & Levinson, 2018), all require social coordination.

Various skills may set needs for *specific* forms of communication, so I add here the notion of *micro-protolanguages*. Early humans with different responsibilities within social groups may have developed small protolanguages specific to communicating about their own activities (while still relying greatly on context, gesture, and pantomime) long before the emergence of larger protolanguages integrating features shared by the whole community. (See Arbib, 2024, for a discussion of how such microprotolanguages might together form the basis for a shared protolanguage for a community, yet possibly preserve distinct aspects within different subcommunities.)

As noted before, but here with no restriction to pedagogy, the fact that pantomime may be performed in the absence of objects suggests an adaptive pressure for the invention of pantomimes to better express objects and affordances. In a *pantomime-for-request*, such as "get me another core," there are two notable differences:

- the details of motion during the pantomime are not important so long as they are distinctive; and
- the pantomime may now be indicating an object rather than an action or sequence of actions.

As the skill becomes more complex, so the cumulative mastery of larger chunks, and the automatization of parts of them emerges. Being able to refer to chunks provides a great step in the interwoven evolution of pantomime-for-teaching and pantomime-for-communication, as in more rapidly coordinating complex behaviors (unavailable to nonhumans) – in each case providing adaptive pressures toward protosign. In pedagogy, this can encourage the mastery of action within action "chunks" rather than having learning diffused over diverse actions in separate parts of the skill being taught. However, the distinction between putting the chunks together and the learning of when and how to match effectivities to affordances should be borne in mid during our later discussions of grammar and narrative.

But now we need to attend to a crucial issue in language origins that is not addressed elsewhere in this volume: the emergence of grammar.

MSH: The emergence of grammar

The transition from protolanguages (note the plural) to languages is a continuum, as protowords yield to words governed by constructions; with lexicon and grammar growing to provide the ability to express a widening range of novel meanings (recall Figure 1). MSH posits that there were no syntactic categories when protolanguages first began to emerge from pantomime – and that many "protowords" were more akin in meaning to phrases or sentences of modern language than to modern words. Instead, there was a long period of cultural evolution for syntactic categories to emerge from semantic categories. This proposal is subject to debate – see, e.g., Arbib and Bickerton (2010) and the companion paper (Arbib, 2024). The main counter-proposals hold that protowords referred to objects and actions (they were noun-like and verb-like) and so the emergence of language involved finding ways to combine them. In somewhat related fashion, Gärdenfors (2021) sees pantomime-for-communication emerging from pantomime-for-teaching in a way that already establishes protosyntactic categories:

> pointing ⇒ protodemonstratives; object properties ⇒ protonouns and protoadjectives; and pantomime (in his sense of direct mimesis) ⇒ protoverbs.

In relation to protodemonstratives, see the discussion of the debate between Diessel and Heine & Kuteva at the end of the next section.

The co-evolution of words and constructions

With Wray (1998, 2000), MSH insists that many protowords may have been *holophrases* – utterances that combined separate meanings even though there were originally no (protowords) to express them. MSH focuses less on "How do we get protonouns and protoverbs?" and more on "How do we *simultaneously* build protoconstructions and the protosigns they combine?" It posits that the general ability for *complex action recognition* came (perhaps after tens of millennia) to support *fractionation* of protowords – breaking them into pieces that "were not there before" but came to be associated with their own meanings. The complementary process yielded constructions as a way to "put the pieces back together" – but now with the advantage that they could also combine pieces that had never been combined before. There is no claim in MSH that this is the only way protowords form.

This approach shares its general framework with *construction grammar* to hold that languages have a multitude of diverse constructions that combine form and meaning, rather than the approach of *generative linguistics* that, at least in its early stages, emphasized the search for a relatively universal set of rules for syntax that operated separately from semantics (Arbib, 2012: 43–65; Croft, 2000; Kemmerer, 2005). The point is that, if we consider pantomime as playing a crucial role on the path to protosign (whether or not we regard protosign as providing a scaffolding for protospeech) then it is inevitable that many protowords would have been neither protonouns nor protoverbs. Indeed, these terms are themselves misleading – the same protoword might, in our terms, be interpreted as *explode* or *explosion – depending on the context* – and this frames a quest to understand how protowords and contexts that helped disambiguate them evolved (culturally) together. (Hartmann & Pleyer, 2021; and Pleyer, 2023, also develop a usage-based construction grammar framework for their study of protolanguages.)

For an anachronistic example, consider a pantomime for *open-a-door*. The pantomime contains no explicit component for *door*. How then might fractionation of the pantomime into two pieces, one a protosign for *door* and the other for *open*, yield a simple construction such as *open-X* to allow free extension of the notion of opening to other objects for which opening is applicable? A possible solution is that the pantomime of turning the handle becomes fractionated out as the protosign for *door* while the two directions of moving the hand yields protosigns for *open* and *close*.

Aa a related example, note that both a protosign for *spear* and a protoconstruction for *throw-X* might arise from fractionation of a conventionalization of the same pantomime, whereas a different path may have led to the construction *give-X* and the subsequent recognition that *spear* could also serve as a slot-filler for *give-X.* Note that to employ *open-X,* the slot-filler X must meet a *semantic* criterion of being something-that-opens. We are a long way from generalized constructions whose slot-fillers are defined by syntactic categories like "noun" or "verb," but even at this early stage, we see that protowords are beginning to become words since they are now enriched by their linkage to constructions. Moreover, the existence of even primitive constructions might scaffold the invention of new (proto)words to complement their emergence through fractionation. For example, a rapid opening and closing of the mouth might become adopted as the protosign for *mouth* that could provide a new X to be available to fill the slot in *open-X* and *close-X.* The gesture of opening and closing the mouth could also be interpreted as *eating* – but in the context of the *open-X* construction it must mean *mouth.*

This example marks an important elision of pantomime of manual gesture with pantomime of oro-facial gesture and is thus, perhaps, indicative of opening up a path to evolution of mechanisms that support protospeech. Indeed, although the key example here has operated on pantomime, the processes of conventionalization and fractionation can operate in the auditory-vocal domain as vocalization, sound symbolism, and onomatopoeia extend the realm of protowords.

Arbib (2012: 303–304) presents an illuminating present-day example of these processes from the emergence of Nicaraguan Sign Language (NSL).

> The complex motion event of "rolling" down a hill includes a *manner* of movement (rolling) and a *path* of movement (descending). These characteristics of motion are simultaneous aspects of a single event and are [pantomimed] as a unity. ... Senghas et al. (2004) found that ... [successive cohorts of NSL signers made increasing use of separate signs for] path and manner in describing such an event ... [However, if] manner and path are expressed separately, it may no longer be clear that the two aspects of movement occurred within a single event. *Roll* followed by *downward* might mean "rolling, and then descending." However, a key finding of Senghas et al. (2004) is that not only did NSL signers come to fractionate path and manner, they also developed a way to put the pieces back together again. NSL now has the X-Y-X construction, such as *roll-descend-roll,* to express simultaneity. This string can serve as a structural unit within a larger expression like *cat [roll descend roll],* or it can even be nested, as in *waddle [roll descend roll] waddle.*
>
> This example shows that the general process of following fractionation with a construction to put the pieces back together, and then be available to combine other pieces as well ... is still operative in the modern brain when the need to expand a communication system demands it.

The earlier example from ASL of how two different conventionalizations of the same pantomime could yield signs for AIRPLANE and FLY suggests another process that could have operated at the earliest stages of the protolanguage-language continuum to respond to context in creating novel words – and note again that it would be misleading to label the original pantomime as a protonoun or a protoverb. Let's turn, then, to the notion of (proto)word categories. Over time, MSH suggests, constructions became merged or generalized, and complemented by new ones, and so the "slot fillers" went from having highly limited semantic variation to becoming abstract enough to form syntactic categories. Lexicon and grammar continued to evolve (culturally) together. Note, though, that the slot-fillers in present day constructions need not be general syntactic categories but may be restricted by semantic range – we only understand the phrase "woman in red" because we know that the general construction "PERSON in COLOR" has the interpretation that the person is wearing garments primarily of the given color.

We close the section with a brief note on pointing and *deixis*. Diessel (2013) emphasizes its importance in the emergence of language and thus of demonstratives (words like *this* and *that*), whereas in their account of the historical emergence of linguistic categories by processes of successive grammaticalization over the recent span of the last few thousand years, Heine and Kuteva (2007: 111) suggest that nouns, verbs and adverbs all had to emerge as syntactic categories before demonstratives emerged through further grammaticalization. A possible resolution is to note that the development of protosigns from pantomimes did not block the continued use of pantomimed trajectories as *cospeech gestures*, so that the parametric properties of pantomime serve even today as a complement to the words of spoken language whose relation to conventionalized pantomime is far less direct. Moreover, Deaf signers employ *cosign gestures* that can be distinguished from the signs of the signed language. Thus it may be that the availability of pointing as a *co-protolanguage gesture* obviated the early need for demonstratives in early stages of grammaticalization – just as someone might say today "the fish was yay big" and spread their hands to indicate (or exaggerate) how big the fish was.

The prehistory of language change

In terms of the notion of a language-ready brain, we must continue to ask: What processes operative now might have operated (but much more slowly, given the limited extent of protolanguages) in prehistoric times? To avoid burdening what is already a long paper, I offer here a challenge with only the merest outline of how I address it:

Schmid (2015) sketches the Entrenchment-and- Conventionalization Model for language change, building on 7 axioms:

1. Speakers use language in order to communicate.
2. For speakers to be able to do so, they need linguistic knowledge.
3. Linguistic knowledge is represented in individual language users' minds and brains.
4. Members of a speech community share linguistic knowledge.
5. No two members of a speech community have identical linguistic knowledge.
6. Individual and shared linguistic knowledge are both stable and subject to change.
7. Linguistic structure is shaped by language use.

These axioms are extended by Schmid to define mechanisms support *usualization*– i.e., the implicit agreement on how to solve communicative tasks. Here is the framework for the rapprochement. The challenge is to adapt these to apply to the capabilities charted above for the language-ready brains of a community that has a protolanguage, but for which many generations of cultural evolution will be required to yield communities that support languages. The sketch here simply addresses the axioms. The basis step is to use the term *(proto)language* to apply to any communal communication system that falls along the language-protolanguage continuum. Since we emphasize that (proto)language is not necessarily spoken, we use "(proto)speakers" with the understanding that their communication between members of a given (changeable) (proto)language community need not be vocal-auditory. I adjust Schmid's axioms as follows (with a few preliminary qualifications in [...]). My claim is that MSH already covers the various contingencies that Schmid presents in exploring mechanisms that would support language change:

1. (Proto)speakers use (proto)language in order to communicate.
2. For (proto)speakers to be able to do so, they need (proto)linguistic knowledge and readiness. [The addition "and readiness" stresses that the knowledge – which takes the form of (proto)lexicon and (proto)constructions-must build on a general understanding of how to generate and comprehend novel as well as familiar communicative acts.]
3. (Proto)linguistic knowledge is represented in individual (proto)language users' minds and brains. [I don't see the need for the mind-brain distinction here.]
4. Members of a (proto)language community share (proto)linguistic knowledge. [This is redundant to the MSH insistence that such knowledge is particular to a community.]
5. No two members of a (proto)language community have identical (proto)linguistic knowledge. [Perhaps this is too strong as stated. I prefer "members of a (proto)language community may have different (proto)linguistic knowledge,

but to belong to that community must share enough knowledge to make it possible to communicate effectively in many cases and also be able (on occasion) to recognize communicative failures and act to repair them. Such repair is a key driver of (proto)linguistic change.]

6. Individual and shared (proto)linguistic knowledge are both stable and subject to change. [This would seem implicit in the reformulation of 5.]

7. (Proto)linguistic structure is shaped by (proto)language use.

These "axioms" would seems to be a general consequence of the MSH framework which is an exemplar of a usage-based and emergentist approach to explaining how the linkage of form and meaning in lexicon as well as grammar emerges. One may place all this within a larger framework studying cultural evolution as affecting artefacts, social relations and skills as well as communication.

Was narrative prior to language in human evolution?

For Ferretti (2021),

> pantomimic movements refer to whole events or sequences of events, which are not divisible into individual parts. Pantomime is a means of expression capable of representing the narrative character of mental representations of which humans are capable. As such, it constitutes a transition point for the advent of language.

Unfortunately, discussion of narrative has not made its way into my previous efforts to "evolve" MSH to incorporate fresh data and concerns, despite my efforts elsewhere to link language to our self-narratives and consciousness as modern humans.[12] MSH focused on the emergence of languages at the level of words and the grammars that evolved to combine them with little concern for how sentences might be combined to yield overall narratives. This section begins to rectify this shortcoming by reflecting on the writings of Francesco Ferretti and

---

12. One referee observed of an earlier draft of (Arbib, 2016a) that – as cited in the paper – "the claim that language decisively contributes to the emergence of fully developed human consciousness leads to the conclusion that consciousness is [in great part] *narrative* or *discursive*. ... This is important in so far as it goes against a long tradition (especially in the continental philosophy) to speak of consciousness as a – more or less coherent – chain of mental images. Moreover, Arbib's theory seems also to undermine the idea of mentalese (language of thought). ... [He asserts that] there are aspects of mental states that cannot be expressed in language, but at the same time he rejects the thesis that there exists a language of thought substantially different from the language we speak." More specifically, I reject the notion that our mental processes are language-like save in limiting cases, with mental processing better defined at the level of schemas and the even less language-like dynamics of brain states (Arbib, 1989).

Chapter 1. Pantomime within and beyond the evolution of language

colleagues on pantomime, narrative and language origins (e.g., Ferretti, 2021; Ferretti, Adornetti, & Chiera, 2022; Ferretti, Chiera, & Adornetti, this volume) and the experimental study of modern ad hoc pantomime by Zlatev et al. (this volume).

Ur-pantomime supports only simple protonarratives

Ferretti argues for the "narrative first hypothesis" that narrative preceded language, opposing the "language first hypothesis" that language preceded narrative. Barnard (2013) argues that the evolution of narrative, and especially of myth, pushed the evolution of linguistic complexity, with language coevolving with mythology in symbolic frameworks which extended the capacity for verbal expression "to the limits of cognition." My only demurrals are that narrative can perform valuable social functions without (or prior to) the emergence of myth, and that cognition co-evolved with means for verbal expression, rather than providing pre-existing limits. However, the relevant point here is that Barnard claims that the evolution of narrative pushed the evolution of linguistic complexity. Thus, just as I have postulated a spectrum from protolanguages to languages of greater complexity and expressivity, so I argue that the full exploration of narrative needs an account of precursors, protonarratives, and then the increasing range of narratives with cultural evolution of "co-narrative processes." (Proto)language and (proto)narrative constitute another expanding spiral.

Let's imagine a time when protohumans had mastered ur-pantomime but had not as yet developed protolanguage. A hunter returns with the carcass of an animal he has killed and wants to tell the tribe about the successful hunt. To do so in pantomime, he might perhaps alternate between miming his movements stalking the prey and then stabbing it with his spear and the movements of the prey seeking to evade him, then turning on him, and finally succumbing to his spear thrusts. This narrative works because the tribe can see that he has just completed a successful hunt and that the pantomime must be a re-enactment of the hunt and the actions of its two protagonists. Similarly, we can envision pantomimes that invite tribe members to join the mimer in scavenging or hunting for prey. However, these primitive extensions of pantomime into the recent past or possible near future succeed only because *these protonarratives are clearly related to the current context* that holds for those who witness the performance.

Sibierska et al. (2023) have actors mime a transitive event (kissing, pushing, slapping, waving) as shown in one of 20 drawings. Observers then watch videotapes of these performances and specify which of the drawings was the basis for the video they observed. Some videos were not classified correctly by any observer, some were classified correctly by all observers, and most had intermediate guessability. The full paper analyzes the various strategies used, but the point I want to make here is that, even for modern humans skilled in language and pictorial representation, pantomime is an unreliable medium. This holds even here when the main action should be easy to mime so that the observer has only five scenes to choose from. In this study, even the single scene sets challenges for identifying which characters are involved and then who does what to whom. Contrast the "hunting narrative" where the two protagonists and the general nature of their encounter is already known to the observers, and so attribution of actions to agents is unlikely to be ambiguous. In assessing the power of "protonarrative," one might further suggest that experience with the disposition of a group during a hunt would be a prerequisite for the initial development of pantomimic narratives about the hunt – compare the role of the teacher's experience with a tool in pantomiming to teach an apprentice. Specifically, the communication needed for a hunting expedition or other behaviors can contribute to embedding the pantomime of a skill into a narrative. We can relate this to the notion of microprotolanguages as being limited to, and thus most effective in, limited domains (as in the hunter's recounting).

But what then of temporally extended narratives rather than single scenes? In the study by Zlatev et al. (this volume), a "Director" is presented with three simple sentences (in Polish) that together tell a simple story such as (in translation):

"A man reached for an apple on a tree. The apple was bad. The man was sad."

The Director then reenacts the story in a pre-designated space in front of the "Matcher" and the camera, having been Instructed to rely on whole-body movements and not use words. The "Matcher" is then asked to match what they saw with one of 4 comic strips, each with three panels. Two show the correct story, but one is in chronological order of the simple events described by the three sentences whereas the other's order is achronological. The other two strips show another story, in chronological and achronological orders. The study involves modern humans skilled in language and pictorial representation, and with the simple task of choosing between two stories (presented in 2 orders) and yet, although the correct choice was made for 92% of chronological narratives, the score was only 31% for achronological narratives! I find this surprising. It suggests that "pure" pantomime may readily express a simple chronological narrative (even if subject to the constraint of a highly focused topic) but that *we need to pass from pantomime of story events to more abstract protosigns to begin to develop more advanced techniques of story telling.* For example, given a sequence of pantomime-complexes (recall that even a minimal subscene may require several basic pantomimes to be communicated) S1, S2, S3 that convey three episodes of a story in chronological order, the inference offered by Zlatev et al. is that a formula, call it F, was needed in the protolanguage, so that its role in S3, F, S1, S2 would be something like "But how did this come to be?" with S1 and S2 then providing the background to S3.

The suggestion, then, is that purely pantomimic narratives would have been severely limited. Protonarratives would then increase in subtlety as protolanguage developed (i) a vocabulary of protosigns large enough to allow the recognition of the As, Xs and Bs of "A does X to B" without strong reliance on a limited context and, crucially, (ii) new protosigns became available that could support achronological narratives of increasing complexity. One such set of protosigns would provide the equivalent of pronouns to remind us that the agent or object now described has already been introduced *earlier in the narrative* (and note that this is earlier in the telling of the story, whether or not the story is presented in chronological order).

We may have a "pantomimic fossil" here: in a *sign* language, one need not use an explicit sign for a pronoun, but can instead use the position in signing space where the agent or object was first introduced to anchor later signing that invokes it. Intriguingly, Almor, Smith, Bonilha, Fridriksson, and Rorden (2007) used functional MRI to show that reading repeated names elicited more activation than pronouns in the middle and inferior temporal gyri and intraparietal sulcus and argue that that the temporal lobe activation suggests that repeated names but not pronouns evoke multiple representations that have to be integrated, whereas (a signature of our "fossil"?) the intraparietal sulcus activation may reflect the role in this integration of brain regions used for spatial attention and perceptual integration. In other words, as we comprehend a narrative, the "characters" may be "imagined" in a conceptual space that is externalized in the narratives of Deaf signers.

The triadic system and the narrative-ready brain

In summary, I agree with Ferretti that, harking back to language origins, ur-pantomime could have supported *simple, context-limited* protonarratives before the emergence of "post-pantomimic" protosigns and constructions but, in line with Barnard, I see extending the scope of narrative as providing one of the drives for the enrichment of protolanguages and the passage to language. Displacement in space and time and change of character being described would be key elements of this enrichment. What are the implications for a language-ready brain that is narrative-ready?

Ferretti's (2021) concern with narrative leads him to privilege a *triadic system* – navigation in space, navigation in time, and mindreading – as "the cognitive equipment by which our ancestors were able to emancipate themselves from animal communication." This obliges me to investigate whether triadic system must be added to the MSH summary of the language-ready brain if we are to encompass narrative as a major form of language use.

MSH hypotheses which features of brain function are present in early humans but not in LCA-ga. It thus leaves implicit in characterizing the language-ready brain diverse features that are shared across many species, including the linkage of multi-modal perception to action, navigation in space, diverse forms of learning, and basic forms of communication linked to social coordination. MSH emphasizes complex action recognition and imitation, pantomime that introduces the shared understanding that this provides an open system for shared communication with parity, the conventionalization that leads to protosign, and flexible vocal control and learning as "add-ons." Inspired by Ferretti, I argue that because a language-ready brain must (as MSH has glossed over) be a narrative-ready brain, "mental time travel" (see the discussion of Suddendorf and Corballis below) must be added as a novel variation on the theme of spatial navigation but that mindreading should not. In this chapter, I can but briefly (and tentatively, pending further study) seek to justify these claims.

First, however, some words of caution about brain evolution.

1. The brain is not organized in terms of separable circuits devoted to separate (e.g., cognitive) functions – rather such functions are mediated by the competition and cooperation of activity in diverse regions. Yes, brains have regions whose lesion can destroy specific abilities, and we can find regions with "primary functions" such as the role of primary visual cortex in preprocessing signals forwarded from the retina via thalamus – but even here we must add that this region can respond to auditory signals, and that visual experience depends on its interaction with diverse regions, including regions that do not depend on information routed via thalamus (Humphrey, 1970).

2. Brain regions that evolved to help support ancestral functions can be rewired on the basis of new functions. This general insight underlies the posited notion that it took cultural evolution to convert a *language-ready* brain to a brain that would become *language-using* once children could develop in a language-using community. In similar vein, consider the idea of a "reading-ready" brain – Dehaene et al. (2010) found that an area serving face recognition becomes adapted for the recognition of visual word forms through experience of reading, not through genetic change.

3. The English neurologist Hughlings Jackson (1878–79) viewed the brain in terms of levels of increasing evolutionary complexity. Observing his neurological patients, he argued that damage to a "higher" level of the brain caused

Chapter 1. Pantomime within and beyond the evolution of language

the patient to use "older" brain regions in a way disinhibited from controls evolved later, to reveal behaviors that were more primitive in evolutionary terms. As the brain evolves, it exhibits new patterns of neural activity which can provide new "ecological niches" for the evolution of new neural circuitry to exploit those patterns. But once such new circuitry evolves, there is a new "information environment" for the earlier circuitry – so it may evolve in turn to exploit these new patterns. Arbib (1989, Section 7.2) offers an evolutionary model of computing optic flow that exemplifies this view, while Iriki and Taoka (2012) assess the inter-relation of ecological, neural, and cognitive niche construction in biocultural evolution.

4. Genes can change the growth potential for cell morphology and connectivity, but these changes may affect whole regions of the brain, rather than a single region. For example, Barton (2012) argues that genetic specification of cerebellum and neocortex are closely coupled, and so we may link expansion in cerebral functions to the co-evolved expansion of cerebellum to provide the resources for the effective tuning and coordination of these capabilities (see Arbib, Schweighofer, & Thach, 1995, for related – but non-evolutionary – modeling)

With these cautions in mind, I offer a brief appetizer for a full course on the evolution of mindreading and navigation in time.

Tellingly, the word "conversation" has not appeared till now in this chapter and does not occur in the chapters by Gärdenfors or by Zlatev et al., so let me close this section by noting that conversation may be at least as important as narrative in the evolution of language. Ferretti et al. (this volume) assert that

> in order to reach the goal of communication, it is not enough to inform someone of something, but it is also required that interlocutors accept what is being said (Sperber et al., 2010) [and recall our earlier discussion of platform of trust]. The most effective solution to this problem lies in conversation as a form of persuasive reciprocity, founded on argumentative strategies of persuasion. However, as we will see in the last part of the [Ferretti et al.] chapter, this type of conversation is not useful to investigate the initial stages of human communication since it presumes syntactically complex verbal codes. Persuasive reciprocity characterizing argumentative persuasion is a late product of evolution which probably constitutes the hallmark of *Homo sapiens*' communication ....

Accepting this, we may nonetheless seek roots for persuasive reciprocity in the sorts of protoconversations needed for people to coordinate their behaviors in a limited set of skills – a propensity suggested earlier as a source of diverse microprotolanguages that might arise within a larger community.

Mindreading

Mindreading (≈ Theory of Mind, ToM), encompasses the cognitive capacity to interpret behavior by attributing mental states to others. Ferretti cites Herman (2013:74) who states "Storytelling also affords a basis for registering and making sense of the intentions, goals, feelings, and actions that emerge from intelligent agent's negotiation of appropriately scaled environments." The issue here is whether the skill of modern humans in mindreading that distinguishes us from other animals required biological evolution post-LCA-ga that had attributes missing in the MSH account of the language-ready brain, or whether it was the cultural evolution of increasing complex protolanguages (in concert with an expanded capacity for narrative) that supported this skill. Can one really separate Herman's listed qualities from already having language?

Gärdenfors (this volume) sees theory of mind as an important extension of human causal cognition, raising the issue of just what mechanisms related to causal cognition must be included in the definition of the language-ready brain, and whether cultural evolution would suffice to yield humans who exhibit a rich theory of mind. Leslie (1987) devized a theoretical model of the cognitive mechanisms underlying the key abilities of shared attention and pretense underlying ToM, relating it to two different types of representations:

– *First-order representations* are in charge of describing visible bodies and events, while
– *Second-order representations* describe invisible minds and mental events[13] and serve to make sense of otherwise contradictory or incongruous information (i.e., engaging simultaneously in an imaginary activity and a real one).

A famous test for ToM is the Sally–Ann task (Baron-Cohen et al., 1985): The child sees the following scenario: "Sally has a basket and Anne has a box. Sally puts a marble into her basket, and then she goes out for a walk. While she is outside, naughty Anne takes the marble from the basket and puts it into her own box. Now Sally comes back from her walk and wants to play with her marble. Where will she look for the marble?" The 4 year old child will assert, correctly, that Sally will look

---

13. Gärdenfors (this volume) offers an account of causal reasoning and event cognition, with expression of the former seen as a driver for increasing complexity of language as part of the transition from showing (as in demonstration) to telling. His account of event cognition focuses on the notion that "[a]n action is modelled as a force vector [and the] result of an event is modelled as a change vector representing the change of properties of the patient." By contrast, Arbib et al. (2021) characterize events in terms of a P[S]Q notation – when suitable preconditions P are available (including affordances), performance of action S can result in establishing postcondition Q (which may include achievement of a goal).

inside her basket – because that is where Sally thinks it is. However, a 2-year-old child (or an autistic 4-year-old-child) will expect Sally to look inside Anne's box because that is where *the child knows it is.*

Based on this, I suggest that the child's exposure to stories of increasing complexity is what makes the emergence of ToM possible, rather than an additional component of post-LCA-ga brain-readiness. I have not developed a rigorous basis for this suggestion, but here I offer some possible lines of support.

First, consider that emotions have both internal roles and external, social roles (Arbib & Fellous, 2004):

– *Internally, emotions support the organization of behavior.* Emotions affect prioritization, action selection, attention, and learning.
– *Externally, emotional expression serves social coordination,* communicating clues as to one's possible course of behavior, allowing others to adjust their behavior accordingly.

For example, anger may mobilize the body's resources in preparation for a fight while the *expression* of anger warns others that a fight may be imminent, so they should prepare to fight, to submit, or to flee – or, in terms of a behavior more specifically human, to conciliate. Internal and external aspects of emotion have co-evolved in animals.

Charles Darwin's (1872) concern with relating facial expressions of certain animals to human emotional expression placed the *external role* of emotion within a comparative, and thus implicitly evolutionary, framework. This in turn set the stage for the notion that the internal role of emotions in affecting behavior has an evolutionary base with a strong social component. In terms of our present concerns, in view of the Sally-Anne task, the suggestion here is that the capacity for mindreading is not a separate human biological evolute but, rather, emerges in modern humans as a cultural extension of the ancient prehuman and even preprimate ability to read the behavioral disposition of others from both their emotional expressions and their behavioral "tells." For modern humans, the stories we hear (and the accompanying pictures) can expose us to a range of human and nonhuman behaviors and an otherwise scarcely accessible understanding of "what the other person is thinking and how that will affect their behavior."

Navigation in time

Any animal that needs to forage for its food, find places to sleep at night, or know where it may be safe from prey must be capable of navigation in space. In particular, this involves, at least in simple form, having brain structures (and not just a hippocampus: Arbib, 2021b, Section 6.3) that support a cognitive map: knowing an increasing number of significant places in its environment and the means to get from one to another. Navigation may involve both the memory of habitual routes and the ability to get to a suitable place via a detour when the habitual route is disrupted (for example, by the presence of a predator). In addition, we know that such a cognitive map is malleable. Certain animals can cache food at specific places during one season and recover them at another season, and this cognitive map is updated each time they animal empties one of its caches or visits the cache and discovers that another animal has removed the food (see Olton et al., 1980, for a related lab study of rats in mazes; while Smith & Reichman, 1984, review studies of the evolution of food caching by birds and mammals).

However, what I doubt (but lack the literature review to assess) is that non-human animals can explicitly remember the relationship between the "when" of each caching or the neural capability – even were it able to pantomime or flexibly communicate in some other way – to create a narrative concerning its search for food. Certainly, animal behavior is regulated internally by their circadian rhythm and externally by the ability – in many cases thanks to genetic underpinnings – to adapt to the changing seasons. But this is very different from the sort of time *modern* humans have become enculturated to, in which the time of year is specified by the date on a calendar, and the time of day is specified down to the minute or even more precisely by a clock.

The issue, then, is to what extent biological changes are required to extend a support for cognitive mapping and navigation in space to support the form of mental time travel (Corballis, 2013, 2018, 2019; Suddendorf & Corballis, 1997, 2007) that is exhibited in the human ability to tell autobiographical narratives based on episodic memory.[14] The key point is that for most of human history, time could be related to the season of the year, the phase of the moon, and the time of day as determined by the position of the sun. Thus the first step towards autobiographical memory would have been to expand the sort of memory involved in food caching to associate particular events not only with the place where they occurred but also with the approximate time they occurred, in the above limited sense. The catch of course is that this is still far from a precise chronology. Our everyday experience equips us with the ability to know that certain events must precede certain others, just as birds know in what order to build their nests, or early humans knew that they must set the fire before they could cook, and find the food by foraging or hunting before they could cook it.

---

14. My suggestion is that this ability underwrites the broader ability for fictional or third person narrative. Steps towards analysis of the relevant cognitive neuroscience relating memory and imagination may be found in (Arbib, 2020a, 2021b, Chapter 10).

But how do we get from that to the ordering of several events over longer time periods? Perhaps the answer is that the development of autobiographical memory and the development of narrative constitute yet another expanding spiral. We may place events in some sort of order because we realized when a later event occurred how it was made possible in part by an earlier event – where later and earlier have no basis in an abstract chronology – or because our memory expanded (and perhaps this required genetic change) to allow a memory of one event to incorporate the fact that we could remember another event at that time.

A cognitive map must link significant places to what it is that makes them significant and to the means to get from one place to another, and must also include the ability to update that significance into the cognitive map. Autobiographical memory may depend in part on having access to the current cognitive map but by being able to recall, additionally, how it relates to earlier versions of the map and even events related to some of the changes. It will be further enriched by including an understanding of how various episodes might be related, an understanding that can be enriched when a new episode evokes associatively some earlier episode which then triggers contemplation of the relationship between those episodes which may, or may not, in due course offer a new linkage within autobiographical memory.

The above sketch, for both mindreading and navigation in time, suggests how these skills may have built upon brain resources shared with other creatures. The challenge for future research is to understand to what extent these depended on the evolution of novel genetic specifications for neural circuitry, enlargements of coupled brain regions, and/or the impact of cultural evolution on circuitry already in place in LCA-ga. In any case, it is clear that the full capacity of modern humans for these two skills could only have been achieved through an expanding spiral that links them with language in all its diversity and with our expanding capacity for narrative in particular.

Conclusion

The paper has had a two-fold purpose: To develop a critique of the strengths and weaknesses of the Mirror System Hypothesis (MSH) of the evolution of language, a hypothesis that assigns great importance to pantomime in providing the basis for a visuo-manual scaffolding for the emergence of language; and to locate the MSH view of pantomime within the context of other studies of pantomime presented at the Toruń meeting, the majority of which formed the basis for papers in this volume. We reiterated that different studies use certain key terms in different ways. Thus MSH distinguishes complex and simple imitation (and the imitation literature offers further nuances) while the Toruń talks explored different aspects of pantomime which the taxonomy in this paper labels *great-ape pantomime, "basic" pantomime, ad hoc pantomime, ur-pantomime, theatrical pantomime*, and *modern ad hoc pantomime*. In the same spirit, the reader is urged to note the specific definitions of *ritualization, conventionalization, protosign* and *protolanguage* since they may differ from those used elsewhere.

A basic exposition of MSH recalls the key distinction between a language-ready brain and a language-using brain (the transition involves cultural evolution along a continuum from protolanguages to languages), and revisits issues such as the relation of hand and voice in the emergence of language. We focus on the processes that took our ancestors from ur-pantomime to protolanguages (and introduce the notion of micro-protolanguages), with a brief discussion of the emergence of grammars (sets of constructions that build upon the lexicon). We modulate the hypothesis by offering a more nuanced assessment of the difference between ritualization and conventionalization, with the latter marking a translation toward parity in the use of gestures as shared by a community.

A discussion of pedagogy related to the chapter by Gärdenfors clarifies the difference between cases where the trajectory of movement of a pantomime is modulated flexibly to convey variations in application of a skill and where the pantomime loses that flexibility in assuming a form that conveys some useful meaning – a process that may rest on ritualization that yields private variants and conventionalization that yields protosigns shared within a community. Finally, responding to ideas on ur-pantomime and modern ad hoc pantomime summarized by Ferretti et al. and studies of modern ad hoc pantomime by Zlatev et al. (this volume), respectively, we note that prior work on MSH has assessed the evolution of lexicons and constructicons but has neglected issues related to narrative. We suggest that ur-pantomime could support only "protonarratives" and that the challenge of telling more complex stories was one of the drivers for developing new words and constructions. Finally, we debate whether the MSH account of the language-ready brain needs to be augmented to support mindreading and navigation in time – it certainly supports navigation in space.

Acknowledgements

This talk is based in great part on talks presented by the author and others at the Workshop "Perspectives on Pantomime" at Nicolaus Copernicus University in Toruń, November 18–19, 2021. My thanks to Sławomir Wacewicz and Przemysław Żywiczyński for inviting me to take part, to Monika Boruta-Żywiczyńska and Przemysław Żywiczyński for their hospitality in Toruń, and to Johan Blomberg for his work on both the meeting and this book. Further thanks to Przemysław Żywiczyński for extensive and constructive comments on an earlier draft, and to

References

Aboitiz, F. (2013). How did vocal behavior "take over" the gestural communication system? *Language and Cognition*, 5, 167–176.

Abramova, E. (2018). The role of pantomime in gestural language evolution, its cognitive bases and an alternative. *Journal of Language Evolution*, 3(1), 26–40.

Almor, A., Smith, D.V., Bonilha, L., Fridriksson, J., & Rorden, C. (2007). What is in a name? Spatial brain circuits are used to track discourse references. *NeuroReport*, 18, 1215–1219.

Arbib, M.A. (1989). *The Metaphorical Brain 2: Neural Networks and Beyond*. New York: Wiley-Interscience.

Arbib, M.A. (2005a). From monkey-like action recognition to human language: an evolutionary framework for neurolinguistics. *The Behavioral and brain sciences*, 28(2), 105–124; discussion 125-167-105–124; discussion 125–167. Retrieved from http://www.ncbi.nlm.nih.gov/pubmed/16201457.

Arbib, M.A. (2005b). Interweaving protosign and protospeech: Further developments beyond the mirror. *Interaction Studies: Social Behavior and Communication in Biological and Artificial Systems*, 6, 145–171.

Arbib, M.A. (2012). *How the brain got language: The mirror system hypothesis*. Oxford University Press.

Arbib, M.A. (2013). Complex Imitation and the Language-Ready Brain. *Language and Cognition*, 5(2–3), 273–312.

Arbib, M.A., Ganesh, V., & Gasser, B. (2014). Dyadic Brain Modeling, Ontogenetic Ritualization of Gesture in Apes, and the Contributions of Primate Mirror Neuron Systems. *Phil Trans Roy Soc B*, 369 (1644), 20130414.

Arbib, M.A. (2016a). How language evolution reshaped human consciousness. In R.R. Poznanski, J.A. Tuszynski, & T.E. Feinberg (Eds.), *Biophysics of Consciousness: A Foundational Approach* (pp. 87–128). Singapore: World Scientific.

Arbib, M.A. (2016b). Towards a computational comparative neuroprimatology: Framing the language-ready brain. *Physics of Life Reviews*, 16, 1–54.

Arbib, M.A. (2018). In support of the role of pantomime in language evolution. *Journal of Language Evolution*, 3(1), 41–44.

Arbib, M.A. (2020a). From spatial navigation via visual construction to episodic memory and imagination. *Biological Cybernetics*, 114, 139–167.

Arbib, M.A. (2021a). The aboutness of language and the evolution of the construction-ready brain. In A. Lock, C. Sinha, & N. Gontier (Eds.), *The Oxford handbook of symbolic evolution*. Oxford University Press.

Arbib, M.A. (2021b). *When brains meet buildings: A conversation between neuroscience and architecture*. Oxford University Press.

Arbib, M.A. (2024). From the protolanguage spectrum to the underlying bases of language. In D. Adone & A. Gramatke (Eds.), *On the evolution, acquisition and development of syntax* (pp. to appear). Cambridge University Press.

Arbib, M.A. (Ed.) (2020b). *How the brain got language: Towards a new road map.* John Benjamins.

Arbib, M.A., & Bickerton, D. (Eds.). (2010). *The emergence of protolanguage: Holophrasis vs compositionality.* John Benjamins Publishing Company.

Arbib, M.A., & Fellous, J.M. (2004). Emotions: from brain to robot. *Trends Cogn Sci*, 8(12), 554–561. Retrieved from http://www.ncbi.nlm.nih.gov/entrez/query.fcgi?cmd=Retrieve &db=PubMed&dopt=Citation&list_uids=15556025.

Arbib, M.A., Fragaszy, D.M., Healy, S.D., & Stout, D. (2023). Tooling and Construction: From Nut-Cracking and Stone-Tool Making to Bird Nests and Language *Current Research in Behavioral Sciences*, 5, 100121.

Arbib, M.A., Liebal, K., & Pika, S. (2008). Primate Vocalization, Gesture, and the Evolution of Human Language. *Current Anthropology*, 49(6), 1053–1076. http://www.journals.uchicago .edu/doi/abs/10.1086/593015.

Arbib, M.A., & Rizzolatti, G. (1997). Neural expectations: a possible evolutionary path from manual skills to language. *Communication and Cognition*, 29, 393–424.

Arbib, M.A., Schweighofer, N., & Thach, W.T. (1995). Modeling the Cerebellum: From Adaptation to Coordination. In D.J. Glencross & J.P. Piek (Eds.), *Motor Control and Sensory-Motor Integration: Issues and Directions* (pp. 11–36). Amsterdam: North-Holland Elsevier Science.

Armstrong, D.F., Stokoe, W.C., & Wilcox, S.E. (1995). *Gesture and the Nature of Language.* Cambridge: Cambridge University Press.

Baron-Cohen, S., Leslie, A.M., & Frith, U. (1985). Does the autistic child have a "theory of mind"? *Cognition* 21, 37–46.

Barnard, A. (2013). Cognitive and social aspects of language origins. In C. Lefebvre, B. Comrie, & H. Cohen (Eds.), *New perspectives on the origins of language* (pp. 53-71). John Benjamins.

Barton, R.A. (2012). Embodied cognitive evolution and the cerebellum. *Philosophical Transactions of the Royal Society B: Biological Sciences*, 367(1599), 2097–2107.

Bergman, T.J., Beehner, J.C., Cheney, D.L., & Seyfarth, R.M. (2003). Hierarchical classification by rank and kinship in baboons. *Science*, 302(5648), 1234–1236. Retrieved from http://www.ncbi.nlm.nih.gov/entrez/query.fcgi?cmd=Retrieve&db=PubMed&dopt =Citation&list_uids=14615544.

Bergman, T.J., Beehner, J.C., Painter, M.C., & Gustison, M.L. (2019). The speech-like properties of nonhuman primate vocalizations. *Animal Behaviour*, 151, 229–237.

Bickerton, D. (2009). *Adam's Tongue. How Humans Made Language, How Language Made Humans.* Hill & Wang.

Brown, S. (this volume). The Pantomimic Origins of the Narrative Arts. In P. Żywiczyński, S. Wacewicz, M. Boruta-Żywiczyńska, & J. Blomberg (Eds.), *Perspectives on pantomime: evolution, development, interaction.* John Benjamins.

Butterworth, G. (2003). Pointing is the royal road to language for babies. In S. Kita (Ed.), *Pointing: Where language, culture, and cognition meet* (pp. 9–33). Erlbaum.

Byrne, R. W. (1999). Imitation without intentionality. Using string parsing to copy the organization of behaviour. *Animal cognition*, 2, 63–72.

Byrne, R. W. (2003). Imitation as behaviour parsing. *Philos Trans R Soc Lond B Biol Sci*, 358(1431), 529–536.

Byrne, R. W., & Russon, A. E. (1998). Learning by imitation: a hierarchical approach. *Behav Brain Sci*, 21(5), 667–684; discussion 684–721. Retrieved from http://www.ncbi.nlm.nih.gov/entrez/query.fcgi?cmd=Retrieve&db=PubMed&dopt=Citation&list_uids=10097023.

Corballis, M. C. (2002). *From hand to mouth, the origins of language*. Princeton University Press.

Corballis, M. C. (2013). Wandering tales: evolutionary origins of mental time travel and language. *Frontiers in Psychology*, 4.

Corballis, M. C. (2018). Mental travels and the cognitive basis of language. *Interaction Studies*, 19(1–2), 352–369.

Corballis, M. C. (2019). Language, memory, and mental time travel: An evolutionary perspective. *Frontiers in Human Neuroscience*, 13.

Coudé, G., & Ferrari, P. F. (2018). Reflections on the differential organization of mirror neuron systems for hand and mouth and their role in the evolution of communication in primates. *Interaction Studies*, 19(1–2), 38–53.

Croft, W. (2000). *Explaining language change: An evolutionary approach*. Longman.

Darwin, C. (1872). *The expression of the emotions in man and animals (republished in 1965)*. University of Chicago Press.

Dediu, D., & Levinson, S. C. (2018). Neanderthal language revisited: not only us. *Current Opinion in Behavioral Sciences*, 21, 49-55.

Dehaene, S., Pegado, F., Braga, L. W., Ventura, P., Filho, G. N., Jobert, A., ... Cohen, L. (2010). How Learning to Read Changes the Cortical Networks for Vision and Language. *Science*, 330(6009), 1359–1364.

Diessel, H. (2013). Where does language come from? Some reflections on the role of deictic gesture and demonstratives in the evolution of language. *Language and Cognition*, 5(2-3), 239-249.

Donald, M. (1991). *Origins of the modern mind: Three stages in the evolution of culture and cognition*. Harvard University Press.

Fay, N., Arbib, M., & Garrod, S. (2013). How to bootstrap a human communication system. *Cognitive Science*, 37(7), 1356–1367.

Fay, N., Lister, C. J., Ellison, T. M., & Goldin-Meadow, S. (2014). Creating a communication system from scratch: gesture beats vocalization hands down. *Frontiers in Psychology*, 5, 354.

Ferrari, P. F., Gerbella, M., Coudé, G., & Rozzi, S. (2017). Two different mirror neuron networks: The sensorimotor (hand) and limbic (face) pathways. *Neuroscience*.

Ferretti, F. (2021). The narrative origins of language. In N. Gontier, A. Lock, & C. Sinha (Eds.), *Oxford Handbook of Human Symbolic Evolution* . Oxford University Press.

Ferretti, F., Adornetti, I., & Chiera, A. (2022). Narrative pantomime: A protolanguage for persuasive communication. *Lingua*, 271 103247.

Ferretti, F., Chiera, A., & Adornetti, I. (this volume). Narrative and Pantomime at the Origin of Language. In P. Żywiczyński, S. Wacewicz, M. Boruta-Żywiczyńska, & J. Blomberg (Eds.), *Perspectives on pantomime: evolution, development, interaction*. John Benjamins.

Fitch, W. T. (2010). *The evolution of language*. Cambridge University Press.

Fogassi, L., Coudé, G., & Ferrari, P. F. (2013). The extended features of mirror neurons and the voluntary control of vocalization in the pathway to language. *Language and Cognition*, 5, 145–155.

Gärdenfors, P. (2021). Demonstration and pantomime in the evolution of teaching and communication. *Language & Communication*, 80, 71–79.

Gärdenfors, P. (2023). The relations of demonstration and pantomime to causal reasoning and event cognition. In P. Żywiczyński, S. Wacewicz, M. Boruta-Żywiczyńska, & J. Blomberg (Eds.), *Perspectives on pantomime: evolution, development, interaction*. John Benjamins.

Gärdenfors, P. (this volume). The relations of demonstration and pantomime to causal reasoning and event cognition. In P. Żywiczyński, S. Wacewicz, M. Boruta-Żywiczyńska, & J. Blomberg (Eds.), *Perspectives on pantomime: evolution, development, interaction*. John Benjamins.

Gärdenfors, P., & Högberg, A. (2017). The Archaeology of Teaching and the Evolution of Homo docens. *Current Anthropology*, 58(2), 188–208.

Gibson, J. J. (1979). *The ecological approach to visual perception*. Houghton Mifflin.

Ghazanfar, A. A., & Eliades, S. J. (2014). The neurobiology of primate vocal communication. *Current Opinion in Neurobiology*, 28(0), 128–135.

Ghazanfar, A. A., Liao, D. A., & Takahashi, D. Y. (2019). Volition and learning in primate vocal behaviour. *Animal Behaviour*, 151, 239–247.

Girard-Buttoz, C., Zaccarella, E., Bortolato, T., Friederici, A. D., Wittig, R. M., & Crockford, C. (2022). Chimpanzees produce diverse vocal sequences with ordered and recombinatorial properties. *Communications Biology*, 5(1), 410.

Halina, M., Rossano, F., & Tomasello, M. (2013). The ontogenetic ritualization of bonobo gestures. *Animal cognition*, 16(4), 653–666.

Hartmann, S., & Pleyer, M. (2021). Constructing a protolanguage: reconstructing prehistoric languages in a usage-based construction grammar framework. *Philosophical Transactions of the Royal Society B: Biological Sciences*, 376(1824), 20200200.

Heine, B., & Kuteva, T. (2007). *The genesis of grammar: A reconstruction*. Oxford University Press.

Heintz, C., Karabegovic, M., & Molnar, A. (2016). The co-evolution of honesty and strategic vigilance. *Frontiers in Psychology*, 7.

Herman, D. (2013). *Storytelling and the sciences of mind*. The MIT Press.

Hewes, G. W. (1973). Primate communication and the gestural origin of language. *Current Anthropology*, 12(1–2), 5–24.

Humphrey, N. K. (1970). What the frog's eye tells the monkey's brain. *Brain Behavior and Evolution*, 3, 324–337.

Iriki, A., & Taoka, M. (2012). Triadic (ecological, neural, cognitive) niche construction: a scenario of human brain evolution extrapolating tool use and language from the control of reaching actions. *Philosophical Transactions of the Royal Society B: Biological Sciences*, 367, 10–23.

Itti, L., & Arbib, M.A. (2006). Attention and the minimal subscene. In M.A. Arbib (Ed.), *Action to language via the mirror neuron system* (pp. 289–346). Cambridge University Press.

Jackson, J. H. (1878–79). On affections of speech from disease of the brain. *Brain*, 1, 304–330.

Kemmerer, D. (2005). Against innate grammatical categories. *Behavioral Brain Sciences*, http://www.bbsonline.org/Preprints/Arbib-05012002/Supplemental/.

Kendon, A. (1980). Gesticulation and speech: Two aspects of the process of utterance. In M.R. Key (Ed.), *Relationships of the verbal and nonverbal communication* (pp. 207–228). Mouton.

Kline, M.A. (2015). How to learn about teaching: An evolutionary framework for the study of teaching behavior in humans and other animals. *Behavioral and Brain Sciences*, 38, 10.1017/S0140525X14000090, e14000031 (14000071 pages with commentaries).

Leslie, A.M. (1987). Pretense and representation: The origins of "theory of mind. *Psychological Review*, 94, 412–426.

MacNeilage, P.F., & Davis, B.L. (2005). The frame/content theory of evolution of speech: A comparison with a gestural-origins alternative. *Interaction Studies*, 6(2), 173–199. Retrieved from http://www.sign-lang.uni-hamburg.de/BibWeb/LiDat.acgi?ID=63566.

Marentette, P., Inaba, C., & Petrie, R. (this volume). Symbolic Distancing in Three-Year-Old Children's Pantomime. In P. Żywiczyński, S. Wacewicz, M. Boruta-Żywiczyńska, & J. Blomberg (Eds.), *Perspectives on pantomime: evolution, development, interaction.* John Benjamins.

McNeill, D. (1998). Speech and gesture integration. In J.M. Iverson & S. Goldin-Meadow (Eds.), *The nature and functions of gesture in children's communication* (pp. 11–27). Jossey Bass.

Mineiro, A., & Moita, M. (this volume). The pantomime roots of Sao Tome and Principe Sign Language In P. Żywiczyński, S. Wacewicz, M. Boruta-Żywiczyńska, & J. Blomberg (Eds.), *Perspectives on pantomime: evolution, development, interaction.* John Benjamins.

Müller, C. (2014). Gestural modes of representation as techniques of depiction. In C. Müller, A. Cienki, E. Fricke, S. Ladewig, M.D., & S. Tessendorf (Eds.), *Body-language-communication: An international handbook on multimodality in human interaction* (pp. 1687–1702). De Gruyter Mouton.

Müller, C. (2016). From mimesis to meaning: A systematics of gestural mimesis for concrete and abstract referential gestures. In J. Zlatev, G. Sonesson, & P. Konderak (Eds.), *Meaning, mind and communication: Explorations in cognitive semiotics* (pp. 211–226). Peter Lang.

Olton, D.S., Becker, J.T., & Handelmann, G.E. (1980). Hippocampal function: Working memory or cognitive mapping? *Physiol. Psychol.*, 8, 239–246.

Pleyer, M. (2023). The role of interactional and cognitive mechanisms in the evolution of (proto)language(s). *Lingua*, 282, 103458.

Poizner, H., Klima, E., & Bellugi, U. (1987). *What the hands reveal about the brain.* MIT Press.

Polich, L. (2005). *The emergence of the deaf community in Nicaragua: "With sign language you can learn so much".* Gallaudet University Press.

Rizzolatti, G., & Arbib, M.A. (1998). Language within our grasp. *Trends in Neurosciences*, 21(5), 188–194. Retrieved from http://www.ncbi.nlm.nih.gov/pubmed/9610880.

Russon, A. (2016). Reconsidering great ape imitation and pantomime: Comment on "Towards a computational comparative neuroprimatology: Framing the language-ready brain" by M.A. Arbib. *Physics of Life Reviews*.

Russon, A. (2018). Pantomime and imitation in great apes: Implications for reconstructing the evolution of language. *Interaction Studies*, 19(1–2), 200–215.

Russon, A., & Andrews, K. (2010). Orangutan pantomime: Elaborating the message. *Biology Letters*.

Russon, A., & Andrews, K. (2011). Pantomime in great apes: Evidence and implications. *Communicative & Integrative Biology*, 4(3), 315–317. Retrieved from http://www .landesbioscience.com/journals/cib/article/14809/.

Sandler, W. (2013). Vive la différence: Sign language and spoken language in language evolution. *Language and Cognition*, 5(2–3), 189–203.

Schmid, H.-J. (2015). A blueprint of the Entrenchment-and- Conventionalization Model. *Yearbook of the German Cognitive Linguistics Association*, 3(1), 3–26.

Senghas, A., Kita, S., & Özyürek, A. (2004). Children creating core properties of language: Evidence from an emerging sign language in Nicaragua. *Science*, 305, 1779–1782.

Sibierska, M., Boruta-Żywiczyńska, M., Żywiczyński, P., & Wacewicz, S. (2023). What's in a mime? An exploratory analysis of predictors of communicative success of pantomime *Interaction Studies*, 23:2, 289–321,

Slocombe, K. E., Waller, B. M., & Liebal, K. (2011). The language void: The need for multimodality in primate communication research. *Animal Behaviour*, 81(5), 919–924. Retrieved from http://www.sciencedirect.com/science/article/pii/S0003347211000558.

Smith, C. C., & Reichman, O. J. (1984). The evolution of food caching by birds and mammals. *Annual Review of Ecology and Systematics*, 15, 329–351. Retrieved from http://www.jstor .org/stable/2096952.

Sperber, D., Clément, F., Heintz, C., Mascaro, O., Mercier, H., Origgi, G., & Wilson, D. (2010). Epistemic vigilance. *Mind & Language*, 25(4), 359–393.

Stokoe, W. C. (2001). *Language in hand: Why sign came before speech*. Gallaudet University Press.

Stout, D. (2010). Possible relations between language and technology in human evolution. In A. Nowell & I. Davidson (Eds.), *Stone tools and the evolution of human cognition* (pp. 159–184). University Press of Colorado.

Stout, D. (2011). Stone toolmaking and the evolution of human culture and cognition. *Philosophical Transactions of the Royal Society B: Biological Sciences*, 366, 1050–1059.

Stout, D. (2018). Archaeology and the evolutionary neuroscience of language: the technological pedagogy hypothesis. *Interaction Studies*, 19(1–2), 256–271.

Stout, D., Toth, N., Schick, K., & Chaminade, T. (2008). Neural correlates of Early Stone Age toolmaking: technology, language and cognition in human evolution. *Philos Trans R Soc Lond B Biol Sci*, 363(1499), 1939–1949. Retrieved from http://www.ncbi.nlm.nih.gov /entrez/query.fcgi?cmd=Retrieve&db=PubMed&dopt=Citation&list_uids=18292067.

Suddendorf, T., & Corballis, M. C. (1997). Mental time travel and the evolution of the human mind. *Genet Soc Gen Psychol Monogr*, 123(2), 133–167. Retrieved from http://www.ncbi .nlm.nih.gov/entrez/query.fcgi?cmd=Retrieve&db=PubMed&dopt=Citation&list_uids =9204544

Chapter 1. Pantomime within and beyond the evolution of language 57

Suddendorf, T., & Corballis, M.C. (2007). The evolution of foresight: What is mental time travel, and is it unique to humans? *Behavioral and Brain Sciences*, 30, 299–351.

Tomasello, M., & Call, J. (1997). *Primate Cognition*. Oxford University Press.

Tomasello, M. (2008). *Origins of Human Communication*. The MIT Press.

Wacewicz, S., & Żywiczyński, P. (2018). Language origins: The platform of trust, cooperation, and turn-taking. *Interaction Studies*, 19(1–2).

Wray, A. (1998). Protolanguage as a holistic system for social interaction. *Language & Communication*, 18, 47–67.

Wray, A. (2000). Holistic utterances in protolanguage: The link from primates to humans. In C. Knight, M. Studdert-Kennedy, & J. Hurford (Eds.), *The evolutionary emergence of language: Social function and the origins of linguistic form* (pp. 285–202). Cambridge University Press.

Zlatev, J., Persson, T., & Gärdenfors, P. (2005). Bodily mimesis as "the missing link" in human cognitive evolution. *Lund University Cognitive Studies*, 121, 1–45.

Zlatev, J., Sibierska, M., & Żywiczyński, P. (this volume). Can pantomime narrate? A cognitive semiotic approach. In P. Żywiczyński, S. Wacewicz, M. Boruta-Żywiczyńska, & J. Blomberg (Eds.), *Perspectives on pantomime: evolution, development, interaction*. John Benjamins.

Zlatev, J., Żywiczyński, P., & Wacewicz, S. (2020). Pantomime as the original human-specific communicative system. *Journal of Language Evolution*, 5(2), 156–174.

Zukow-Goldring, P. (2012). Assisted imitation: first steps in the seed model of language development. *Language Sciences*, 34(5), 569–582.

Zukow-Goldring, P., & Arbib, M.A. (2007). Affordances, effectivities, and assisted imitation: Caregivers and the directing of attention. *Neurocomputing*, 70, 2181–2193.

Żywiczyński, P., Wacewicz, S., & Sibierska, M. (2018). Defining Pantomime for Language Evolution Research. *Topoi*, 37(2), 307–318.

CHAPTER 2

The relations of demonstration and pantomime to causal reasoning and event cognition

Peter Gärdenfors
Lund University

This article deals with the role of showing in the evolution of human communication and how it has developed into telling. When a communicator is showing, she is performing, not just doing. Demonstration is a combination of doing and showing, while pantomime is only showing. I make a distinction between pantomime used for teaching and pantomime for communication and argue that this is central for the transition from showing to telling. Telling involves describing an event or a series of events. The evolutionary question then becomes: Which selective forces made hominins extend their communication from doing to showing and then to telling? My answer is that showing and, to a larger degree, telling require advanced forms of causal cognition and event representation that are not found in other species. I analyze how event cognition is relevant for demonstration and pantomime and how this type of cognition influences the structure of language.

Keywords: demonstration, pantomime, cognitive evolution, causal cognition, event representation

1. Introduction: From doing to showing to telling

Consider a homely scene where a wife expresses the following in front of her husband: "I am dead tired of all your <makes snoring sound> and your <makes farting sound>. I am leaving you <walks out through the door and slams it>." This example illustrates that three kinds of communication can occur more or less simultaneously: *Doing* (walking out, slamming door), *showing* (imitating snoring and farting sounds) and *telling* (informing husband that she is leaving).

From an evolutionary point of view, doing is universal in all animals, but showing and telling are more limited. In this article, I will be concerned with the

https://doi.org/10.1075/ais.12.02gar
© 2024 John Benjamins Publishing Company

role of showing in the evolution of human communication and how it has developed into telling. My focus will be on demonstration and pantomime. Earlier, I have made a distinction between pantomime used for teaching and pantomime used for more general communication and argued that the former is evolutionarily older than the latter (Gärdenfors, 2021a). I shall show that this step is central for the transition from showing to telling.

Of course, most forms of doing in animals (including humans) are not communicative. A communicative form of doing requires that the actor *intends* that other individuals observe the action and uses the observation to draw pragmatic consequences. Demonstration fits into the communicative form of doing. The distinction between showing and telling is something that many people learn in kindergarten. Haiman discusses the transitions from doing to showing and then to telling. He writes that "before showing became telling, doing had to become showing" (Haiman, 2018: 73). When a communicator is showing something, she is *performing*, not just doing, and she often becomes one with what she depicts (Quinto-Pozos, 2007). As I will argue later in the article, demonstration is a combination of doing and showing, while pantomime is only showing. The communicator is playing a role on the world's stage (Haiman, 2018: 47) by not just doing something, but by *representing* doing something. In contrast, when the communicator is telling, she is inviting the listeners to share mental representations of some events. In other words, she expresses her inner "event stage." As I shall argue, demonstration is showing but pantomime can be both showing and telling.

Apes show by using gestures, for example, showing where they want to be groomed or which copulation posture they prefer (Pika & Mitani, 2006; Tanner & Byrne, 1996). However, they seldom tell, that is, describe an event or a series of events. Lyn et al. (2014) provide a list of examples of declarative gestures produced by encultured apes. These gestures, however, almost exclusively correspond to one-word utterances and are therefore limited as cases of telling.

In contrast, telling is ubiquitous in humans, even from a very young age. From an evolutionary point of view the question then becomes: What selective forces made hominins extend their communication from doing to showing and then to telling? A follow-up question is why the process did not occur among other apes.

In brief, my answer to these questions is that showing, and to a larger degree telling, require advanced forms of causal cognition and event representation that are not found in other apes. I have argued that demonstration and pantomime have been central for the evolution of teaching among hominins (Gärdenfors & Högberg, 2017; Gärdenfors, 2017; Gärdenfors, 2021a).

I have, together with Marlize Lombard, argued that human tool use and tool manufacture lead to a development of human causal cognition (Lombard & Gärdenfors, 2017; Gärdenfors & Lombard, 2018; Gärdenfors & Lombard, 2021;

Lombard & Gärdenfors, 2021) and then to mental representations of events. My main goal here is to expose the relations between demonstration and pantomime on the one hand and causal cognition and event cognition on the other. In this way, the evolutionary prerequisites for demonstration and pantomime to appear among hominins will become clearer.

In Sections 2 and 3, I give brief presentations of the aspects of causal cognition and event representations, respectively, that are relevant for my arguments. In Section 4, characteristic features of demonstration and pantomime are described. Section 5 then analyses how event cognition is relevant for demonstration and pantomime. Section 6, finally, shows how the role of event cognition in demonstration and pantomime influences the structure of language.

2. Causal cognition

2.1 Non-human primate reasoning about causes

As background to the evolution of causal cognition in hominins, I present a summary of some of the findings concerning the abilities of non-human primates to reason with causes. It is useful to distinguish between *cued* (externally signaled) and *detached* mental representations Gärdenfors (1995; 2003). A cued representation refers to something in the current (or recently experienced) external situation of the experiencer. When, for example, a chimpanzee uses two stones to crack nuts, it represents one of them as support (anvil) and the other as the hammerstone. By contrast, detached representations stand for objects or events that are not present in the subject's current or recent external context and thus cannot trigger the representation directly. An individual that has detached representations can create an inner world where consequences of different actions or events can be simulated (Decety & Grèzes, 2006; Gärdenfors, 2003; Grush, 1997). Such simulations are central to abstract causal reasoning.

Being able to reason from inanimate effects to non-present causes seems, at present, to be unique to humans. There exist a plethora of experiments and observations that indicate that primates cannot infer physical causes from their effects (e.g., Cheney & Seyfarth, 1990; Povinelli, 2000). For example, Cheney & Seyfarth's (1990) experiments with vervet monkeys showed that when catching sight of a predator, they emit warning cries. However, the same monkeys do not react to detached visual signs such as the trail of a snake or the carcass of an antelope in a tree, which indicates a leopard in the vicinity. Thus, while non-human primates are dependent on direct physical effects, it seems that the aptitude for causal understanding based on inanimate or indirect sensory cues evolved only in the hominin species (Calvin & Bickerton, 2000; Shaw-Williams, 2014; Stuart-Fox, 2015).

In a study comparing the nut-cracking performances of humans and chimpanzees (Boesch et al., 2017), the result was that humans understood how to apply force to extract numerous nut species through using hammerstones. In contrast, chimpanzees only applied hammerstones to Panda nuts, although they regularly eat hard Irvingia nuts using their teeth. Chimpanzees in other groups and regions cracked different nut types with hammerstones (Hannah & McGrew, 1987; Morgan & Abwe, 2006), but a single group does not use hammerstones to obtain several food sources. This example illustrates how humans, in contrast to chimpanzees, reason more abstractly about the causal effects of applying tool-assisted forces. This allows humans to generalize a particular solution to a wider range of problems.

2.2 Human reasoning about forces

The human capacity to reason about physical forces develops early in infants. Michotte (1963) showed that if one object moving on a screen came into contact with another object and the other object began moving in the same direction, then adults perceived a causal relation between the two movements. If the second object only began moving 500 milliseconds after the collision, however, the time difference eliminated the impression of causality. Michotte's experiments were performed with six-month-old infants by Leslie and Keeble (1987). The result was that the infants reacted differently to the two types of events. Leslie (1995) argues that infants have a special system in their brains for mapping the "forces" of objects. Wolff and his collaborators (Wolff, 2008, 2012; Wolf & Shepard, 2013; Wolff & Thorstad, 2017; Wolff et al., 2010) have collected further evidence supporting that people can directly perceive the forces that lie behind different kinds of events. The upshot is that the sensory input generated by the movements of an object is sufficient for the brain to automatically calculate the forces that lead to the movements (Runesson, 1994).

As humans, we do not only reason about physical forces but also about how *psychological* and *social* factors influence us. The increasing complexity of hominin societies has generated a highly developed "theory of mind," that is, an understanding of how our emotions, desires, intentions and beliefs lead to different kinds of interactions between people (Gärdenfors, 2003, 2007; Premack & Woodruff, 1978, Tomasello 2014, Tomasello et al. 2007; see also Arbib (this volume) and Ferretti (this volume)). By observing the actions of ourselves and others and through various processes of social learning, we infer the state of mind of other humans under the hypothesis that their minds are similar to our own.

In such cases, we do not perceive the cause of another's actions physically, but use our understanding of their inner state as a detached causal variable for their behaviors. This involves a separation of perceptual similarities from the causal ones that are determined from emotions, desires, intentions and beliefs. A theory of mind is, therefore, an important extension of human causal cognition (Lombard & Gärdenfors, 2021).

3. Event cognition

3.1 A cognitive model of events

I next turn to the relation between causal thinking and event cognition. A considerable part of human cognition depends on representations of events (Gärdenfors, 2014; Gärdenfors et al., 2018; Gärdenfors and Warglien, 2012; Radvansky & Zacks, 2014; Warglien et al., 2012). We use events in causal reasoning, planning and communication.

An event typically contains information about an agent who is the *cause* of an action that leads to a result related to a patient (see also Zlatev, (this volume)). Agents and patients are object categories with different properties. It is assumed that an agent is able to act, which amounts to exerting forces. Although event representations generally contain an agent, some do not involve any, for example, events of raining, falling and growing. A representation of an event may also contain other "thematic roles" such as instrument, recipient and beneficiary (Dowty, 1991; Levin & Rappaport Hovav, 2006).

The core idea of the event model presented in Gärdenfors (2014) and Gärdenfors and Warglien (2012) is that an event is represented by two vectors – the force of an action that drives the event, and the result of the force (see Figure 1). The first vector is determined by the strength and direction of the force and the second by the beginning and end states of an object undergoing a change. More formal details of the model can be found in Gärdenfors (e.g., 2014; Gärdenfors et al., 2018; & Gärdenfors & Warglien, 2012)

Figure 1. The main components of an event representation

An action is modelled as a force vector (or a pattern of force vectors as in running). The result of an event is modelled as a change vector representing the change of properties of the patient (Gärdenfors, 2014; Warglien et al., 2012). For example, when Karl (the agent) lifts (the force vector) a heavy stone (the patient),

Chapter 2. Demonstration and pantomime relations to causal reasoning and event cognition

the force exerted makes the stone move in a vertical (the result vector). Or, when Victoria cooks the pasta, the result is that the pasta becomes soft. When the result vector is just a point (a null vector), that is, when the result is no change, then the event is a *state*. An important feature of the event model is that it captures a basic sense of causation: The action of the agent causes the change in the patient. The distinction between forces and changes of states (Wolff, 2007, 2012) results in the fundamental division between causes and effects.

3.2 Event cognition and planning

A central question is what were the evolutionary selective factors that resulted in the extended human dependence on mental representations of events. A main part of the answer is that detached event cognition allows us to speculate about potential outcomes of actions, test and re-adjust our imaginative hypotheses, and shift attention from one target to another (see e.g., Donald, 1991; Gärdenfors, 2003). It thereby allows generalization by comparing the force and result in one event with those of another (Gärdenfors et al., 2018).

In particular, different forms of *planning* involve event cognition. A plan consists of a series of imagined actions as causes together with the expected effects of the actions. For example, a hunter imagines a series of events, some related to the previous movements of an animal, some as part of a plan to kill or catch it. An anthropological example is that when hunting with poisoned arrows, Kalahari San engage in "speculative tracking," using working hypotheses gained from the signs left by an animal, socially and experientially gained knowledge about the behaviors of the animal and of the landscape in which the tracking is taking place (Liebenberg, 1990). This imagination may also involve an understanding of the mental state of the animal, for example, that it is exhausted because it is overheated or dehydrated or that it is afraid because it is hunted. Based on these imagined reconstructions, the hunter creates predictions in ever changing circumstances involving a continuous cognitive process (Lombard & Gärdenfors, 2017). The upshot is that event cognition allows for more complex causal thinking to evolve.

4. Demonstration and two kinds of pantomime

Relating causal thinking and event cognition on the one hand and demonstration and pantomime on the other may seem tenuous. In this and the following section, however, I argue that demonstration and pantomime depend crucially on the two related forms of cognition.

Demonstration and pantomime are present, from an early age, in all human societies (Csibra & Gergely, 2009). Showing a child what can be done with a toy, how to tie her shoelaces or how to eat with fork and knife, are well-known everyday examples. The properties of demonstration and, in particular, pantomime have been analyzed in a series of articles (Abramova, 2018; Arbib, 2012, 2018, this volume; Brown et al., 2019, this volume; Gärdenfors, 2017, 2020, 2021a; Zlatev et al., 2020; Żywiczyński et al., 2018). Here I present a summary of my own work together with some further aspects.

4.1 Characteristics of demonstration

When a teacher demonstrates to a learner how to perform a certain task, the following criteria are characteristic:

1. The demonstrator *actually performs* the actions involved in the task.
2. The demonstrator makes sure that the learner *attends* to the series of actions.
3. The demonstrator's *intention* is that the learner perceives the right actions in the correct sequence.
4. The demonstrator *exaggerates* and slows down some of the actions in order to facilitate for the learner to perceive important features.

In comparing animal communication and demonstration, it is not difficult to find several striking differences (Żywiczyński et al., 2018). Demonstration is

5. voluntary in the sense that the act is realized by bodily motion that is under conscious control,
6. honest since there is no point in deceiving a learner,
7. directed to one or a few individuals.
8. involves an intention on part of the teacher that the learner *imitates* what is demonstrated.

In other words, the actions of the teacher "points to" the actions that the learner is supposed to perform later (see also Zlatev, this volume).

Doing something practical is performing an action. Demonstrating how to do the same thing is *showing* (as well as doing). In both cases, the actions are causes that lead to perceptually available results. For the onlooker, the causal relation between the actions and the effect is therefore manifest and no advanced causal cognition is involved. In other words, for demonstration, causal cognition concerns directly perceived effects of the actions. Furthermore, a demonstration is an event that simultaneously points to a future event (the action sequence to be performed by the learner).

Chapter 2. Demonstration and pantomime relations to causal reasoning and event cognition **65**

To be sure, the learning effect can be obtained without explicit demonstration. An individual can by emulation (Tomasello, 1999; Heyes, 2021) strive to obtain the same result. This is what happens when young chimpanzees emulate the behavior of the adults when, for example, cracking a nut. However, the intentional teaching aspects of conditions (2), (3), (4) and (7) ensure that demonstration is more efficient for learning than mere emulation.

4.2 Characteristics of pantomime

Turning to pantomime, it also fulfills criteria (2)–(7). The crucial difference concerns criterion (1) (see also Zlatev, this volume, and Wacewicz & Żywiczyński, this volume), since what characterizes pantomime is:

1'. The teacher performs the *movements* of the actions in the task without actually performing the actions.

Consequently, in pantomime, the actual actions are not performed, but some more or less simplified version of them. For example, if I am teaching someone how to knap a Levallois flake, I cannot perform the crucial strike of the hammer stone, because there will then be nothing left to do for the learner. Or, if I am teaching how to harpoon fish, I cannot complete the thrust of the harpoon, because then the fish will be caught (or it will be gone) and, again, there is no practicing opportunity left for the learner (see also Arbib, this volume).

Demonstration and pantomime are, when they are used in a teaching context, *triadic* in that there is an actor (the teacher), an intended recipient (the learner) and a referent (cf. Zlatev, this volume; and Żywiczyński et al., 2018). In both cases the referent is the action that the teacher wants the learner to perform. In the case of demonstration, the intended action by the learner should be *as similar as possible* to the action performed by the teacher.

An important property of both demonstration and pantomime is that they are *productive*, that is, new forms can easily be introduced and understood by the recipients. No animal communication system seems to have this property. In line with this, Arbib (2012: 217, also this volume) writes:

> [B]uilding on the skill for complex imitation, pantomime provided the breakthrough from having just a few gestures to the ability to communicate freely about a huge variety of situations, actions, and objects. Where imitation is the generic attempt to reproduce movements performed by another, whether to master a skill or simply as part of a social interaction, pantomime is performed with the intention of getting the observer to think of a specific action or event.

4.3 Theory of mind and communicative intentions

Demonstration as well as pantomime build on components of a theory of mind both for the teacher and for the learner. It presumes that the teacher understands the lack of knowledge in the learner and that the learner experiences that there is something to learn from the teacher. Criterion (2) – that the teacher makes sure that the learner attends the demonstration or the pantomime – entails that the teacher sees that the learner sees the action. The learner also sees that the teacher sees the act performed. Hence, demonstration and pantomime both presume that the interactors can achieve *joint attention* (Brinck, 2004; Gärdenfors, 2007; Tomasello, 1999) to the act performed by the teacher. As regards non-human animals, the ability to engage in joint attention is limited and has not, so far, been established conclusively. Thus, the evolution of joint attention is one of the factors behind why humans are, more or less, alone in exhibiting intentional teaching by demonstration and pantomime. Another factor related to a theory of mind is that when the learner tries to imitate the demonstrated action, the teacher can also react with evaluative feedback, and, if necessary, with renewed demonstration (Gärdenfors & Högberg, 2017).

For a pantomime, the learner must also understand that the teacher intends the pantomime to *stand for* a real action. This means that the teacher intends that the learner realizes that the action to be performed by the learner should be *different from* the one performed by the teacher. Seemingly, this is a small difference between demonstration and pantomime, but one that is crucial for the evolution of communication. This difference can be analyzed in relation to the following criterion (Zlatev et al., 2005):

Communicative sign function: The agent intends for the act to stand for some action, object or event for an addressee, and for the addressee to realize that the act is a representation.

The representational relation is different in demonstration compared to pantomime. For demonstration, the act performed by the teacher is a representation only to the extent that the teacher demonstrates what is *characteristic* for the actions to be performed. Demonstration therefore fulfills the communicative sign function only as a marginal case. On the other hand, in pantomime, the learner must realize that the action intended by the teacher is *not* the one performed by the teacher but a similar one, often involving tools or other objects.

As a consequence, pantomime does not fulfill condition (8) for demonstration, but rather the following:

8ʹ. Pantomime involves an intention that the learner performs a different action than what is demonstrated, but an action that involves the same bodily movements as in the pantomime.

Pantomime for teaching is not acting, but it is still showing (although this does not hold for pantomime for communication as will be seen). The crucial difference compared to demonstration is that in pantomime the learner only observes a representation of a cause (the mimed actions), but does not perceive the effects of the action. Therefore, learners must *imagine* the effects on their own. Consequently, the effects are represented in a detached way. In cases where instruments used in the action or the object affected is not part of the pantomime, reasoning about forces and their effects become necessary. Hence, this form of causal cognition is required for correctly interpreting a pantomime. The upshot is that more extensive causal cognition is involved in interpreting pantomime.

If the learner has previously witnessed a real action or a demonstration involving the same action as in the pantomime, it may be comparatively easy to imagine the effects and thereby understand the causal connection. In cases where the *goal* of the actions performed in a pantomime is shared between teacher and learner, the situation is ameliorated since the learner will assume that the actions will lead to effects that satisfy the common goal. If, however, the pantomime represents actions that are new to the learner, then the causal reasoning is more complicated and the learner may not be certain concerning which effects will follow. For example, you may want to pantomime how to start your old-fashioned boat motor that has a string that is pulled, but if the learner is not familiar with strings on boat motors, she may fail to understand the pantomime.

From an evolutionary perspective, an interesting question is whether non-human animals, in particular apes, can pantomime. Researchers are divided on whether other apes (wild or in captivity) have the capacity. On the one hand, some researchers are skeptical, for example Zuberbühler (2013:136), who claims about apes that "pantomiming is conspicuously absent, apart from isolated anecdotes." On the other hand, Russon and Andrews (2011) have collected evidence for pantomiming in orangutans. Their subjects lived in a rehabilitation camp and were used to communicate with humans. They conclude that "pantomime could have been within the grasp of the common human-great ape ancestor" (2010:316). Their notion of pantomime is broader than the one used here and includes cases of deception (Wacewicz & Żywiczyński, this volume). Furthermore, most of the evidence they analyze conforms to the observation by Gibson (2013:209) that apes only gesture about requested actions of the addressee. In line with this, 17 out of 18 examples in Russon and Andrews (2010) were classified as imperative so that what is referred to by the gesturer is the behavior of the addressee (see e. g. Boesch & Tomasello, 1998). Hence these cases are pantomimes for instruction. Only one case – enacting a shared memory – is classified as declarative: This is the case of the female Kikan acting out how the person next to her had doctored her foot the previous week, when it was cut. This episode, however, may also be interpreted as an apprentice showing that she has learnt what to do. Hence, it is not unequivocal that it is a case of pantomime for communication.

4.4 Pantomime for communication

My position is that the evolutionary origin of pantomime is an extension of demonstration in teaching contexts. However, pantomime can also be used for other more directly *communicative* purposes, for example, in describing a plan, in narrating, or as part of telling a joke (for narrative uses of pantomime, see also the chapters by Arbib, Brown, Ferretti, & Zlatev in this volume). Of course, pantomime for teaching is a form of communication, but its pragmatic function is that of *showing* that leads to a *request*: "Please copy these movements when you do the real thing!" Pantomime for communication, in contrast, has the function of *telling*. The shift from one type of pantomime to the other may be difficult to perceive, but it is a crucial step in the evolution of communication.

The distinction between the two types also shows up when determining what is the *intention* of a pantomime. There seem to be two different forms: Firstly, I can pantomime an *action* that I want you to perform. This is the typical case in a teaching situation. Secondly, I can pantomime an action as part of a *message* (statement, command, warning, narrative, play element, etc). In the gesture literature, the second type of pantomime (communicative act) has been in focus. A demonstration can also be seen as a gesture, but it is only used for the first type of intention. However, since pantomime can also be used for the second type, it has a broader use than demonstration.

I have previously suggested that pantomime for teaching is evolutionarily prior to pantomime for communication. In this section, I present some arguments for this claim. More detailed versions of these and other arguments are presented in Gärdenfors (2021a) together with a table summarizing the differences between demonstration, pantomime for teaching and pantomime for communication.

In the more communicative uses of pantomime, the detachment is more extensive. In narrating, the reference of a pantomime can be far detached in space and time, and may refer to imaginary events (see also Ferretti, this volume). Hence, using pantomime in communication involves a widening of the mental horizons in space and time, and therefore involves more extended cognitive capacities. Such a widening of horizons is necessary for planning for cooperation (Gärdenfors, 2010, 2012).

A second difference is that when pantomime is used for teaching it is *proto-imperative*, that is, it functions as an injunction for the learner to perform a similar action, while, when a pantomime is used in narration, it is a *proto-declarative* that functions as information for the persons attending to the pantomime. In terms of the four levels of communication proposed by Winter (1998) (see also Gärdenfors 2014), pantomiming in a teaching context functions as an instruction, while pantomiming in a narrative context is part of forming a *common ground* (Clark, 1992) which is a more advanced form of communication.

Brown et al. (2019) propose a distinction between *egocentric* and *allocentric* pantomimes. In egocentric pantomime, the reference is determined in relation to the miming person's own body. This is the typical form used in a teaching context (Brown, this volume). In contrast, in allocentric pantomime the body of the mimer enacts another person or object located at another place. For example, one can pantomime a galloping horse by a full body movement or by using a hand to show a galloping movement.

What is important here is that allocentric pantomimes are more detached than egocentric, since in egocentric pantomime the body of the mimer is representing itself, while in allocentric pantomime the mimer uses the body as a representation of another person, animal or object. Therefore, egocentric pantomime requires less cognitive processing than allocentric forms.

Finally, pantomime for communication opens up for more advanced forms of pretense (Marentette, this volume). For example, I can exploit allocentric pantomime to enact two different individuals in narrating or in a play sequence. Pretense play, which appears around 12 months of age in human children, is strongly connected to the ability to pantomime (Leslie, 1987). When you pretend, you use two perspectives on the same object or action – your perception (of the object or action) and an imagined version of it (Leslie, 1987, Nielsen, 2012). For example, when a boy pretends that a box is a car, he knows that it is a box but she simultaneously "sees" it as a car that he 'drives' with. By suppressing his perception, he uses his imagination instead. The pantomimes that are part of pretense play is an enactment of a *story* that unfolds during the activities. Play stories are *participatory* rather than narrative. Furthermore, play often involves turn-taking, which seldom occurs in pantomime. It should be noted that pretense typically does not involve any form of teaching.

In contrast, demonstration does not presume the double worlds that are required for pantomime. Pantomime can therefore be described as a combination of demonstration and pretense (see also Pleyer et al., 2021). This indicates that demonstration puts less demand on the cognitive capacities of the demonstrator.

5. The role of event cognition in pantomime for communication

In linguistics, the components of events have mainly been modeled in terms of *thematic roles* such as agent, patient, recipient, goal, instrument, etc (Dowty, 1991). Rissman and Majid (2019) note about such roles that "[t]o some they are universal components of core knowledge, to others they are scholarly fictions without psychological reality." In their analysis of thematic roles, they find strong evidence that there is a universal bias to represent agent and patient, while for other roles there is only mixed evidence. This result fits well with the model of event cognition presented in Section 3, where agents and patients are central components.

Sometimes the different components of an event are *explicit* in a communicative situation, since they can be directly perceived, but sometimes they are *implicit* in the sense that they must be inferred by the attendee. In demonstration, the agent and patient are both explicit, since they are both part of the demonstrated action. The agent of the action that is intended to be performed is the learner. This means that a demonstration is both an event in itself and a communicated event since the communication contains an agent, a patient, an action and a result. In brief, all these four components are *shown* in a demonstration – and thus explicit, so there is no need to tell about them. This also means that both cause and effect are visible in a demonstration, so only basic causal cognition is required.

When pantomime is used for teaching, the agent is similarly explicit in the pantomime (and is understood to be the learner in the intended action). In most cases, the result of the action, that is the change in the patient, cannot be observed. Since the intended action is not performed but just represented, the pantomime can then be made clearer by *telling* about the result – and thus making it explicit – by an additional gesture or by a word (or conventional sign). Sometimes the patient is part of the pantomime (and then it is clear that the same or a similar patient is supposed to be part of the intended action). In some cases, however, the patient is not part of the pantomime. Typical examples of absent patients are when boxing, fencing or golf swings are taught.

In contrast, when pantomime takes on its communicative function, the represented actor need not be the individual performing the pantomime, as it is in pantomime for teaching, but can be another individual or even a non-human animal or a non-animate object. The pantomime is then allocentric and it is often the case that neither the intended agent, nor the patient is explicit. There is then a need to tell *who* is the agent of the communicated action and sometimes also *what* is the object acted on or *where* it is performed (Brown et al., 2019). In order to achieve a representation of an event, the action depicted in the pantomime must thus be complemented with signs (gestures or sounds) that make the agent, the object and the location explicit (for comparisons with sign languages, see Mineiro

Chapter 2. Demonstration and pantomime relations to causal reasoning and event cognition 71

& Moita, this volume). Since the miming is allocentric, the actions (force patterns) represented in the pantomime must be interpreted in a broader way than in pantomime for teaching where the action always is that of the mimer. Therefore, a more abstract form of causal cognition is required when interpreting pantomimes with communicative function.

A final comment is that a difference between pantomime for communication and protolanguage is that in protolanguage every component of the event is implicit and either the action or the result (or both) must be communicated (see also Arbib, this volume). The typical linguistic tools to express actions and results are *verbs*. Linguists have argued that verbs can be divided into manner verbs (expressing actions) and result verbs (Levin & Rappaport Hovav, 2005; Gärdenfors, 2014). The causal cognition involved in understanding a narrative is therefore even more abstract than in pantomime for communication since not even the force patterns are perceivable but only represented by manner verbs.

The arguments of this section are summarized in Table 1.

Table 1. The explicitness of the components of event cognition in different forms of communication

	Agent	Patient	Action	Result
Demonstration	explicit	explicit	explicit	explicit
Pantomime for teaching	explicit	sometimes implicit	explicit	often implicit
Pantomime for communication	implicit	implicit	explicit	implicit
Protolanguage	implicit	implicit	implicit	implicit

In the table, the components that are marked as explicit can be shown, while those that are marked as implicit must be told (by gesture or speech). I submit that the ordering of the rows corresponds to the evolutionary order of the four forms of communication. The upshot is that, as one goes down the rows in the table, the required form of communication gradually shifts from showing to telling.

6. Influence on the structure of language

In contrast to demonstration and pantomime, where the actions are represented by continuous movements, the structure of language (spoken or sign language) contains representations which are discrete. Talmy (2006) views this as an argument against gestural origins of language. He argues that if language had evolved from gestures, it would be expected that a continuation of analogue representations was found. Since spoken languages almost exclusively depends on recombinations of discrete elements, this suggests, according to Talmy, that language is grounded in the vocal and auditory channels.

I do not agree. In this section, I present a sketch of how and why this discretization took place as a part of a story of how language evolved out of demonstration and pantomime.

In line with the arguments in the previous section, I suggest that the discretization of language can be derived from the structure of event cognition (cf. fractionation in Arbib, this volume). My hypothesis is that as a consequence of cognitively representing events in terms of the four main factors of the model presented in Section 3 – agent, patient, action, result – the structure of communication is to a large extent determined by these factors.

One piece of evidence supporting the hypothesis is that, unlike adolescents and adults, children segment and linearize their gestures and thereby make them more language-like (Clay et al., 2014; see also Marenetette, this volume). Adolescents and adults simultaneously express manner and path when gesturing, while the children more often temporally separate manner and path. "Path" is a form of result, representing changes in the spatial domain (Gärdenfors, 2014). In this way, children bring fundamental structural elements of their event thinking into their communication mechanisms. This tendency can also be seen in sign language. For example, in the Nicaraguan Sign Language, simultaneously representing manner and result has been replaced by discrete representations so that "rolling down" is expressed by a combination of a sign for "roll" and another for "down" (Kegl et al., 1999; Senghas et al., 2004; see also Mineiro & Moita, this volume). Such discretization may be a fundamental generator of syntactic structures, since the order and the structure of the components become increasingly dependent on conventions.

A second form of support may come from conventionalization processes. Before there was proto-language with an emphasis on speech, there might have been proto-sign with an emphasis on gestures (I do not believe that there ever was a human communication system that was purely gestural or purely vocal). Here proto-sign refers to a communication system that is conventional and combinatorial. In the transition to proto-sign, pantomimes were exapted from their original function as a request to copy in a teaching situation (an imperative) to having an informative function as part of a planning process, as part of a narrative, or as an element in a play sequence (see Arbib, 2018; Brown et al., 2019). In this way, they formed the seeds for a larger set of conventionalized gestures. Unlike a pantomime, a convention must be *learned*.

The result of a communicative convention is a *label* (gesture or word). Gelman and Roberts (2017) analyze the role of labels in cultural inheritance. They argue that "category labels work in an almost paradoxical way to ensure stability in the transmission process, but simultaneously to permit and even foster conceptual change" (2017: 7900). Sabbagh and Henderson (2007) argue that children's understanding that words meanings are conventional makes their word learning more efficient. What has been called the *principle of conventionality* (E. V. Clark, 1992) states that words are efficient tools for communication when the form–meaning associations are known, shared, and expected within a language community. Already one-and-a-half-year-old children exploit this principle in their learning of language (Graham et al., 2016; Sabbagh & Henderson, 2007).

7. Conclusion

This article has been concerned with how human communication crossed the Rubicon from showing to telling. According to the analysis presented here, this occurred when pantomime was exapted from being used in teaching to a more general communicative use. I have argued that these transitions would not be possible unless there had been an evolution of causal cognition and event representation that, among other things, allow human reason about forces and their effects. I have also given examples of how the role of event cognition determines certain components of syntax.

References

Abramova, E. (2018). The role of pantomime in gestural language evolution, its cognitive bases and an alternative. *Journal of Language Evolution*, 3(1), 26–40.

Arbib, M. A. (2012). *How the brain got language: The mirror system hypothesis* (Vol. 16). Oxford University Press.

Arbib, M. A. (2018). In support of the role of pantomime in language evolution. *Journal of Language Evolution*, 3(1), 41–44.

Boesch, C., Bombjaková, D., Boyette, A., & Meier, A. (2017). Technical intelligence and culture: Nut cracking in humans and chimpanzees. *American Journal of Physical Anthropology*, 163(2), 339–355.

Boesch, C., & Tomasello, M. (1998). Chimpanzee and human cultures. *Current Anthropology*, 39(5), 591–614.

Brinck, I. (2004). The pragmatics of imperative and declarative pointing. *Cognitive Science Quarterly*, 3(4), 429–446.

Brown, S., Mittermaier, E., Kher, T., & Arnold, P. (2019). How pantomime works: Implications for theories of language origin. *Frontiers in Communication*, 4, 9.

Calvin, W.H., & Bickerton, D. (2000). *Lingua ex machina: Reconciling Darwin and Chomsky with the human brain*. MIT Press.

Cheney, D., & Seyfarth, R. (1990). Attending to behaviour versus attending to knowledge: Examining monkeys' attribution of mental states. *Animal Behaviour*, 40(4), 742–753.

Clark, E.V. (1992). Conventionality and contrast: Pragmatic principles with lexical consequences. *Lehrer and Kittay, 1992a*, 171–188.

Clark, H.H. (1992). *Arenas of language use*. University of Chicago Press.

Clay, Z., Pople, S., Hood, B., & Kita, S. (2014). Young children make their gestural communication systems more language-like: Segmentation and linearization of semantic elements in motion events. *Psychological Science*, 25(8), 1518–1525.

Csibra, G., & Gergely, G. (2009). Natural pedagogy. *Trends in cognitive sciences*, 13(4), 148–153.

Decety, J., & Grèzes, J. (2006). The power of simulation: imagining one's own and other's behavior. *Brain Research*, 1079(1), 4–14.

Donald, M. (1991). *Origins of the modern mind: Three stages in the evolution of culture and cognition*. Harvard University Press.

Dowty, D. (1991). Thematic proto-roles and argument selection. *Language*, 67(3), 547–619.

Gärdenfors, P. (1995). Cued and detached representations in animal cognition. *Behavioural Processes*, 35(1–3), 263–273.

Gärdenfors, P. *How homo became sapiens: On the evolution of thinking*; Oxford University Press: Oxford, UK, 2003.

Gärdenfors, P. (2007). Evolutionary and developmental aspects of intersubjectivity. In H. Liljenström, & P. Århem (Eds.), *Consciousness transitions* (pp. 281–305). Elsevier Science BV.

Gärdenfors, P. (2010). What are the benefits of broad horizons? In *The Benefit of Broad Horizons: Intellectual and Institutional Preconditions for a Global Social Science* (pp. xiii–xx). Brill Academic Publishers.

Gärdenfors, P. (2012). The cognitive and communicative demands of cooperation. In J. van Eijck, & R. Verbrugge (Eds.), *Games, actions and social software* (pp. 164–183). Springer.

Gärdenfors, P. (2014). *The geometry of meaning: Semantics based on conceptual spaces*. MIT Press.

Gärdenfors, P. (2017). Demonstration and pantomime in the evolution of teaching. *Frontiers in Psychology*, 8, 415.

Gärdenfors, P. (2020). From pantomime to protolanguage. *Paradigmi*, 38(2), 251–268.

Gärdenfors, P. (2021). Causal reasoning and event cognition as evolutionary determinants of language structure. *Entropy*, 23(7), 843.

Gärdenfors, P., & Högberg, A. (2017). The archaeology of teaching and the evolution of Homo docens. *Current Anthropology*, 58(2), 188–208.

Gärdenfors, P., Högberg, A. (2021) Evolution of intentional teaching. In N. Gontier, A. Lock & C. Sinha (Eds.), *The Oxford Handbook of Human Symbolic* Evolution. Oxford University Press. .

Gärdenfors, P., Jost, J., & Warglien, M. (2018). From actions to effects: Three constraints on event mappings. *Frontiers in Psychology*, 1391.

Gärdenfors, P., & Lombard, M. (2018). Causal cognition, force dynamics and early hunting technologies. *Frontiers in Psychology*, 9, 87.

Gärdenfors, P., & M. Lombard. (2021). 'The Evolution of Human Causal Cognition, In T. Wynn, K.A. Overmann, & F.L. Coolidge (Eds), *The Oxford Handbook of Cognitive Archaeology*.(pp. .

Gärdenfors, P., & Warglien, M. (2012). Using conceptual spaces to model actions and events. *Journal of Semantics*, 29(4), 487–519.

Gelman, S.A., & Roberts, S.O. (2017). How language shapes the cultural inheritance of categories. *Proceedings of the National Academy of Sciences*, 114(30), 7900–7907.

Gibson, K.R. (2013). Talking about apes, birds, bees, and other living creatures: Language evolution in the light of comparative animal behaviour. *The Evolutionary Emergence of Language: Evidence and Inference*, 17, 204.

Gómez, J.C. (2007). Requesting gestures in captive monkeys. *Gestural Communication in Nonhuman and Human Primates*, 10, 83.

Graham, S.A., Gelman, S.A., & Clarke, J. (2016). Generics license 30-month-olds' inferences about the atypical properties of novel kinds. *Developmental Psychology*, 52(9), 1353.

Grush, R. (1997). The architecture of representation. *Philosophical Psychology*, 10(1), 5–23.

Haiman, J. (2018). *Ideophones and the Evolution of Language*. Cambridge: Cambridge University Press.

Hannah, A.C., & McGrew, W.C. (1987). Chimpanzees using stones to crack open oil palm nuts in Liberia. *Primates*, 28(1), 31–46.

Heyes, C. (2021). Imitation and culture: What gives? *Mind & Language*, 1–22.

Kegl, J., Senghas, A., & Coppola, M. (1999). Creation through contact: Sign language emergence and sign language change in Nicaragua. *Language creation and language change: Creolization, diachrony, and development*, 179–237.

Leslie, A.M. (1995). A theory of agency. In D. Sperber, D. Premack & J.A. Premack (Eds.), *Causal Cognition: A Multidisciplinary Debate* (pp. 121–141). Oxford University Press.

Leslie, A.M. (1987). Pretense and representation: The origins of "theory of mind.". *Psychological review*, 94(4), 412.

Leslie, A.M., & Keeble, S. (1987). Do six-month-old infants perceive causality? *Cognition*, 25(3), 265–288.

Levin, B., & Hovav, M.R. (2005). *Argument realization*. Cambridge University Press.

Liebenberg L. (1990). *The art of tracking: The origin of science*. David Philip Publishers.

Lombard, M., & Gärdenfors, P. (2017). Tracking the evolution of causal cognition in humans. *Journal of Anthropological Sciences* 95, 1–18.

Lombard, M., & Gärdenfors, P. (2021). Causal cognition and theory of mind in evolutionary cognitive archaeology. *Biological Theory*, 1–19.

Lyn, H., Russell, J.L., Leavens, D.A., Bard, K.A., Boysen, S.T., Schaeffer, J.A., & Hopkins, W.D. (2014). Apes communicate about absent and displaced objects: methodology matters. *Animal Cognition*, 17(1), 85–94.

Michotte, A. (1963) *The Perception of Causality*. Methuen

Morgan, B.J., & Abwe, E.E. (2006). Chimpanzees use stone hammers in Cameroon. *Current Biology*, 16(16), R632–R633.

Nielsen, M. (2012). Imitation, pretend play, and childhood: Essential elements in the evolution of human culture? *Journal of Comparative Psychology*, 126(2), 170.

Pika, S., & Mitani, J. (2006). Referential gestural communication in wild chimpanzees (Pan troglodytes). *Current Biology*, 16(6), R191–R192.

Pleyer, M., Wacewicz, S., & Żywiczyński, P. (2021). Shared evolutionary and developmental foundations of pretence and pantomime, abstract for *Protolang 7*, Düsseldorf.

Povinelli, D.J. (2000). *Folk physics for apes: The chimpanzee's theory of how the world works*. Oxford University Press.

Premack, D., & Woodruff, G. (1978). Does the chimpanzee have a theory of mind?. *Behavioral and brain sciences*, 1(4), 515–526.

Quinto-Pozos, D. (2007). Can constructed action be considered obligatory? *Lingua*, 117(7), 1285–1314.

Radvansky, G.A., & Zacks, J.M. (2014). *Event cognition*. Oxford University Press.

Rissman, L., & Majid, A. (2019). Thematic roles: Core knowledge or linguistic construct? *Psychonomic Bulletin & Review*, 26(6), 1850–1869.

Runesson, S. (1994). Perception of biological motion: The KSD-principle and the implications of a distal versus proximal approach. In G. Jansson, S.S. Bergström & W. Epstein (Eds.), *Perceiving Events and Objects* (pp. 383–405). Lawrence Erlbaum Associates.

Russon, A., & Andrews, K. (2011). Orangutan pantomime: elaborating the message. *Biology Letters*, 7(4), 627–630.

Sabbagh, M.A., & Henderson, A.M. (2007). How an appreciation of conventionality shapes early word learning. *New Directions for Child and Adolescent Development*, 2007(115), 25–37.

Senghas, A., Kita, S., & Özyürek, A. (2004). Children creating core properties of language: Evidence from an emerging sign language in Nicaragua. *Science*, 305(5691), 1779–1782.

Shaw-Williams, K. (2014). The social trackways theory of the evolution of human cognition. *Biological Theory*, 9(1), 16–26.

Stuart-Fox, M. (2015). The origins of causal cognition in early hominins. *Biology & Philosophy*, 30(2), 247–266.

Talmy, L. (2006). Recombinance in the evolution of language. In A. Cangelosi, A.D.M. Smith, & K. Smith (Eds.), *The evolution of language: Proceedings of the 6th International Conference* (pp. 449–451). World Scientific Publishing Company.

Tanner, J.E., & Byrne, R.W. (1996). Representation of action through iconic gesture in a captive lowland gorilla. *Current Anthropology*, 37(1), 162–173.

Tomasello, M. (1999). *The cultural origins of human cognition*. Harvard University Press.

Tomasello, M. (2014). *A natural history of human thinking*. Harvard University Press.

Tomasello, M., Carpenter, M., & Liszkowski, U. (2007). A new look at infant pointing. *Child Development*, 78(3), 705–722.

Warglien, M., Gärdenfors, P., & Westera, M. (2012). Event structure, conceptual spaces and the semantics of verbs. *Theoretical Linguistics*, 38(3–4), 159–193.

Winter, S. (1998). *Expectations and linguistic meaning*. Lund University Cognitive Science 73.

Wolff, P. (2007). Representing causation. *Journal of Experimental Psychology: General*, 136(1), 82.

Wolff, P. (2008). Dynamics and the perception of causal events. In S. Thomas & J. Zacks. (Eds.), *Understanding events: How humans see, represent, and act on events* (pp. 555–587). Oxford University Press.

Wolff, P. (2012). Representing verbs with force vectors. *Theoretical Linguistics*, 38, 237–248.

Wolff, P., Barbey, A. K., & Hausknecht, M. (2010). For want of a nail: How absences cause events. *Journal of Experimental Psychology: General*, 139(2), 191.

Wolff, P., & Shepard, J. (2013). Causation, touch, and the perception of force. In *Psychology of learning and motivation* (Vol. 58, pp. 167–202). Academic Press.

Wolff, P.; Thorstad, R. (2017). Force dynamics. In M. R. Waldmann (Ed.), *The Oxford handbook of causal reasoning* (pp. 147–167). Oxford University Press.

Zlatev, J., Persson, T., Gärdenfors, P. (2005). Bodily mimesis as 'the missing link' in human cognitive evolution, Lund: *Lund University Cognitive Studies* 121.

Zlatev, J., Żywiczyński, P., & Wacewicz, S. (2020). Pantomime as the original human-specific communicative system. *Journal of Language Evolution*, 5(2), 156–174.

Zuberbühler, K. (2013). Acquired mirroring and intentional communication in primates. *Language and Cognition*, 5(2–3), 133–143.

Żywiczyński, P., Wacewicz, S., & Sibierska, M. (2018). Defining pantomime for language evolution research. *Topoi*, 37(2), 307–318.

CHAPTER 3

Narrative and pantomime at the origin of language

Francesco Ferretti
Roma Tre University

The present chapter proposes a pantomimic account of language origin resting on a persuasive/narrative conception of human communication. Relying on the twofold constraint of the cognitive architectures responsible for the processing of the mental content and of the material resources for expressing that content, I suggest that pantomime represented an ideal means to convey proto-narrative representations in the absence of verbal language. Although representing an early effective form of protolanguage because of its narrative persuasive power, pantomime shows its limits in sustaining a more sophisticated type of communication characterizing face-to-face conversation. In this context, the need to engage in an arguing-counterarguing dialectics might have created new selective pressures towards complex syntactic structures able to support argumentative forms of persuasion.

Keywords: pantomime, narrative, language origin, persuasion, protolanguage

1. Introduction

The present chapter deals with the idea that language origin is related to two main intertwined topics: (i) the cognitive resources responsible for processing mental content and (ii) the expressive resources in charge of communicating mental content. In general, my idea is that the way humans mentally represent reality (the way they think) constrains the way they communicate. More schematically, my claim is that the form of mental representation constrains the form of the expressive system through which humans communicate their thoughts to others. In light of these considerations, understanding how humans think (how they represent reality) is a precondition for the study of language origin. In this chapter, my aim is twofold: to analyze the systems devoted to the processing of mental content and

https://doi.org/10.1075/ais.12.03fer
© 2024 John Benjamins Publishing Company

to determine to what degree the form of representations realized by those systems can act as a constraint on the evolution of an effective communicative system.

My specific claim is that humans, unlike other animals, represent reality through story-like thoughts (for a different perspective on this topic see Arbib, this volume; Brown, this volume; Gärdenfors, this volume; Zlatev et al., this volume). The hypothesis that human thought is inherently narrative in its structure has important consequences for our view on how humans communicate their own thoughts to others: if thought has a narrative form, then the most effective way to express thoughts should be by means of a system suitable for telling stories. In the present work, I claim that in the early stages of human communication, long before the advent of verbal language, pantomime was the expressive system used to convey narrative forms of thought. Since my proposal is that the specific way in which humans express their thoughts is deeply constrained by the kind of thoughts they can entertain, the first step of my argument is linked to the study of the nature of the mental representations characterizing the form of human thoughts.

2.   Mental stories

The nature of mental representation has been a central topic in cognitive science since its beginning (e.g., Fodor, 1975). A major question of the debate on this topic concerns understanding what kind of representational format can convey the content of thoughts. Such a question is crucial for the origin of language since it relies on both the nature of the content that has to be expressed in communication and the issue of the expressive system able to convey that content.

In this chapter, it is my claim that humans, unlike other animals, represent reality in the form of stories. A growing body of models has supported the hypothesis that there exists a narrative basis behind mental representation. For example, Niles (1999) defines humans in terms of *Homo narrans*, while Thompson (2010) considers them storytellers. Dennett (1991) highlights the crucial role of narrative in shaping consciousness, White (1980; 1981) its importance in the representation of reality, while Tomasello (2019) proposes that storytelling contributes to making us specifically humans. That said, Bruner (1991) is the scholar who most decisively contributed to the debate on the narrative foundation of thought. In his view, "we organize our experience and our memories of human happenings mainly in the form of narratives – stories, excuses, myths, reasons for doing and not doing, and so on" (Bruner, 1991: 4).

From an adaptive perspective, the ability to represent experience in a narrative form has clear cognitive advantages, especially concerning the possibility to extend knowledge beyond the here-and-now, a phenomenon known in linguistic terms as "displacement" (see also Arbib, this volume; Gärdenfors, this volume; Zlatev et al., this volume; for a perspective of the communicative costs involved in displacement see Wacewicz & Żywiczyński, this volume). In line with Aristotle, Corballis (2015, 2017) emphasizes that stories are extraordinarily powerful means of knowledge compared to other forms of mental representations because they allow us to imagine possible worlds that are different from the current one. In his view, indeed,

> if there is anything that defines our species as unique (...) it is the telling of stories, and the invention of language as the means of doing so. (...) Other animals, even rats, may well undertake limited mental travels through limited domains, but stories allow us to expand our mental lives to unlimited horizons.
>
> (Corballis, 2015: 107)

Consistent with Corballis, I will propose a twofold hypothesis. First, narrative thought predates storytelling; second, humans invented storytelling to share narrative thoughts with others.[1]

That said, the thesis of the primacy of thought over language is anything but uncontroversial. Before exploring in more detail how this thesis can be placed in the context of language origins, it is worth examining the arguments of those who oppose it. The first challenge for my proposal comes from the idea that the ability to represent reality in a narrative form depends on the capacity to tell stories through language, i.e., the idea that the narrative foundation of representation originates from the linguistic practices characterizing human communication As this is a widely prevailing idea, my argument starts with an analysis thereof.

---

1. In emphasizing the constraints that the form of mental representation imposes on the form of the expressive system, in this chapter we do not intend to underestimate the feedback effect of the expressive system on thought. This is an important effect involving the transformation of mental content from its proto-narrative structure (the result of the direct functioning of the narrative brain) into a fully-fledged narrative form (the result of the restructuring of the mental content exerted by the expressive system). That said, from the cognitive perspective assumed in this chapter, the constraints imposed by thought on the construction of the expressive system precede, both temporally and logically, the role of the expressive system in the construction of thought. For an alternative proposal to the one advocated for in this chapter, see Zlatev et al., this volume).

2.1 Narrative as a social practice

The first issue to be addressed is whether the ability to tell stories constitutes the product or the precondition of a narrative representation of reality. In general, in the context of language origins, there is this idea that language is communication-driven (Gärdenfors, this volume), or more generally, interaction-driven (Levinson, 2006). In the context of the narrative perspective, there seems to be something of a consensus that the capacity to represent experience in the form of stories is the result of narrative practices which characterize the communicative exchanges of humans as members of social communities (Bruner, 1990; Hutto 2007, 2008; Gallagher & Hutto, 2008). On this perspective, the way in which humans represent reality depends on the cultural values of their social group that are transmitted through stories. An example from this line of thought is the Narrative Practice Hypothesis (NPH) advanced by Hutto (2007, 2008). An illustrative case to understand how NPH considers mental representation is the critique of the hypothesis according to which the intentional stance makes exclusive reference to cognitive systems. The intentional stance (Dennett, 1987) is the way in which humans interpret their own and other's behavior in terms of mental properties (see also Arbib, this volume). In the cognitive oriented philosophy of mind, this capacity depends on the activity of innate processing systems implemented in specific brain structures (Abu-Akel et al., 2020). Leslie and colleagues (2004) define these systems in terms of Theory of Mind Mechanisms (Arbib, this volume; Gärdenfors, this volume). Hutto's thesis is that, while admitting the existence of similar cognitive systems, referring exclusively to them is not enough to explain how humans interpret their own or other people's behavior. This kind of explanation would require theoretical models that consider the intentional stance (IS) as highly determined by cultural narrative practices (Hutto, 2007, 2008; Gallagher & Hutto, 2008). Interpreting other people's behavior means, indeed, situating those people in a story: only through the plot of a story is it possible to understand the reasons behind people's actions. In fact, as Hutto (2009: 13) holds explicitly,

> the NPH must be distinguished from the softer claim that narrative engagements merely add finishing touches and refinement to pre-existing mindreading capacities that are best explained by these familiar theories. The NPH is interesting precisely because it makes a stronger claim than the one cited above. It says that appropriate engagement in narrative practices is what normally engenders IS competence. Consequently, we do not just refine our pre-existing IS understanding by means of narrative engagements – on the contrary, we do not begin to exhibit IS skills proper until we have had the right sorts of encounters with the right sorts of narratives. Children are not IS competent until they have mastered certain narrative skills. Engaging in narrative practice is the source of our IS understanding.

With Hutto's view, Herman (2013:74) argues that:

> more than just requiring adoption of the intentional stance for its interpretation, storytelling also affords a basis for registering and making sense of the intentions, goals, feelings, and actions that emerge from an intelligent agent's negotiation of appropriately scaled environment. ... Stories allow ... reasons, which are analyzable into interlocking set of beliefs and desires ... to be configured into internally coherent and situationally appropriate accounts of why someone has acted – or failed to act – in the way he or she has.

What emerges here is a theoretical perspective according to which social practices, along with their acquisition in ontogeny, are the primary condition to interpret another's behavior. According to NPH, in fact, the intentional stance has mainly a social character, given that "narratives are a distinctive and characteristic feature of human cultural niches, just as dams are for beavers" (Hutto, 2009:27). Hutto fits into a consolidated trend in research (cultural constructivism) that has at its center Bruner's (1990) proposal, according to which stories are largely the product of the cultural values that children begin to encounter in their social environment starting at birth. Within this line of research, representational abilities are governed by learning processes (see also Marentette, this volume) that allow for the internalization of a social group's communicative practices.

That said, the result of this perspective is a loss of the explanatory value of the role played by cognitive architectures in the interpretation of intentional behaviors. Describing the mind exclusively as the result of a process of apprenticeship, i.e., an internalization of external practices, in fact, means strengthening the role of language as an external scaffolding capable of structuring thoughts autonomously and independently of the role of internal processing systems. This is particularly relevant for my purposes since, in such a view, the narrative structure of thought relies on the idea that narrative is a product of language. An important hypothesis in this direction is the so-called Language First Hypothesis (LFH), strongly supported by Scalise Sugiyama (2001, 2005).

2.2 The language first hypothesis

According to Scalise Sugiyama (2001, 2005), the role assigned to language (verbal language, specifically) in narrative derives from the fact that language is able to tell stories through an expressive appropriateness that other expressive systems are not capable of. In this perspective, images, for example, are too vague to ensure the correct interpretation of a story. Following Scalise Sugiyama, the argument that distinguishes images from narrative is clear; what is less clear, however, is how to distinguish language per se from narrative. The problem to be addressed, as Scalise Sugiyama herself acknowledges, is how to avoid the conclusion that narrative's specific power is merely a side effect of the representational power of language. Her answer to this problem is that narrative cannot be identified with language; indeed, "although cognitive psychologists have had only limited success in their efforts to delineate story grammar, it is clear that such a grammar must exist, since stories are not simply random conglomerations of sentences" (Scalise Sugiyama, 2005: 183).

The distinction between story grammar and the grammar of sentences is convincing and consistent with the hypothesis of the present chapter. However, justifying this distinction appears to be challenging in the context of LFH. Claiming that language evolved for reasons that are separate from narrative and then, after its appearance, permitted humans to tell stories through verbalization is entirely plausible. Notwithstanding, in this perspective it seems unclear how to distinguish between (a) what derives from language and (b) what derives from narrative. It must be one or the other: either language has intrinsic narrative properties, or it does not have those properties. In the latter case, however, it is unclear why and how being endowed with language should make humans able to tell stories. Scalise Sugiyama argues that story grammar exists and is different from the grammar of sentences. Thus, if narrative depends on language (and if the grammar of stories has specific characteristics that distinguish it from the grammar of sentences), how does story grammar emerge and become distinct from the grammar of sentences? Where do narrative properties come from if language does not already possess them? Arguing that narrative presumes language without corresponding to it is an unsuccessful way of solving the difficulty. The LFH seems to foster a vicious circle: language accounts for narrative but the grammar of sentences is not capable of explaining the distinctive traits of story grammar.

One way to overcome the vicious circle is to consider the ability to tell stories as more ancient than language and to frame the origin of language with reference to this early capacity (see Arbib in this volume for "Ur-pantomime supports only simple protonarratives" and the motivation of the study in Zlatev et al., this volume). This is a way to ascribe intrinsic narrative properties to language, thus weakening the thesis of the primacy of language over narrative. When trying to combine the thesis of the narrative representation of reality with the topic of language origin, a specific hypothesis arises since language has a narrative character much more than narrative has a linguistic nature, which suggests abandoning the Language First Hypothesis in favor of the Narrative First Hypothesis. This reversal of perspective has important implications for the issue of the relationship between thought and language: the primacy of language is replaced by the primacy of thought over language (Ferretti 2022, 2021).

One way to take seriously the idea that story grammar is distinct from the grammar of sentences is to identify the characteristic features of narrative, showing that they are processed by cognitive systems that are different from those involved in the processing of sentences. The adherence to the Narrative First Hypothesis leads us to analyze the cognitive systems capable of processing the narrative structure of language. It is time to focus on the functional and structural components underlying the narrative brain.

3.   The narrative brain and the proto-narrative representation of experience

What makes story grammar so different from the grammar of sentences? More generally, what makes story a story? In research in narratology several aspects of story properties have been emphasized, promoting a lively debate. Although the properties characterizing narrative are the subject of controversy, there is consensus on a general definition which describes narrative as "a primary resource for configuring circumstances and events into more or less coherent scenarios involving the experience of persons" (Herman 2013:74; see Brown this volume and Zlatev et al. this volume for their approaches to the problem). Moreover, there is wide support for the idea that at least three elements contribute to define a story: time, plot, and characters. To mention some examples: plot and time are at the center of Ricoeur's (1983) proposal; with explicit reference to Aristotle, who exalts plot structure over characters, Brook (1984) emphasizes the role of the plot; at odds with the Aristotelian perspective, Fludernik (1996) highlights the role of characters. I will not examine in detail the various narratological proposals. My interest here is understanding if there is a correspondence between the properties that are commonly acknowledged as distinctive of stories and the cognitive architectures recruited for their processing – and if so, to what degree the idea of a narrative brain makes sense. The existence of a narrative brain is, indeed, the only way to break the vicious circle underlying LFH and to give shape to the idea that the origin of storytelling depends on the ability to represent reality in a narrative form.

Several studies have corroborated the idea of a narrative brain (for an overview, see Ferretti & Adornetti, 2021; Ferretti et al., 2022). For example, the role of characters is widely supported by experimental investigations focusing on the ability to take another's perspective (through forms of attachment to a protagonist, for example) in the comprehension of stories (e.g., Chiera et al., 2022; Yuan et al., 2018). Many studies have also revealed the role of the plot, a dimension of narrative governed by global coherence (the property that presides over the causal and temporal relationship between events). In fact, as emphasized by Herman (2013:237), "from a structural standpoint, one of the hallmarks of narrative is this linking of phenomenon into causal-chronological wholes; stories provide a resource for connecting otherwise isolated occurrences onto elements of episodes or 'scenes', whose components can then be represented as systematically interrelated via causal networks." Along with the holistic dimension determined by the causal relations between events (see also Gärdenfors, this volume), the extended character of narrative is strictly connected with the time factor. Ricoeur (1983) has highlighted the intertwining of plot and time, referring to Augustine's concept of the threefold present.

The role of the temporally extended dimension in stories has been empirically supported. Corballis (2011: 110–111) holds that "the same constructive process that allows us to reconstruct the past and to construct possible futures also allows us to invent stories." In line with this intuition, we conducted some studies on the ability of children with Autism Spectrum Disorder (ASD) to perform mental projection in time, showing the role of Mental Time Travel – the cognitive systems allowing us to project backward and forward in time – in the processing of narrative global coherence (Ferretti et al., 2018; Marini et al., 2019). Consistently with our findings, an investigation by Race and colleagues (2015) on hippocampal amnesic patients has corroborated the link between the processing of global coherence and the brain systems (especially the hippocampus) involved in spatio-temporal representation (see the section "Navigation in time" in Arbib, this volume).

The fact that the mechanisms underlying the narrative brain are cognitive systems capable of processing the extended dimension of stories contributes to the idea that the cognitive underpinnings of stories should be identified with a functional macrosystem designed to allow for contextually relevant behaviors through detachment from the here-and-now, which I have termed *Triadic System of Grounding and Projection* (Ferretti, 2010, 2015). Offering credence to this idea is the existence of a brain network – the Default Mode Network (DMN) – composed of systems closely bound to one another and responsible for projection in space, time and the minds of others (Buckner & Carroll, 2007). Specifically, my idea is that the abilities of projection governed by such systems are the skills we need to produce a narrative representation of reality (Ferretti, 2022; Ferretti & Adornetti, 2021). Since these projection abilities are crucial for the processing of stories, it is possible to consider the DMN as the neurological substrate of the narrative representation of experience.

Narrative is the way in which human beings represent mental content, which is a necessary constituent of any form of communication. To distinguish narrative mental content from the content of storytelling (as it is expressed in communication), I will use the term proto-narrative representation (see also Arbib this volume, Gärdenfors this volume, Brown, this volume, and Marentette et al., this volume for narrative in children). In this regard, it is required that (i) proto-narrative representations be independent from communication (even a single human being, isolated from the social context, could generate similar representations which are implemented by the brain and human cognitive devices) and that (ii) the attempt to account for protonarrative representations with reference to projective systems comprising the narrative brain be an interpretive strategy capable of overcoming the difficulty of the constructivist perspective about the origin of narrative competence. In my opinion, in fact, mental proto-narrative representations are the evolutionary preconditions of the ability to communicate by means of stories. That said, the transition from cognition to communication is not a simple and direct one: proto-narrative representation, particularly fruitful at the cognitive level, at the communicative level entails a problem needing to be addressed.

4. Splendor and misery of the narrative brain

From the above considerations, the role of the narrative brain in the construction of proto narrative representations has been emphasized. While a similar apparatus has a clear adaptive advantage in cognitive terms, accounting for the reference to proto-narrative representations in communication is not equally straightforward. Let's imagine that I am looking at something which, on the basis of my memories, I interpret in a specific way, and you are looking at the same object or scene: your interpretations will differ from mine since you engage in your personal temporal projections related to that thing. It becomes clear that even the simple perception of the same object entails very different points of view in the observers. This affects the sharing of knowledges that are required for communication.

Projection characterizing each proto-narrative interpretation of experience provides representations that are always framed from an individual perspective. Therefore, even when interlocutors essentially agree, communication is necessarily marked by disparity. Without questioning the role of cooperation (Wacewicz & Żywiczyński, this volume) and shared beliefs in human communication, this element of disparity emphasizes the role of a *competitive* dimension. It is an important aspect characterizing the conversational context in which interlocutors, beyond sharing information, are engaged in an attempt to convince each other of their own opinions. The necessity to overcome this disparity characterizes communication in terms of persuasion: in order to reach the goal of communication, it is not enough to inform someone of something – it is also required that interlocutors accept what is being said (Sperber et al., 2010). The most effective solution to this problem lies in conversation as a form of persuasive reciprocity, founded on argumentative strategies of persuasion. However, as we will see in the last part of the chapter, this type of conversation is not useful to investigate the initial stages of human communication since it presumes syntactically complex verbal codes. Persuasive reciprocity characterizing argumentative persuasion is a late product of evolution which probably constitutes the hallmark of *Homo sapiens* communication (Ferretti, 2022; Ferretti & Adornetti, 2021).

How to cope with the disparity of perspectives in the early stages of communication when syntactically complex expressions were not present to permit argumentative forms of persuasion? One possible answer has to do with pre-argumentative forms of persuasion that were narrative in character (Ferretti, 2022; Ferretti et al., 2022). From a phylogenetic point of view, it is plausible that scavenging and hunting contexts triggered the evolution of a typically human form of communication (e.g., Bickerton, 2009; Számadó, 2010). In such contexts, one-to-many communication might have prevailed compared to face-to-face interactions characterizing fully-fledged conversation (see Dunbar & Levinson for a competing view). In a hunt story, the chief's instructions to be followed on the basis of the specific role of each member rely on persuasive strategies aimed at making them act in a certain way: the power of stories lies in their persuasive effect (Ferretti, 2022; see Gärdenfors, this volume for the case of demonstration), not in mere description of facts.

Dessalles (2007) links language origin to the political, rather than generically social, nature of the human animal. It is an important thesis which adds the role of sexual selection, beyond that of natural selection, to the evolution of language (e.g., Foolen, 2002). Along with the theory of social prestige (Zahavi & Zahavi, 1997), central to Dessalles' hypothesis is the idea that language evolved to form large coalitions governed by the granting of status, which is widely determined by the persuasive abilities of the leader. For my purposes, particularly interesting is the idea that a more effective speech for the granting of social status should contain storytelling characteristics: the persuasive power of stories, in fact, makes a leader able to convince others that she/he is speaking for the group's benefit (Burling, 1986). As Shaw-Williams (2017: 206) points out, "new ethnographic evidence has shown good storytellers have higher reproductive success, even more than expert hunters. In addition, bands with more skilled storytellers remain more cooperative and egalitarian during times of stress" (Smith et al., 2017, cited in Boyd, 2018). As is clear from this quote, stories (because of their persuasive power) can be an effective tool for cooperation and social equality.

These considerations make the strict link between leadership and storytelling evident: the ability to tell stories is crucial for leadership and social coalitions since narrative is extraordinarily persuasive. Bilandzic and Busselle (2013) define narrative persuasion as "any influence on beliefs, attitudes, or actions brought about by a narrative message through processes associated with narrative comprehension or engagement" (2013: 201). What makes stories effective tools of persuasion? In addition to the tradition of classical rhetoric, nowadays the study of the persuasive power of stories relies on the cognitive mechanisms underlying narrative processing.

While the mechanisms underlying the persuasive power of stories are multiple and act in different ways, in general, transportation and engagement play a primary role in a persuasive perspective mainly based on emotional aspects, rather than argumentative ones. Listening to a story (even reading or watching a movie) implies one's being transported into the narrated events. To account for the persuasive power of stories, Green and Brock (2000) reworked the classical model by Gerrig (1993), proposing the Transportation Imagery Model (TIM). At its basis is the idea that "to the extent that individuals are absorbed into a story or transported into a narrative world, they may show effects of the story on their real-world beliefs" (Green and Brock, 2000:701). Green and Brock identify three consequences of transportation.

The first one concerns the fact that the reader loses access to some real-world facts in favor of accepting the narrative world that the author has created. This loss of access may occur on a physical level (...) or, more importantly, on a psychological level, a subjective distancing form reality. While the person is immersed in the story, he or she may be less aware of real-world facts that contradict assertions made in the narrative (Green and Brock, 2000:702).

The second consequence is that "transported readers may experience strong emotions and motivations, even when they know the events in the story are not real" (Green and Brock, 2000). The third consequence is that "people return from being transported somewhat changed by the experience" (Green and Brock, 2000).

Imagery in the form of the construction of scenarios is among the essential mechanisms involved in transportation. In their model, Green and Brock (2002) place imagery at the center of narrative persuasion. Through imagery, individuals experience a virtual reality by means of perceptions that are similar to those involved in the experience of reality – images are, indeed, the vicarious substitute for real event perception. Bilandzic and Busselle (2013:212) claim that "we do not need an argument when we have an image." The persuasive power of stories largely depends on the fact that "images have specific implications for beliefs, and by leading readers to infer these, images may oppose and change existing beliefs" (Bilandzic & Busselle, 2013:211). This latter consideration is particularly relevant for our purposes as it emphasizes the role of non-argumentative forms of persuasion.

Its persuasive character makes narrative a valuable tool for facing the difficulty of a communication characterized by different points of view as consequence of a prospective narrative brain. Since narrative, before being a tool for communication, is the way in which the brain represents reality, the persuasive power of stories largely depends on the fact that stories "enchant the brain" (Storr, 2019): the human brain is sensitive to narratives because they represent its natural way of representing reality (Ferretti, 2022; Ferretti & Adornetti, 2021). Overall, my argument can be outlined as follows: interlocutors participate in communication through a narrative perspective of experience which constrains their point of view; mediation between different points of view characterizes human communication in persuasive terms; stories act as points of contact between the various points of view in a communicative context not equipped with argumentative persuasive strategies. This framework provides a plausible scenario of language origin in a one-to-many communicative context characterizing scavenging or hunting.

We have reached the heart of the matter. If it is true that our ancestors introduced persuasive forms of communication to overcome the difficulties of their prospective brain, the remaining difficulty to be addressed is understanding how they could actually realize a similar kind of communication. Along with structural and functional preconditions, it is important to account for material conditions – how our predecessors gave rise to a typically human form of communication. My claim is that pantomime is the ideal means to persuasively tell stories in the absence of verbal language and that our ancestors exploited it in the initial stages of human communication.

5. The proto-stories of bodily mimesis

The issue of the expressive system used by our predecessors to communicate is strictly related to the issue of which system is most effective to express thought. A guiding principle is that some expressive forms work better than others depending on the type of thoughts they are required to convey. In light of the considerations developed in previous sections, this principle fits with the selection of the expressive system most effective to convey narrative representations. Traditionally, verbal language appears as the best system to express stories. For example, Scalise Sugyiama (2005) considers the ability to tell stories as strictly associated with verbalization. Notwithstanding, since all requirements necessary for speech emerged not before *Homo heidelbergensis* (Dediu, & Levinson, 2013), an alternative hypothesis to account for the communication of early members of genus *Homo* draws attention to the gestural forms of expression (Fay et al., 2022). More specifically, I suggest considering pantomime as the first typically human expressive means (see also Arbib this volume; Gärdenfors, this volume; Zlatev et al., this volume; Mineiro & Moita, this volume) since it embodies two key aspects of the communicative use of the narrative brain: pantomime meets the constraint exerted by the need to convey proto-narrative thoughts and pantomime meets the criterion of persuasion as telling stories through pantomime has effects on conviction (Ferretti et al., 2022).

When it comes to stories, traditionally – since Aristotelian times – their mimetic character has played a primary role (for a different perspective see Brown, this volume). At the same time, mimesis is a fundamental characteristic of pantomime since "pantomime is at the heart of what Donald (1991) and Zlatev (2008) have influentially called mimetic communication" (Żywiczyński et al., 2018: 312). Bodily mimesis is a powerful expressive tool for initiating language, mainly because of its interpretive transparency, which helps to bypass the problem of conventionalization in the early stage of communication (see Arbib's chapter in this volume).

Donald (1991) argues that a mimetic-based culture is the point of transition from episodic to symbolic culture. While not being intrinsically communicative, mimesis is therefore a basic condition for the evolution of specifically human communication. Indeed, "although mimesis may not have originated as a means of communication and might have originated in a different use of reproductive memory, such as toolmaking, mimetic acts by their nature are usually public and inherently possess the potential to communicate" (Donald, 1991: 172). Zlatev (2014) revised Donald's proposal, in support of the bodily mimesis hypothesis, "stating that an adaptation for improved volitional control of the body gave our ancestors advantages in the domains of imitation, empathy and (gestural) intentional communication. It is assumed that this paved the way for the evolution of language, with no other adaptations being required apart from improved vocal control" (Zlatev, 2014: 166).

The transition from something that is not communicative to something that has the potential for communication is decisive for the topic of language origin. McBride (2014: 3) adds an important piece to the idea of mimesis as a precursory form of language:

> Mimes are not language. The proposal is that mimes come into being as a way of telling stories long before any possibility of language existed or was even anticipated. Mime was a complete storytelling process well within the talents of the hominins in whose bands it occurred. These individuals had zero concept of language, but they could manage mimed stories and understand them. Mimes and their understanding required nothing that every hominin did not already have.

McBride's proposal to consider mimesis as the best tool for telling stories in the absence of language is completely consistent with my hypothesis, but a lexical clarification is required: the emphasis on the communicative character of mimesis should go hand in hand with the reference to pantomime, as "pantomime is performed with the intention of getting the observer to think of a specific action or event. It is essentially communicative in its nature" (Arbib, 2012: 217–18).

A general definition advanced by Arbib (for a revision, cf. his chapter in this volume) describes pantomime as "a performance that resembles an action of some kind and can thus evoke ideas of the action itself, an associated action, object, or event, or a combination thereof" (Arbib, 2012: 217) or, alternatively, as the ability of "expressing a situation, object, action, character, or emotion without words, and using only gestures, especially imitative gestures, and other movements" (Arbib, 2012: 217). Referring to Stokoe (2001), Arbib (2012: 219) highlights that pantomime "provides open-ended possibilities for communication that work without prior instruction of convention." Pantomime is easy to understand (its mimetic character makes it transparent) and it does not involve specialized cognitive systems for its processing (concerning transparency, see also Miniero, this volume and Marenette, this volume). It is sufficient that the nervous system can interpret the bodily movement in terms of action meaning and that "motor knowledge of our own acts is a necessary and sufficient condition for an immediate understanding of the acts of others" (Rizzolatti & Sinigaglia, 2008: 106).

That said, although the use of the term pantomime is variable and can include the narrative factor or not (e.g., Arbib, 2012; Corballis, 2017; Gärdenfors, 2017; Tomasello, 2008), my idea is that the ability to tell stories should be included in the definition of pantomime. McBride (2014) takes the example of a tribal chief that stops the group members rushing to eat the prey, gains their attention (...) and starts miming the hunt story. In this case, according to McBride (2014: 3), "what had been transmitted was something gestures alone could never do, present a whole story, a metaphor of an event. Every watcher understood how this hunt had been organized and why it was so special."

The reference to a whole story has to be considered the distinctive trait of pantomime for a proto-narrative origin of language, since this trait equips it with features of protolanguage (concerning the problem of what level of story complexity pantomime can express see Zlatev et al., this volume; Arbib, this volume). This occurs for two main reasons: first, because through pantomime it is possible to express proto-narrative contents (as shown, the main function of language is expressing thoughts through the telling of stories); second, because of its proto-narrative nature, pantomime has effects on the persuasive level (proto-stories, as well as stories, are powerful tools for persuasion). In the light of these considerations, I posit that the proto-narrative dimension is a core feature of pantomime that should be included in its definition. Paradoxically, in this vein the most relevant definition has been proposed by a scholar who considers pantomime as an evolutionary dead-end. McNeill (2005), in effect, describes pantomime as "a gesture or sequence of gestures conveying a narrative line, with a story to tell, produced without speech" (2005: ivi, 2). In his opinion, however, the "silent" character makes it impossible for pantomime to be a precursor of language because language is an integrated system of gesture and speech from its very beginning. In McNeill's view, the thesis of "equiprimordiality" is useful to overcome a major difficulty of the gestural hypothesis of language origin: the transition "from hand to mouth" (Corballis, 2002), namely, from mimetic to symbolic forms of expression. Burling (2005) considers the modality transition problem a serious weakness of the gestural theories of language origin.

The first strategy to solve the problem is to renounce the sharp distinction between the "purely" symbolic and the "purely" gestural, to consider "the possible transition from a predominantly mimetic form of communication to a predominantly symbolic one" (Zlatev, 2014:166), thus acknowledging the multimodal nature of linguistic communication (Ahlner & Zlatev, 2010). In line with this proposal, Zlatev et al. (2020) reformulated the previous definition of pantomime proposed by Żywiczyński and colleagues (2018) highlighting the polysemiotic character of this expressive system. In this new proposal, the authors define pantomime as a nonverbal, mimetic, and non-conventionalized polysemiotic communicative system which holistically refers to events displaced from the here and now by means of coordinated movements of the whole body.

Making explicit reference to the polysemiotic character of pantomime, this definition rules out the limitations of a mere gestural (hence, silent) conception (in line with this is Minerio, this volume; against it Arbib, this volume). However, while referring to the holistic capacity to represent events (the basic components of stories), such a definition omits the essential feature of any narrative structure: the causal connection of events in time.

In an empirical study with children exhibiting typical development, we corroborated the hypothesis of the efficacy of pantomime to tell stories (Adornetti et al., 2023). If pantomime can tell stories, then the ability to represent sequences of events connected in time should be a defining characteristic of this expressive system. On this view, I suggest revising the definition by Zlatev and colleagues (2020) as follows:

> A nonverbal, mimetic, and non-conventionalized polysemiotic communicative system, which holistically refers to events *and/or to sequences of events causally connected in time and* displaced from the here and now by means of coordinated movements of the whole body.

While pantomime is not exclusively associated with narrative, the intrinsic potential for communicating proto-narrative thoughts to others clearly emerges from this definition. Emphasizing the proto-narrative nature of pantomime is a way to consider it a form of protolanguage – an evolutionary platform from which the evolution of storytelling as a peculiar dimension of human communication began (for a critique of the hypothesis of pantomime as protolanguage see Arbib, this volume and Gärdenfors, this volume). This is a relevant point fueled by the fact that storytelling, in addition to being an effective way to express thoughts, is also an effective way to convince others to act in a certain way.

6. From gesture to speech (from stories to conversation)

In the light of the above considerations, to conclude, a final step is required. If certain abilities can be considered in terms of protolanguage when they represent an evolutionary prerequisite of language, then the analysis of the transition from pantomime to verbal language is a necessary step to understand whether pantomime was the evolutionary platform for the emergence of a fully-fledged language.

Several scholars have claimed that this transition is mainly linked to the need to overcome the expressive difficulty of pantomime. As Corballis (2015: 91; see also Arbib, this volume; Mineiro & Moita, this volume) argues, although it is likely that in the early stages of human communication stories were pantomimic, it should be noted that "pantomime is inefficient and often ambiguous and needed to be developed into a system of symbols whose meanings were clear and understood by members of the community." In this perspective, the transition to verbalization (a less iconic and more abstract tool of expression) consists in the transition to a more precise and expressively effective symbolic system.

Even acknowledging the expressive difficulties of pantomime in accounting for the transition from the mimetic to the symbolic (or, more accurately, from the mainly mimetic to the mainly symbolic), my idea is that the selective pressures in favor of this transition should be identified in another phenomenon. I claim that the difficulty which acted as selective pressure towards verbal and syntactically complex expressions was represented by the transition from one-to-many communication (characterizing our more ancient predecessors) to the face-to-face conversation of modern humans. Pickering and Garrod (2004: 169) argue that "the most natural and basic form of language use is dialogue."

In a similar vein, Chafe also (2008: 686) considers conversation as the characteristic feature of human communication, in terms of

> a uniquely human and extraordinarily important way by which separate minds are able to influence and be influenced by each other, managing to some extent, and always imperfectly, to bridge the gap between them, by constructing any kind of lasting object but through a constant interplay of constantly changing ideas.

The persuasive power of pantomimic storytelling is particularly effective in one-to-many communication, typically involving a leader who needs to bring together a social group for a common goal (for example, in hunting contexts). In this case, pantomime is highly persuasive because it exploits the trust and respect of members toward the chief's authority.

Correctly, Wacewicz and Żywiczyński (2018; see also their chapter in this volume) interpret pantomime within the theoretical framework of the Platform of Trust (PoT; Knight, 1998): the cooperative trait of human communication based on the ability to overthrow "the default settings from manipulation expectations to honesty expectations" (Wacewicz & Żywiczyński, 2018: 170). But modern communication, governed by the reduction of aggression in the context of self-domestication (Benitez-Burraco & Progovac, 2020), is largely founded on face-to-face conversation in which interlocutors, beyond cooperating, are in competition with each other to assert their reasons and defend their own point of view. If in one-to-many communication the persuasive intent is unidirectional, in conversation it takes the bidirectional character of persuasive reciprocity. Therefore, given the constant alternation of roles between interlocutors in the attempt to mutually persuade, conversation puts speaker and listener in competition with each other.

The difficulty of pantomime to convey conversational exchanges guided by persuasive reciprocity is its major limitation (for a different perspective on the difficulties of pantomime see Arbib, this volume; Gärdenfors, this volume; Zlatev et al., this volume). In the conversational context governed by persuasive reciprocity, argumentation, beside narrative, becomes crucial. The transition to argumentation raises the problem of expressive codes, which need to be sufficient for this new form of communicative persuasion to succeed. Argumentation, in fact, requires a verbal language structured on the syntactic level, capable of giving rise to propositional inferences characteristic of arguments (Ferretti, 2022; Ferretti et al., 2022; Ferretti & Adornetti, 2021; Benitez-Burraco et al., 2021). As argumentation implies computational processes that apply to the propositional forms of representation, the evolution of syntactically complex structures becomes an important factor in such a communicative model. The pressure towards effective argumentative strategies required by persuasive reciprocity is a crucial factor in the origin of grammar and, specifically, of syntax (Ferretti, 2022; Benítez-Burraco et al., 2021; see also Arbib, this volume; Gärdenfors, this volume; Mineiro & Moita, this volume; Zlatev et al., this volume).

My idea about the origin of syntax is consistent with the model of grammaticalization and, in particular, with the arguments used by interactional linguistics in favor of "grammar in everyday talk" (Thompson, Fox, & Couper-Kuhlen, 2015). In such a perspective, "syntax cannot be fully understood without an account of its interactional inhabitant in a turn" (Lindström, 2009: 99). The interactive nature of grammar at work can be analyzed from different perspectives. For my purposes, of particular interest is the dependence of clause construction on the conversational context, since Thompson and Couper-Kuhlen

(2005) consider the clause as a locus of interaction in everyday conversation. In their view, the clause can be considered "the crystallization of solutions to the interactional problem of signaling and recognizing social actions" (Thompson & Couper-Kuhlen, 2005: 484). In such a perspective, the conversational context creates an evolutionary pressure for grammatical complexity, a process in constant change, as clauses are shaped in contingent situations of interaction and "grammar is constantly being shaped and re-shaped, constantly undergoing revision and redesign as it is deployed in everyday talk" (2005: 482). Furthermore, grammar involved in the enhancement of persuasive abilities is thought of as the product of the conversational context in which the exchange of arguments strongly affects the ongoing adjustment of inferential structures and processes (Ferretti, 2022; Benítez-Burraco et al., 2021).

7. Conclusions

In this chapter, within a perspective about language origin founded on the ability to tell stories, I argued for the thesis that pantomime is a form of protolanguage. Pantomime can be considered in these terms not only because it predates language, but mostly because it embodies the evolutionary preconditions of fully-fledged language. Indeed, pantomime is an ideal means to express typically human thoughts because of the proto-narrative character of human thoughts which pantomime is ideally suited to express. Moreover, capable of telling stories in the absence of verbal language, pantomime can be considered as the early tool used by our ancestors to give rise to persuasive forms of communication – the first means through which humans attempted to communicate in one-to-many contexts. However, the persuasive power of pantomime in these contexts also represented its major disadvantage when communication switched to face-to-face conversation. In this type of communication governed by persuasive reciprocity, narrative persuasion needs to be complemented with argumentative persuasion based on turn-taking and the dialectics of arguing and counterarguing. The need to enhance similar argumentative abilities constituted the selective pressure towards complex syntactic structures. The underlying processes in argumentation are different from those involved in narrative but they respond to the same selective pressures that favor persuasive effectiveness, strengthening the view that pantomime is the evolutionary foundation of modern language.

References

Abu-Akel, A.M., Apperly, I.A., Wood, S.J., & Hansen, P.C. (2020). Re-imaging the intentional stance. *Proceedings of the Royal Society B*, 287(1925), 20200244.

Adornetti, I., Chiera, A., Deriu, V., Altavilla, D., Ferretti, F. (2023), Comprehending stories in pantomime. A pilot study with typically developing children and its implications for the narrative origin of language. *Language & Communication*, 93, 155-171. .

Ahlner, F., & Zlatev, J. (2010). Cross-modal iconicity: A cognitive semiotic approach to sound symbolism. *Sign Systems Studies*, 38(1/4), 298–348.

Arbib M. (this volume) Pantomime within and beyond the evolution of language.

Arbib, M. (2012). *How the brain got language. Towards a new road map*. Oxford University Press.

Benítez-Burraco, A., Ferretti, F., & Progovac, L. (2021). Human self-domestication and the evolution of pragmatics. *Cognitive Science*, 45(6), e12987.

Benítez-Burraco, A., & Progovac, L. (2020). A four-stage model for language evolution under the effects of human self-domestication. *Language & Communication*, 73, 1–17.

Bickerton, D. (2009). *Adams' tongue: how humans made language, how language made humans*. McMillan.

Bilandzic, H., Busselle, R. (2013). Narrative persuasion. In J.P. Dillard & L. Shen. (Eds.), *The Sage handbook of persuasion: Developments in theory and practice*. (2nd ed., pp. 200–219). Sage.

Boyd, B. (2018). The evolution of stories: from mimesis to language, from fact to fiction. *Wiley Interdisciplinary Reviews: Cognitive Science*, 9(1), e1444.

Brooks, P. (1984). *Reading for the Plot*. Harvard University Press.

Bruner, J. (1990). *Acts of Meaning*. Harvard University Press.

Bruner, J. (1991). The narrative construction of reality. *Critical Inquiry*, 18(1), 1–21.

Buckner, R.L., & Carroll, D.C. (2007). Self-projection and the brain. *Trends in Cognitive Sciences*, 11(2), 49–57.

Burling, R. (1986). The selective advantage of complex language. *Ethology and Sociobiology*, 7(1), 1–16.

Burling, R. (2005). *The talking ape: How language evolved*. Oxford University Press, New York.

Chafe, W. (2008). Aspects of discourse analysis, in *Brno studies in English*, 34(s14), pp. 27–37.

Chiera, A., Adornetti, I., Altavilla, D., Acciai, A., Cosentino, E., Deriu, V., ... & Ferretti, F. (2022). Does the character-based dimension of stories impact narrative processing? An event-related potentials (ERPs) study. *Cognitive Processing*, 23(2), 255–267.

Corballis, M.C. (2002). *From hand to mouth*. Princeton University Press.

Corballis, M.C. (2011). *The recursive mind: The origins of human language, thought, and civilization*. Princeton University Press.

Corballis, M.C. (2015). *The wandering mind: What the brain does when you're not looking*. University of Chicago Press.

Corballis, M.C. (2017). *The truth about language: What it is and where it came from*. University of Chicago Press.

Dediu, D., & Levinson, S.C. (2013). On the antiquity of language: the reinterpretation of Neandertal linguistic capacities and its consequences. *Frontiers in Psychology*, 4, 397.

Dennett, D. C. (1987). The intentional stance. MIT Press.

Dennett, D. C. (1991). Consciousness explained. Penguin.

Dessalles, J. L. (2007). *Why we talk: The evolutionary origins of language.* Oxford University Press.

Donald, M. (1991). *Origins of the modern mind: Three stages in the evolution of human culture.* Harvard University Press.

Fay, N., Walker, B., Ellison, T. M., Blundell, Z., De Kleine, N., Garde, M., ... & Goldin-Meadow, S. (2022). Gesture is the primary modality for language creation. *Proceedings of the Royal Society B, 289*(1970), 20220066.

Ferretti, F. (2007). The social mind. In Marraffa M., M. De Caro, F. Ferretti (Eds.), *Cartographies of the Mind* (pp. 295–308). Springer.

Ferretti, F. (2010). *Alle origini del linguaggio umano. Il punto di vista evoluzionistico.*

Ferretti, F. (2015). *La facoltà di linguaggio. Determinanti biologiche e variabilità culturale.*

Ferretti, F. (2022). *Narrative persuasion. A cognitive perspective on language evolution* (Vol 7). Springer.

Ferretti, F. (2021). The narrative origins of language. In N. Gontier, A. Lock, & C. Sinha (Eds.), *The Oxford handbook of human symbolic evolution.* Oxford University Press.

Ferretti, F., & Adornetti, I. (2021). Persuasive conversation as a new form of communication in Homo sapiens. *Philosophical Transactions of the Royal Society B, 376*(1824), 20200196.

Ferretti, F., Adornetti, I., & Chiera, A. (2022). Narrative pantomime: A protolanguage for persuasive communication. *Lingua, 271,* 103247.

Ferretti, F., Adornetti, I., Chiera, A., Nicchiarelli, S., Valeri, G., Magni, R., ... & Marini, A. (2018). Time and narrative: An investigation of storytelling abilities in children with autism spectrum disorder. *Frontiers in Psychology, 9,* 944.

Fludernik, M. (1996). *Towards a 'natural' narratology.* Routledge.

Fodor, J. A. (1975). *The language of thought.* Harvard University press.

Foolen, A. P. (2002). Language origins and sexual selection. In Jacobs H., Wetzels L. (Eds.), *Liber Amicorum Bernard Bichakjian* (pp. 37–58). Shaker.

Gallagher, S., & Hutto, D. (2008). Understanding others through primary interaction and narrative practice. In J. Zlatev, et al. (Eds.), *The shared mind: Perspectives on intersubjectivity* (pp. 17–38). Benjamins.

Gärdenfors, P. (2017). Demonstration and pantomime in the evolution of teaching. *Frontiers in Psychology, 8,* 415.

Gerrig, R. J. (1993). *Experiencing narrative worlds: On the psychological activities of reading.* Yale University Press.

Green, M. C., Brock, T. C. (2000). The role of transportation in the persuasiveness of public narratives. *Journal of Personality and Social Psychology 79*(5), 701.

Herman, D. (2013). *Storytelling and the sciences of mind.* MIT Press.

Hutto, D. D. (2007). The narrative practice hypothesis: Origins and applications of folk psychology. *Royal Institute of Philosophy Supplements, 60,* 43–68.

Hutto, D. D. (2008). The narrative practice hypothesis: clarifications and implications. *Philosophical Explorations, 11*(3), 175–192.

Hutto, D. (2009). Folk psychology as narrative practice. *Journal of Consciousness Studies, 16*(6–7), 9–39.

Knight, C. et al.. 1998 Ritual/speech coevolution: a solution to the problem of deception. In J. Hurford (Ed.), *Approaches to the evolution of language* (pp. 68–91). Cambridge University Press.

Leslie, A.M., Friedman, O., & German, T.P. (2004). Core mechanisms in 'theory of mind'. *Trends in Cognitive Sciences*, 8(12), 528–533.

Lindström, J. (2009). Interactional linguistics. In S. D'hondt, J.-O. Östman & J. Verschueren (Eds.), *The pragmatics of interaction* (pp. 96–103). John Benjamins.

Marini, A., Ferretti, F., Chiera, A., Magni, R., Adornetti, I., Nicchiarelli, S., ... & Valeri, G. (2019). Episodic future thinking and narrative discourse generation in children with Autism Spectrum Disorders. *Journal of Neurolinguistics*, 49, 178–188.

McBride, G. (2014). Storytelling, behavior planning, and language evolution in context. *Frontiers in Psychology* 5, 1131.

McNeill, D. (2005). *Language and gesture.* Cambridge University Press

Niles, J.D. (1999). *Homo Narrans: The poetics and anthropology of oral literature.* University of Pennsylvania Press.

Pickering, M.J., & Garrod, S. (2004). Toward a mechanistic psychology of dialogue. *Behavioral and Brain Sciences*, 27(2), 169–190.

Race, E., Keane, M.M., & Verfaellie, M. (2015). Sharing mental simulations and stories: Hippocampal contributions to discourse integration. *Cortex*, 63, 271–281.

Ricouer, P. (1983). *Temps et récit, tome I.* Édition de Seuil.

Rizzolatti, G., & Sinigaglia, C. (2008). *Mirrors in the brain: How our minds share actions and emotions.* Oxford University Press.

Scalise-Sugiyama, M.S. (2001). Narrative theory and function: Why evolution matters. *Philosophy and Literature*, 25(2), 233–250.

Scalise-Sugiyama, M. (2005). Reverse-engineering narrative: Evidence of special design. In J. Gottshall & D.S. Wilson (Eds.), *The Literary Animal* (pp. 177–196). Northwestern University Press.

Shaw-Williams, K. (2017). The social trackways theory of the evolution of language. *Biological Theory*, 12(4), 195–210.

Smith, D., Schlaepfer, P., Major, K., Dyble, M., Page, A.E., Thompson, J., ... & Migliano, A.B. (2017). Cooperation and the evolution of hunter-gatherer storytelling. *Nature communications*, 8(1), 1–9.

Sperber, D., Clément, F., Heintz, C., Mascaro, O., Mercier, H., Origgi, G., & Wilson, D. (2010). Epistemic vigilance. *Mind & Language*, 25(4), 359–393.

Stokoe, W.C. (2001). *Language in hand: Why sign came before speech.* Gallaudet University Press.

Számadó, S. (2010). Pre-hunt communication provides context for the evolution of early human language. *Biological Theory*, 5(4), 366–382.

Thompson, T. (2010). The ape that captured time: folklore, narrative, and the human-animal divide. *Western Folklore*, 66, 395–420.

Thompson, S.A., Fox, B.A., & Couper-Kuhlen, E. (2015). *Grammar in everyday talk: Building responsive actions.* Cambridge University Press.

Tomasello, M. (2008). *Origins of human communication.* MIT Press.

Tomasello M. (2019). *Becoming Human.* Harvard University Press.

Wacewicz, S., & Żywiczyński, P. (2018). Language origins: Fitness consequences, platform of trust, cooperation, and turn-taking. *Interaction Studies*, 19(1–2), 167–182.

White, H. (1980). The value of narrativity in the representation of reality. *Critical Inquiry*, 7(1), 5–27.

White, H. (1981). The narrativization of real events. *Critical Inquiry*, 7(4), 793–798.

Yuan, Y., Major-Girardin, J., & Brown, S. (2018). Storytelling is intrinsically mentalistic: A functional magnetic resonance imaging study of narrative production across modalities. *Journal of Cognitive Neuroscience*, 30(9), 1298–1314.

Zahavi, A., & Zahavi, A. (1997). *The handicap principle: A missing piece of Darwin's puzzle.* Oxford University Press.

Zlatev, J. (2014). Bodily mimesis and the transition to speech. In M. Pina and N. Gontier (Eds.), *The evolution of social communication in primates* (pp. 165–178). Springer.

Zlatev, J., Żywiczyński, P., & Wacewicz, S. (2020). Pantomime as the original human-specific communicative system. *Journal of Language Evolution*, 5(2), 156–174.

Zywiczyński, P., Wacewicz, S. & Sibierska, M. (2018). Defining pantomime for language evolution research. *Topoi* 37 (2), 307–318.

CHAPTER 4

Two types of bodily-mimetic communication

Distinct design specifications and evolutionary trajectories

Sławomir Wacewicz & Przemysław Żywiczyński
Nicolaus Copernicus University

In this paper, we outline a novel approach to the study of pantomime, through applying the logic of evolutionary signalling theory to analysing the properties of the proposed precursors of language, in particular bodily-mimetic communication. We rely on a classic account by Krebs & Dawkins (1984), who outline two very different trajectories of the evolution of communication: into conspicuous, repetitive, exaggerated, and loud displays (*expensive hype*) versus cheap, subtle, inconspicuous and efficient messages (*conspiratorial whispers*). Pantomimic scenarios of language origins envisage a progression from mimetic to conventional communication, i.e., towards greater efficiency and expressive power, thereby assuming the latter trajectory. We argue that as a default, bodily mimetic communication is instead predicted to follow (or, remain trapped in) the expensive-hype trajectory, resulting in the communicative uses of the body that are defined by a high cost, such as artistic, sexual or ritual displays. The development of such forms of communication into systems increasingly resembling language could not happen on the surface level of communicative properties alone. Such changes could instead only happen as a result of the communication system switching to the efficient trajectory, which requires very special socio-ecological conditions.

Keywords: pantomime, bodily mimesis, platform of trust, rituals, honest signaling, signalling theory, alignment of interests

1. Introduction

Many accounts of the evolutionary emergence of language posit a stage of bodily communication based on pantomimes and gestures preceding the emergence of fully fledged language as we know it today (see Wacewicz & Żywiczyński, 2021 for a review). Pantomimic scenarios of language origins typically apply the canonical logic of "evolutionary stages" (see Arbib, 2012; Arbib, this volume; Brown, this volume; Ferretti, this volume; see also Mineiro & Moita, this volume), envisaging a progression from "simpler" to "more advanced" cognitive capacities that underlie a similar progression towards communication systems of increasing expressive power. A good example is Arbib (2012), who proposes a progression from simple to complex imitation and action recognition, then pantomime of praxic action and then of other action, to conventional gesture. In short, on a standard account bodily mimetic expression gives rise to pantomime as a type of sign-based referential communication, which then undergoes pressures for efficiency that lead to its conventionalisation into some system of proto-sign (see Section 2 below). Such a progression is intuitively plausible and implicitly or explicitly assumed to be favoured by natural selection. With a possible sole exception of Tomasello (2008), its adaptiveness is typically not directly considered.

However, such assumptions are not borne out by evolutionary signalling theory. In the following sections we rely on a classic signalling-theoretic account by Krebs & Dawkins (1984), who outline two very different trajectories of the evolution of communication: *expensive hype* vs *conspiratorial whispers*. Expensive hype are conspicuous, repetitive, exaggerated, and loud displays, while conspiratorial whispers are cheap, subtle, inconspicuous and efficient messages. Language and other types of ostensive communication characteristic of humans embody the latter type. However, a key observation is that the trajectory of conspiratorial whispers, rather than being the default one, is in fact very (if not extremely) rare in nature. Its emergence, far from being obvious, requires very special socio-ecological conditions, such as very close alignment of interests between the communicators (cf. Searcy & Nowicki, 2005). Without those conditions in place, the evolution of bodily-mimetic communication will not follow the efficient trajectory leading to the evolution of systems with increasingly language-like properties, but may instead be trapped in the expensive trajectory, which in turn constitutes a barrier to the development of such language-like properties.

2. Pantomimic scenarios of language origins

Pantomimic scenarios form a family of approaches that emphasise the following characteristics of the bodily-visual communication, which are assumed to have emerged after the separation of the hominin line from the *Pan* line (chimpanzees and bonobos) and later enabled the development of language:

- bodily visual modality: movements of the body, often the whole body, stand for referents;
- self-sufficiency: these body movements are understood without recourse to other signs, which is typically achieved through robust forms of iconicity (cf. Gärdenfors, this volume; Marentette et al., this volume; Mineiro & Moita, this volume);
- holism: these body movements are typically not analysable into smaller compositional units (see Arbib, this volume; Ferretti, this volume; Gärdenfors, this volume; Mineiro & Moita, this volume; Zlatev et al., this volume);
- improvisation: these body movements are produced *impromptu* and are unstandardised;
- semantically advanced: this form of bodily communication has a potential to convey content that is displaced, open-ended, and domain-universal, i.e., capable of expressing a unlimited range of meanings that are not limited to the here- and-now or to a predefined set of semantic domains (Żywiczyński et al., 2021; see Arbib, this volume; Gärdenfors, this volume; Mineiro & Moita, this volume).

We will understand pantomime as a form of communication that exhibits this set of features. This includes the important feature of whole-bodiness. Although the role of whole-bodiness is often misconstrued as a definitional property of individual pantomimes, a crucial point is that it pertains to a whole system (*pantomime*) rather than an individual element (*a pantomime*). It is not necessary that each and every pantomimic sign be performed with the whole-body, and pantomimic communication can include individual signs that are purely manual, purely facial, or indeed multimodal (visuo-vocal), as long as these are integrated into a larger repertoire of signs whose communicative potential substantially draws on the expressive use of the whole body (see the definition in Wacewicz & Żywiczyński 2021, and the discussions in the contribution in this volume by Arbib, Ferretti, Gärdenfors, Mineiro & Moita, and Zlatev et al.).

In modern-day literature on language origins, there is a number of influential approaches that identify pantomimic communication as a crucial stage in the evolution of language, in particular Arbib's Mirror Neuron Hypothesis (2012; this volume), Tomasello's proposal of "pointing and pantomiming" (Tomasello,

2008), Gärdenfors's hypothesis about the evolution of language and pedagogy (2017; this volume), or the proposal of the "original communicative system" by Zlatev and colleagues (2020; this volume). Either explicitly (Gärdenfors, 2017; Zlatev et al., 2020; cf. Donald, 1991) or implicitly (Arbib, 2012; Tomasello, 2008), these hypotheses acknowledge the semiotically novel status of pantomime, which broke away from the dyadic design of ape communication focused on the relation between the communicator and the addressee (Hurford, 2007). In contrast, pantomime uses signs, i.e., semiotic units that involve three entities: an *expression* that stands for a *referent* (an object, quality or an event) for an *interpreter* (cf. Zlatev et al., 2005; see Gärdenfors, this volume; Zlatev et al., this volume). The truly referential function of pantomime is taken to be responsible for its *semantic open-endedness and displacement* (or *detachment*, see Gärdenfors, this volume), something that is considered absent from the communication of non-human great apes (with only very rare exceptions, e.g., Lameira & Call, 2018).

There are two huge advantages that pantomimic scenarios have over purely speech-based scenarios (see Wacewicz & Żywiczyński, 2021 for review): they offer a persuasive explanation of how signs, as defined above, emerge in absence of any pre-existing signs, and how these improvised signs evolve towards more language-like forms (Arbib, this volume; Ferretti, this volume; Gärdenfors, this volume; Mineiro & Moita, this volume; Zlatev et al., this volume; acknowledge this expressly; see Marentette et al., this volume, for a discussion of this point from a developmental perspective). With regard to this first point, the above characterisation of pantomime in terms of self-sufficiency requires that the meaning of a pantomime, i.e., the relation between a (bodily-visual) expression and its referent, be established without the knowledge of other signs. It is assumed that evolutionarily only such signs could bootstrap sign-based communication (Żywiczyński et al., 2021; cf. Harnad, 1990). The solution to the bootstrapping problem is to rely on robust iconicity, or *primary iconicity* (Sonesson, 2007), where the similarity between expression and object is recognizable and in most cases sufficient for understanding that the former represents the latter (though not unmistakeably and not necessarily without effort – see next paragraph). Accordingly, pantomime, understood as the original type of sign-based communication, consisted of body movements that "maximally resemble their intentional object" (Zlatev et al., 2020: 162).

In support of this evolutionary scenario, proponents of pantomimic hypotheses appeal to evidence from the communication of modern humans, most importantly experimental data on improvising communication (e.g., Fay et al., 2013; Zlatev et al., this volume) and the research on emerging signed languages (e.g., Mineiro et al., 2017; Mineiro & Moita, this volume). The same lines of evidence are used to illustrate the evolution of pantomime towards a more language-like form of communication. The same properties that make pantomime an expedient means of bootstrapping signs also make it a cumbersome form of communication once signs have already emerged, which creates pressures for efficiency: "to have a ... system, effortless in terms of articulation and quicker to produce" (Mineiro et al., 2021). The impromptu character of pantomime requires a relatively great effort on the producer's side and the continued use of creative inference on the side of the recipient – as noted by Arbib, "[p]antomime can be both laborious and highly ambiguous" (2016: 13; see also Arbib, this volume). Hence, the first step in the evolution of pantomime is its routinisation or conventionalisation (cf. the notion of usualisation, Schmid, 2020; micro-entrenchment, Hartmann & Pleyer, 2021; or Ur-pantomime, Arbib, this volume). Conventionalisation is a process whereby the meaning of signs increasingly depends on the knowledge shared by a group of communicators and decreasingly on the similarity between the form and meaning (Sulik, 2018); this requires "a shared norm for producing a particular form to express a particular meaning" (Zlatev, 2018). But for these norms to emerge, ad hoc forms of pantomimic expressions must be simplified so that they become replicable and easily recognisable (Roberts et al., 2015; Gärdenfors, 2017; Gärdenfors, this volume). This stage in the evolution of pantomime is encapsulated in Arbib's idea of protosign: a "mixture of iconicity and convention ... [which] required reduced effort both to generate and to interpret" (Arbib, 2012: 222). Once the pressure for efficiency gains momentum, it pushes this pantomime-derived communication further and further towards a language-like system through its segmentation into recombinable elements, cf. grammaticalisation (Ferretti, this volume), fractionation (Arbib, this volume), and discretisation (Gärdenfors, this volume).

Pantomimic scenarios tend to agree that the evolution of pantomime in our evolutionary lines was based on the emergence of a more fundamental ability – bodily mimesis (see Żywiczyński et al., 2018, for review). According to Donald's influential conception of human evolution, mimesis was the first cognitive watershed after the *Homo* and *Pan* lines separated (Donald, 1991). Mimesis depends on intentional representation, with the body performing the role of a representational device. Pantomimic conceptions of language origin tend to stress the communicative role of pantomime, or more precisely the role of pantomime to communicate referential meaning (Zlatev et al., 2020; see the definition of pantomime above). However, the basic function of bodily mimesis is to produce "conscious, self-initiated, representational acts that are intentional but not linguistic" (Donald, 1991). As such, bodily-mimesis does not need to have a primary role of subserving social communication, let alone referential communication. It emerged first as a neuro-cognitive adaptation for tool-production, which allowed the tool-makers to "represent the event to oneself, for the purpose of rehearsing and refining a skill: the act itself may be analyzed, re-enacted and reanalyzed, that is, represented to oneself" (Donald, 1991). Only later did bodily mimesis acquired communicative function and enabled various forms of bodily representational expression, including ritual, dance, games, pretend play, and athletics.

Crucial for our argument is the point, often downplayed by proponents of pantomimic scenarios of language origins (but not Donald himself), that these communicative behaviours evolved along a different trajectory than pantomimic signs used for referential communication. Instead of following the pathway dictated by efficiency, they developed in expressions that are costly to produce, analogue rather than segmented and geared towards communicating social and emotional information rather than referential-proposition content. In what follows, we will explain these two different evolutionary trajectories of bodily-mimetic communication by appealing to signalling theory.

3. Evolutionary signalling theory

Evolutionary signalling theory (Maynard Smith & Harper, 2003; Searcy & Nowicki, 2005) is the received framework for accounting for communication in the evolutionary sciences. Evolutionary theory conceptualises living organisms as fitness-maximising machines, which are not typically expected to be helpful to other, genetically unrelated organisms; in short, "purely selfish alternatives most often provide superior fitness" (Sachs & Rubenstein, 2007). This applies to any form of behaviour, including communication. In most contexts, communicating "dishonestly" and manipulating the receiver to one's own advantage will result in greater fitness benefits than communicating "truthfully," leading natural selection to favor manipulators over "honest" signallers. The presence of manipulators, in turn, puts the receivers at risk of losing fitness from "deceit," and as a result, the receivers are selected to evaluate signals for their reliability and trustworthiness.

Whether signals from another agent can be trusted or not depends first and foremost on game-theoretic constraints, most notably *alignment of interests* (Searcy & Nowicki, 2005; but see Ferretti, this volume, for a complementary view) between the communicators. Following the foundational paper by Krebs and Dawkins (1984), evolutionary signalling theory predicts two main paths of the evolution of communication systems, depending on the presence or absence of alignment of interests: flashy or efficient (see also Knight, 1998).

Close alignment of interests is the exception rather than the rule in nature. Much more frequently, the signaller and receiver compete for resources, resulting in some degree of conflict of interests. This often leads to the evolution of what Krebs and Dawkins (1984) call *expensive hype*, exemplified by roars of red deer stags – conspicuous, repetitive, exaggerated, and loud displays. This is because signallers prove the veracity of their signals by paying a high *strategic cost* (Maynard,

Smith & Harper, 2003), which leads to the emergence of "flashy" signals designed to impress and convince. A typical context is the conflict of interests between males, who typically gain by maximising their mating opportunities, and females, who gain by choosing as mates the males of best biological quality, and a typical way of unequivocally demonstrating their biological quality by males is through the production of mating calls that are highly energetically costly (which is often measurable in the increase of the male's metabolic rate, cf. Bailey et al., 1993).

In the rare scenarios where the interests of the communicating animals align, signals are used to non-deceptively inform the receiver. The alignment of interests eliminates the incentives to manipulate, so the animals can safely trust each other, which in turn obviates the need to certify each signal with a strategic cost. Signals are instead streamlined for maximum communicative efficiency and tend to minimise costs in terms of time, energy and risk. This leads to the evolution of what Krebs and Dawkins (1984) call *conspiratorial whispers*: cheap, subtle, inconspicuous and efficient signals, canonically exemplified by the dance of the honeybee (but also human language).

The above account is necessarily highly simplified and many caveats apply (see e.g., Cronk, 2005). However, at least as a general rule, systems of communication typically evolve along one of two paths: alignment of interests drives communication to be "efficient," whereas a lack of alignment of interests – to be "flashy."

4. Flashy *vs.* efficient bodily mimetic communication

There is a broad range of contexts in which modern humans rely on forms of bodily-mimetic communication that overlap with our concept of pantomime (cf. pantomimic fossils, Żywiczyński et al., 2021). One type of such communicative behaviours is "true pantomime," whose function is to transfer referential-propositional information in the absence of language. True pantomime (cf. Gärdenfors, this volume) is declarative and triadic, and its design is typically optimised for communicative efficiency, which predicts that repeated use will result in conserving energy, in minimising the span of movement, in non-redundancy, and ultimately in washing-away of primary iconicity and in the development of semiotic conventions.

However, there are situations where such transfer is not a communicative priority; contemporary examples include the realms of art, performance and ritual (cf. Brown, this volume), where emotional and social meaning dominates over the efficient transfer of referential information (e.g., the Haka dance, see below). From our perspective, such cases are predicted to form a qualitatively different class of bodily-mimetic communication, distinguished by its primary function and the resulting design specifications. Accordingly, this second class of bodily-mimetic communication involves contexts in which the function to transfer propositional information is either absent or can be offloaded to co-present language. The function of such mimetic acts is instead performative and dyadic, and their design is not optimised for efficiency but rather for emotional impact, not unlike what Krebs & Dawkins (1984) call "expensive hype." Since *retaining a high cost is instrumental to achieving this function*, the prediction is that such bodily mimetic behaviours should involve high redundancy, wasting energy, and maximising the span of movement, and that these characteristics should not be affected by repeated use. Finally, although with repeated use such mimetic expressions may become stereotypic and even achieve some level of normativity, they are not predicted to develop semiotic conventions: as we discuss in Section 4.1 below, rituals can be conventional, but these are not the type of semiotic conventions to refer to actions and objects in interpersonal communication.

A clear example of this category are bodily displays functioning as signals of combat potential or of mating quality, which are guaranteed to be "honest," because the energetic expenditure or the degree of motor skill required for their execution closely correlate with the communicated characteristic. Such displaying often happens in the context of sexual selection (cf. Section 3 above): either intersexual, i.e., mate choice, or intrasexual, i.e., competing within the sex for access to mating opportunities (cf. Ferretti, this volume, for a different account). This in turn links to theories of aesthetic fitness, and sexual selection theory of the origins of art, which posit that artistic virtuosity is sexually selected (Miller, 2001; Boyd, 2009). Historically, artistic forms of pantomime often relied on athletic performance and skill (cf. Brown, this volume). For example, ancient pantomime was often comical, relied on mannerisms and exaggerations, and required precision of facial expression and gesturing, and "[c]alling for great athletic ability, it resembled sports more than arts: it involved boxing and wrestling moves, high jumping, or somersaults (wasting the performers' energy)" (Żywiczyński et al., 2018; cf. Slater, 1994; Barba, 1995: 15).

A similar function may be attributed to bodily mimesis in traditional narratives. For example, the Bayaka nomads of the Western Congo Basin typically incorporate elaborate pantomimes of both the hunter's and game's moves in their accounts of hunting expeditions (Lewis, 2014). Finally, ritualistic and ceremonial uses of mimetic communication, such as the famous Haka dance in Māori culture, link to theories of rituals as costly signals (e.g., Irons, 2001; Sosis et al., 2007; Henrich, 2009; Soler, 2012; Xygalatas et al., 2013).

4.1 Ritual

The case of ritual is particularly interesting, since it plays a pivotal role in several language origins accounts (Hutto, 2008; Power, 2014; Knight, 1998; Gärdenfors, 2018). A good point of departure to discuss ritual in the context of bodily mimesis is the work of Peter Gärdenfors (2018), who posits a sequence of evolutionary steps in the development of bodily mimesis:

– demonstration, or pantomime for teaching was the primary form of bodily mimesis;
– it later gave rise to pantomime, or more specifically pantomime for communication, which was a form of pretense and served the function of referring to events (mainly actions) displaced in space and time;
– finally, ritual evolved through the conventionalisation of pantomime. As noted above (Section 2), the conventionalisation of pantomime is the process that leads to the emergence of proto-sign and is driven by the need for growing efficiency in transmitting referential information. In Gärdenfors's view, the conventionalisation of pantomime into ritual has a wider scope and relates to developing strict norms for performing certain behaviours – "ritualized conventions of behaviour" (2018: 45; cf. Zlatev, 2018) – such as holding a hand above somebody's head to bless this person.

A further difference between pantomime and ritual concerns their functions. The function of pantomime is to transmit the referential content about actions and to do so in the way that is as understandable to the receiver as possible ("The intention behind a pantomime is normally apparent to the onlooker ..." Gärdenfors, 2018: 46). As already noted, the process of conventionalisation of pantomime amplifies the intelligibility of evolving signs (Sulik 2018). In contrast, the core function of religious rituals is to transmit generic, impersonal knowledge, often of "otherwise difficult-to-accept beliefs" such as supernatural explanations of natural causes (Gärdenfors, 2018: 48; cf. Whitehouse & Lanman, 2014: 8).

Explaining the evolutionary significance of ritual, Gärdenfors submits that engaging in common rituals improves group identification and cooperation between group members:

> When you encounter a stranger that turns out to share the same beliefs connected to the same rituals, then this individual is more likely to be a suitable cooperation partner than somebody who does not share these beliefs ... participation in rituals is associated with pro-social in-group behaviour, and will therefore contribute to improving the reputation of the participants. Furthermore, rituals are favoured by cultural evolution since they transmit belief, commitment and thereby promote cooperation. (2018: 50)

Although we are largely in agreement with the above view of the social functions of rituals in regulating intra-group cooperation, below we propose a different analysis of the communicative properties of bodily-mimetic rituals – one that we believe more closely aligns with evolutionary signalling theory as outlined in Section 3. We begin from the formal properties of ritual, in describing which Gärdenfors follows Kapitány and Nielsen's idea of *ritual stance*: "formality, repetition, redundancy, stereotypy, and causal opacity, in which performance is more important than outcome" (Kapitány & Nielsen, 2015; Gärdenfors, 2018: 46). Gärdenfors links some of these properties, mainly stereotypy, to the exaggeration of movement patterns observed in demonstration and pantomime in contrast to relevant praxic actions (e.g., the pantomime and demonstration of hammering vs. the action of hammering). However, we note that these definitional characteristics of rituals, that is repetition, redundancy, and stereotypy, as well as exaggeration, are the hallmarks of the "expensive hype" category of communicative behaviours, which strongly suggests that such properties of rituals are shaped by the underlying high strategic cost component.

Indeed, on a mainstream evolutionary approach to rituals, the essential deep property of rituals is not their semantics, related to beliefs about reality, nor its pedagogical function, but rather the high cost that the performance of ritual involves without bringing any obvious benefit. In particular, performing rituals incurs "time, energetic and/or financial costs that are not directed toward accomplishing somatic or reproductive goals efficiently or that limit an individual's ability to achieve these benefits from nongroup members" (Sosis & Bressler, 2003). A particularly relevant account is the costly signalling theory of religion, which explains rituals as "hard-to-fake signals of commitment to the group and the ideas it represents and that such advertisements promote trust and solidarity among group members" (Soler, 2012: 347). Soler follows Bliege-Bird & Smith (2005), who enumerate four general conditions necessary for a behavior to function as an evolutionarily stable costly signal:

> one, members of a population vary with regard to an attribute that cannot be directly assessed but can be otherwise signaled; two, it is advantageous for others to obtain reliable information about variation in attribute quality; three, there is a conflict of interest between signalers and receivers so that deception (i.e., signaling higher-than-actual quality) benefits signalers at the expense of receivers; and four, the costs of producing or performing the signal are condition-dependent (low-quality individuals pay higher costs to produce the signal, or, ceteris paribus, the benefits of signaling are greater for high-quality individuals).   (Soler, 2012: 347)

Building on the work of Sosis (esp. Sosis et al., 2007), Soler goes on to argue that ritual meets these conditions. Firstly, members of a population differ in the intensity of their faith, a trait that can only be assessed indirectly based on ritual participation. Secondly, information about the intensity of each individual's faith is useful to the observers, who can rely on it as a proxy for estimating that individual's commitment to the group and thus its readiness for in-group cooperation. Further, such readiness to cooperate with in–groups is vulnerable to be exploited by non-believers, whose signalling of religious faith is deceptive (not genuine). Finally, believers and non-believers will differ in the opportunity costs related to signalling faith, which "will be lower for believers (i.e., high-quality signallers) than for nonbelievers because the former have willingly changed or abandoned behaviours in order to comply with the religious doctrine, while the latter have not" (Soler, 2012: 347).

The main upshot of this reasoning is that a high cost is not an accidental property that ritual can lose in the process of evolving into pantomimes as they begin to be used for information transfer. Rather, a high cost is an essential property, fundamental to what a ritual is. This in turn would *prima facie* make pantomime and ritual represent two different evolutionary trajectories of bodily mimetic communication: the former evolving along the trajectory of efficiency; the latter, along the trajectory of expensive hype. Consequently, rituals could not evolve into pantomime and then language, because developing the function of transferring referential-propositional information implies following the efficient trajectory. Thus, even if rituals and pantomimes may superficially rely on similar mechanics of body movement – which might suggest evolutionary continuity – their deep functions and resulting design specifications are very different. In particular, although rituals are highly conventionalised, they do not undergo the type of conventionalisation required by language evolution scenarios. They cannot simplify and streamline for the sake of communicative efficiency, because doing that would also lose the high strategic cost, and thus subvert the very essence of what it means to be a ritual.

5. Conclusion

In standard language origins accounts (e.g., Jackendoff, 2002), including the most popular pantomimic or bodily mimetic theories of language emergence (Arbib, 2012; Zlatev, 2014), the evolutionary logic often amounts to a gradual advancement through stages, each stage incrementally increasing cognitive or communicative complexity. The evolutionary element is thus taken to mean a gradualistic reduction of big – intuitively unbridgeable – discontinuity between language and animal communication into a sequence of smaller – intuitively bridgeable – discontinuities, or "stages" (cf. the contributions in this volume by Arbib, Ferretti, Gärdenfors, and Zlatev et al., who embrace evolutionary continuity). However, evolution through natural selection does not necessarily imply either gradualism or a progression from simple to complex, especially considering that gains in cognitive or communicative complexity cannot be assumed to be adaptive without justification.

In the preceding sections we have argued that actual evolutionary accounts should give proper consideration to the question of the evolutionary stability of communication systems. As first explained by Krebs & Dawkins (1984), misalignment of interests promotes the evolution of expensive, conspicuous, repetitive, exaggerated, and loud displays, while alignment of interests leads to the evolution of cheap, subtle, inconspicuous and efficient signals or signs. Applying this logic to the evolution of bodily-mimetic communication, we contrast the expensive forms, such as artistic or ritual displays, with the conventionalisation of pantomime into simpler signs, which embodies the latter, "efficient" trajectory. As we remarked above, an important corollary of signalling theory is that since misalignment of interests is much more common than alignment, the "efficient" path for the evolution of communication is rare, and its emergence requires very special socio-ecological conditions. Without such conditions in place, bodily-mimetic communication will not evolve from displays to protosign but will instead remain trapped in the "expensive hype" trajectory.

More generally, we argue for a greater prominence of explanations that take away focus from cognitive, semiotic and structural complexity, and place it on the evolutionary constraints such as "trust," which underlie and predict many dimensions of complexity. This would also open the door to new language-origins scenarios, having the advantage of a direct grounding in evolutionary signalling theory.

Funding

This study was supported by grant UMO-2017/27/B/HS2/00642 from the Polish National Science Centre.

References

Arbib, M. (2012). *How the Brain Got Language*. Oxford University Press.

Arbib, M. (2016). Towards a computational comparative neuroprimatology: framing the language-ready brain. *Physics of life reviews*, 16, 1–54.

Bailey, W. J. Withers, P. C., Endersby, M., Gaull, K. (1993). The energetic costs of calling in the bushcricket Requena verticalis (Orthoptera: Tettigonidae: Listroscelidinae). *J. Exp. Biol.*, 178, 21–37.

Barba, E. (1995). *The paper canoe. A guide to theatre anthropology.* London.

Bliege Bird, R., & Smith, E.A. (2005). Signaling Theory, Strategic Interaction, and Symbolic Capital. *Current Anthropology*, 46(2), 221–248.

Boyd, R. (2009). Does an evolutionary perspective help understand environmental degradation?. *Trends in Ecology & Evolution*, 24(2), 71–72.

Cronk, L. (2005). The application of animal signaling theory to human phenomena. *Soc. Sci. Inf*, 44, 603–620.

Donald, M. (1991). *Origins of the modern mind.* Harvard University Press.

Fay, N., Arbib, M., & Garrod, S. (2013). How to bootstrap a human communication system. *Cognitive Science*, 37(7), 1356–1367.

Gärdenfors, P. (2017). Demonstration and pantomime in the evolution of teaching. *Front. Psych.*, 8, 415.

Gärdenfors, P. (2018). Pantomime as a foundation for ritual and language. *Studia Liturgica*, 48(1–2), 41–55.

Harnad, S. (1990). The symbol grounding problem. *Physica D: Nonlinear Phenomena*, 42(1–3), 335–346.

Hartmann, S., & Pleyer, M. (2021). Constructing a protolanguage: reconstructing prehistoric languages in a usage-based construction grammar framework. *Philosophical Transactions of the Royal Society B*, 376(1824), 20200200.

Henrich, J. (2009). The evolution of costly displays, cooperation and religion: Credibility enhancing displays and their implications for cultural evolution. *Evolution and human behavior*, 30(4), 244–260.

Hurford, J.R. (2007). *The origins of meaning: Language in the light of evolution*, Vol. 1. Oxford University Press.

Hutto, D. (2008). First Communions: Mimetic sharing without theory of mind. In J. Zlatev et al.. (Eds.), *The Shared Mind* (pp. 246–276). Benjamins.

Irons, W. (2001). Religion as a hard-to-fake sign of commitment. In R.M. Nesse (Ed.), *Evolution and the capacity for commitment* (pp. 290–309). Russell Sage Foundation.

Jackendoff, Ray (2002). *Foundations of language: Brain, meaning, grammar, evolution.* Oxford University Press UK.

Kapitány, R., & Nielsen, M. (2015). Adopting the ritual stance: The role of opacity and context in ritual and everyday actions. *Cognition*, 145, 13–29.

Knight, C. (1998). Ritual/speech co-evolution: A solution to the problem of deception. In J.R. Hurford, M. Studdert-Kennedy, & C. Knight (Eds.), *Approaches to the evolution of language. Social and cognitive bases* (pp. 68–91). Cambridge University Press.

Krebs, J.R., Dawkins, R. (1984). Animal Signals: Mind-Reading and Manipulation. In J.R. Krebs & R. Dawkins (Eds.), *Behavioral ecology* (pp. 380–402). Blackwell.

Lameira, A.R., & Call, J. (2018). Time-space–displaced responses in the orangutan vocal system. *Science Advances*, 4(11), eaau3401.

Lewis, J.D. (2014). BaYaka Pygmy multi-modal and mimetic communication traditions. In D. Dor, C. Knight, & J. Lewis (Eds), *The Social origins of language* (pp. 77–91). Oxford University Publishing.

Maynard Smith, J., & Harper, D. 2003. *Animal Signals.* Oxford University Press.

Miller, S. (2001). *Social action: A teleological account.* Cambridge University Press.

Mineiro, A., Báez-Montero, I. C., Moita, M., Galhano-Rodrigues, I., & Castro-Caldas, A. (2021). Disentangling pantomime from early sign in a new sign language: window into language evolution research. *Frontiers in psychology*, 12, 1130.

Mineiro, A., Carmo, P., Caroça, C., Moita, M., Carvalho, S., Paço, J., & Zaky, A. (2017). Emerging linguistic features of sao tome and principe sign language. *Sign Language & Linguistics*, 20(1), 109–128.

Power, C. (2014). The evolution of ritual as a process of sexual selection. The social origins of language. In D. Dor, C. Knight, & J. Lewis (Eds), *The social origins of language* (pp. 196–207). Oxford University Publishing.

Roberts, G., Lewandowski, J., & Galantucci, B. (2015). How communication changes when we cannot mime the world: Experimental evidence for the effect of iconicity on combinatoriality. *Cognition*, 141, 52–66.

Sachs, J., Rubenstein, D. (2007). The evolution of cooperative breeding... *Behav. Proc.*, 76(2), 131–137.

Schmid, H. J. (2020). *The dynamics of the linguistic system: Usage, conventionalization, and entrenchment*. Oxford University Press.

Searcy, W., Nowicki, S. (2005). *The Evolution of Animal Communication*. Princeton University Press.

Slater, W. J. (1994). Pantomimes. *Didaskalia*, 1(2).

Soler, M. (2012). Costly signaling, ritual and cooperation: Evidence from Candomblé, an Afro-Bazilian religion. *Evolution and Human Behavior*, 33(4), 346–356.

Sonesson, G. (2007). From the meaning of embodiment to the embodiment of meaning: A study in phenomenological semiotics. In T. Ziemke, J. Zlatev & R. Frank (Eds.), *Body, language and mind. Vol 1: Embodiment* (p. 85–128). Mouton de Gruyter.

Sosis, R., & Bressler, E. R. (2003). Cooperation and commune longevity: A test of the costly signaling theory of religion. *Cross-cultural research*, 37(2), 211–239.

Sosis, R., Kress, H. C., & Boster, J. S. (2007). Scars for war: evaluating alternative signaling explanations for cross-cultural variance in ritual costs. *Evolution and Human Behavior*, 28, 234–247.

Sulik, J. (2018). Cognitive mechanisms for inferring the meaning of novel signals during symbolisation. *PloS One*, 13(1), e0189540.

Tomasello, M. (2008). *Origins of human communication*. MIT Press.

Wacewicz, S., & Żywiczyński, P. (2021). Pantomimic conceptions of language origins. In N. Gontier, A. Lock, C. Sinha (Eds.), *Handbook of human symbolic evolution*. Oxford University Press.

Whitehouse, H., & Lanman, J. A. (2014). The ties that bind us: Ritual, fusion, and identification. *Current Anthropology*, 55(6), 674–695.

Xygalatas, D., Mitkidis, P., Fischer, R., Reddish, P., Skewes, J., Geertz, A. W., ... & Bulbulia, J. (2013). Extreme rituals promote prosociality. *Psychological Science*, 24(8), 1602–1605.

Zlatev, J. (2014). Human uniqueness, bodily mimesis and the evolution of language. Humana. *Mente Journal of Philosophical Studies*, 7(27), 197–219.

Zlatev, J. (2018). Meaning making from life to language: The semiotic hierarchy and phenomenology. *Cognitive Semiotics*, 11(1), 1–18.

Zlatev, J., Persson, T., & Gärdenfors, P. (2005). Bodily mimesis as "the missing link" in human cognitive evolution. *Lund University Cognitive Studies*, 121, 1–45.

Zlatev, J., Żywiczyński, P., & Wacewicz, S. (2020). Pantomime as the original human-specific communicative system. *Journal of Language Evolution*, 5(2), 156–174.

Żywiczyński, P., Wacewicz, S., & Sibierska, M. (2018). Defining pantomime for language evolution research. *Topoi*, 37(2), 307–318.

Żywiczyński, P., Wacewicz, S., & Lister, C. (2021). Pantomimic fossils in modern human communication. *Philosophical Transactions of the Royal Society B*, 376(1824), 20200204.

CHAPTER 5

Can pantomime narrate?
A cognitive semiotic approach

Jordan Zlatev,[1] Marta Sibierska,[2] Przemysław Żywiczyński,[2]
Joost van de Weijer[1] & Monika Boruta-Żywiczyńska[2]
[1] Lund University | [2] Nicolaus Copernicus University

Adopting the conceptual-empirical loop of cognitive semiotics, we define *narrative* as a three-part structure consisting of Narration, Story and Event-sequence and *primary narrativity* as the process of interpreting a narrative from the former to the latter two. We distinguish between simple narratives with chronological mappings between Story and Event sequence, and complex narratives, where this is not the case; for example, by beginning the narration with the final event. Understanding pantomime as a prototype-based concept grounded in iconic gesture, we ask if it affords primary narrativity, in the case of both simple and complex narratives. We proceed by reviewing and elaborating a recent experimental semiotic study where communicators inter-semiotically translated three-event stories from language to pantomime, and interpreters had to match these performances with three-image cartoon strips. The results showed that pantomime was successful when the narratives were simple, but much less so when they were not. To be able to distinguish between the two, the participants spontaneously introduced various *markers of event order*. When they conventionalized these markers, they introduced elements of protolanguage, thus going beyond the narrative potentials of pantomime.

Keywords: cognitive semiotics, bodily mimesis, narration, story, event sequence primary/secondary narrativity, simple/complex narratives

1. Introduction

Most would agree that language is particularly well suited for narrating (Donald, 1991; Ryan, 2012). But what is it that makes it so? And what about other semiotic systems like pictures (single, or in sequences, as in picture books, comic books, and graphic novels), music and pantomime: bodily expressions organized as

https://doi.org/10.1075/ais.12.05zla
© 2024 John Benjamins Publishing Company

sequences of (whole-body) gestures?[1] Which of these can be used for "storytelling without telling" (Sibierska, 2017), or in other words: for communicating "mute narratives" (Sonesson, 1997)? What are the narrative potentials of these semiotic systems when compared to language? These are the questions that we ask in this article, in part by reviewing and elaborating on a recent experimental-semiotic study on the capacity of pantomime to narrate (Sibierska et al., 2023). But to answer such questions we must first delve into conceptual matters and explicate notions like semiotic systems, pantomime, and perhaps the most controversial of them all: *narrative*.[2] In the context of the interdisciplinary field of "narratology" (see Section 2), Ryan (2007) begins an article aiming to provide a comprehensive definition of narrative as follows:

> In the past fifteen years, as "the narrative turn in the humanities" gave way to the narrative turn everywhere (politics, science studies, law, medicine, and last but not least, cognitive science), few words have enjoyed so much use and suffered so much abuse as *narrative* and its partial synonym, *story*.   (Ryan, 2007:22)

Such "abuse" has more recently led to skepticism, as with other notions that have been overused in the past, like "media," "representation," or "multimodality," and in more recent years we have noticed that people, including ourselves, have begun to avoid using "the N-word." But why throw away the proverbial baby with the dirty bathwater? In this article we therefore address head on the conceptual challenges behind the question "can pantomime narrate?" armed with a framework from *cognitive semiotics*, the new discipline combining ideas and methods from semiotics, cognitive science and linguistics, under the synthesizing influence of phenomenology (Konderak, 2018; Sonesson, 2007; Zlatev, 2015; Zlatev, Sonesson & Konderak, 2016). Particularly appropriate is the methodological principle of the *conceptual-empirical loop*, which urges us to seek conceptual definitions that are both intuitive and productive for empirical investigations of a given phenomenon, and then carry out various studies in which we observe and experiment with how the phenomenon manifests itself, thus opening up for revising the definitions that we started with.[3]

Applying this approach to our present concerns, in Section 2 we discuss and define a concept of narrative, linking it to a helpful discussion of "narration in

---

1. For a proper definition of this notion, pivotal in the present context, and for some cross-references to other chapters in this volume, see Section 3.

2. It is characteristic that the relations between this concept and that of pantomime is also the focus of Feretti (this volume). While our understanding of pantomime largely overlaps, we apparently have very different notions of narrative.

3. Of course, more implicit forms of the conceptual-empirical loop can be found more generally, especially within psychology and related fields. For example, Marentette et al. (this volume) relies on empirical research to help explicate (essentially semiotic) notions such as *symbolic distancing* (Werner & Kaplan, 1963).

various media" by Ryan (2012). We find ourselves, for the most part, in agreement with Ryan's argument on the narrative superiority of the semiotic system of language compared to those of depiction, gesture and music. Still, we find this argument somewhat biased in favor of "the primacy of language," leaving gaps for further research. In Section 3 we discuss how best to define pantomime, another prerequisite for addressing the research question in the title.

In Section 4 we turn to the empirical side of the conceptual-empirical loop and review the design and main findings of an experimental study (Sibierska et al., 2023), which addressed the issue of the narrative potential of pantomime by means of two steps of *intersemiotic translation* (Jakobson, 1959; Li & Zlatev, 2021). In this study, a communicator is asked to translate simple three-event narratives from language to pantomime, while an interpreter has to match these pantomimes to one of four pre-given sequences of pictures, thus translating pantomime to pictures. The study showed that in a simpler condition, where the order of events to be narrated was chronological, this intersemiotic communication process was by and large successful. However, it was much less so in the more complex condition where the order of events to be narrated was not chronological. To deal with this the participants begin inventing "markers" to distinguish these conditions and mark the order of events, as we explain in Section 4. As we discuss in the concluding Section 5, this implies that the communicative system used can no longer be characterized as pantomime, but rather constitutes a form of *protolanguage*.[4] Thus, we are brought back to the conceptual side of the loop.

2. Narrative, primary vs. secondary narrativity, and different semiotic systems

The notion of narrative has been defined and redefined many times, and even has its own field known as *narratology* (e.g., Hühn, Pier, Schmid & Schönert, 2009). A commonly cited definition of narrative is that of Prince (2008:19): "the logically consistent representation of at least two asynchronous events that do not presuppose or imply each other." But this begs many questions: what counts as a "representation"? What does it mean that it should be "logically consistent"? This can clearly not be in a standard understanding of logic since that would contradict

---

4. This widely used notion in the language origins literature differs considerably across researchers, depending on the evolutionary scenarios that they propose. This appears also to be the case in the present context, with Feretti (this volume) assuming something more general, while Arbib (this volume) and Gärdenfors (this volume), something more specific than what we mean by protolanguage: a communicative system relying heavily on conventionality, but lacking systematic structure (i.e., grammar).

the final requirement that the events – or rather the propositions that represent them – should not "presuppose or imply one another." The intuition behind the definition seems to be that, for example, (1) would contradict this requirement and thus fail as a narrative given the presuppositional relation between the two sentences, and so would (2) since there is no apparent relation between described events, but (3) would pass, as the events are "asynchronous" and some sort of (causal) relation between them can be imputed.

(1) John's brother is coming to town. John has a brother.

(2) John's brother is coming to town. John kissed Mary.

(3) John kissed Mary. She slapped him.

To some degree this is indeed intuitive, but we need to spell out and elaborate the definition to avoid ambiguities and potential contradictions. In (3) the story is expressed verbally, but it could as well be realized in some other semiotic system, like a sequence of pictures. The generalization to make is that a narrative must be made up of *signs*, where each sign has two poles: denoting *expression* and denoted *object* (in a generalized sense to include individuals, properties, and events, see Sokolowski, 2000; Zlatev, Żywiczyński & Wacewicz, 2020). The *content* of each sign is then the particular way in which the object is represented, a kind of "viewpoint" on the object that may differ even if the object itself stays the in the famous examples of Frege (1948 [1891]): *Evening Star* and *Morning Star* have different contents ("senses") but the same object ("reference"). "John" and "him," and "Mary" and "she" are in this sense co-referential but not synonymous. Thus, we have the three apexes of the "semiotic triangle," or the three levels of signification, with content mediating between expression and object, as shown in (4).

(4) $_{\text{Sign}}$ [Expression – Content – Object]

Applying this logic to the level of narrative implies straightforwardly that a narrative must also consist of three levels: (a) the Expression: in one semiotic system or another, (b) the Object: the sequence of events that are being narrated, and (c) the Content: the way this object is being presented. Many have recognized these three levels (e.g., Genette, 1980), but the terms for them have varied. For example, Bal (1997: 5, our emphasis) states:

> [A] narrative text is a text in which an agent or subject conveys to an addressee ("tells" the reader, viewer, or listener) a story in a *medium*, such as language, imagery, sound, buildings, or a combination thereof. A *story* is the content of that text and produces a particular manifestation, inflection, and "colouring" of a

fabula. A *fabula* is a series of logically and chronologically related events that are caused or experienced by actors.

We may use the following relatively neutral and common-sensical terms and generalize that a narrative consists of three independent parts or levels: (a) Narration in a certain "medium," (b) Story and (c) Event sequence, or "fabula," as expressed in (5).

(5)   _{Narrative} [Narration – Story – Event sequence][5]

That each of these is a necessary condition for the existence of a narrative can be easily appreciated. Say that the Event sequence is the Trojan war, or some other actual or imagined sequence of events. This can be narrated in indefinitely many different ways, and thus give rise to different Stories. And the same Story could be (in principle) narrated using different "media" – orally through speech, like in the original Homeros epos, by written language as we read it today, or polysemiotically and multimodally by a film like *Troy*. A question that arises is if such different Narrations "tell" the *same* story, even if the Event sequence is the same. Very often it will not be so since the differences in "manifestation, inflection, and 'coloring' of the fabula" – in the words of Bal (1997) – or what we can call in one word, *construal* (Möttonen, 2016; Zlatev, 2016) will be too extensive. This is why the inter-semiotic act of translating a story by crossing the borders of semiotic systems (e.g., from text to film), is often referred to as *adaptation* (Hutcheon, 2006) or *transposition* (Sonesson, 2014).

But at least sometimes it can be the same Story, narrated in different semiotic systems, as we discuss below. This is both an argument for distinguishing this level from the two others, and for placing clear criteria on what would count as the "same" Story under different narrations. A general requirement, stated first by Aristotle, and then repeated and elaborated many times (Allen, 2013; Todorov, 1969), is that the Story needs to be organized into a coherent whole, with at least a beginning, middle and end:

> A *whole* [story] is that which possesses a beginning, a middle and an end. A *beginning* is that which itself does not follow necessarily from anything else, but some second thing naturally exists or occurs after it. Conversely, an *end* is that which does itself naturally from something else ... but there is nothing after it. A *middle* is that which itself comes after something else, and some other thing comes after it.
>
> (*Poetics* 5.1) (Aristotle, 1987)

---

5. Since these terms are highly ambiguous, we use them here and in the rest of the paper with initial capitals when they are intended in the present technical sense.

Unlike in the Event sequence itself, however, there is no requirement for the temporal order of events in the Story itself to abide by the sequence beginning-middle-end; one can very well begin *in medias res*, and then go back in time to what led to this, as customary in much fiction (e.g., Currie, 2007). There are many other aspects that define a particular story, such as the subjective viewpoint from which events are being represented,[6] but the order of representing events in the story is a key element of story organization. It is also central for the empirical study that we review in Section 4.

But there is one more ambiguity in the concept of narrative that we need to clarify. By presenting the three elements (or layers) of narrative as in (5) above, a presumed left-to-right order would imply that Narration has temporal primacy. This is indeed the likely perspective of the *audience* of a narrative, going from the Expression to the represented Object (the sequence of events) via the Story, the construal of the Event sequence. But this is not the perspective of the narrator, who would for the most part go in the opposite direction (Diget, 2019). Even from the point of view of the audience, "understanding the narrative by going from narration to the underlying story" (Stampoulidis, 2019:33) is what characterizes *primary narrativity*. But there are many cases, especially when Narration does not use the semiotic system of language, that the Story is already known by the audience. This allows a particular, even very minimal, Expression to be interpreted as a Narration. Stampoulidis (2019) calls this *secondary narrativity*, and argues that single ("monophase") images of Greek street-art can only narrate in this way, by presupposing common knowledge of heroic Stories (e.g., that narrated in the film *300*), according to which Greece is first harmonious, then threatened by a powerful enemy, and finally emerges as victorious. This can be generalized as follows: *single pictures can participate in secondary, but not primary narrativity.*

Li and Zlatev (2021) elaborate the notion of secondary narrativity, emphasizing that it should be seen as a cognitive process operating jointly with primary narrativity, in converse directions and in parallel, with different narratives, contexts and audiences involving different *proportions* of the two processes. But still, some extremely "reduced" forms of Narration, like the *Little Mermaid* statue in Copenhagen, are almost completely reliant on prior knowledge of the "underlying story"; or rather stories, as they are interpreted very differently when these stories differ, as is the case with the H.C. Andersen and Disney versions. The authors offer empirical support for this claim in a study where Chinese and European audiences were to provide "little mermaid stories" in response to a picture of the statue. It tuned out that not only these narrations, but the participants' interpretations of what the *Little Mermaid* statue expresses, correlated with the prior stories which they were familiar with.

---

6. Kurosawa's *Roshomon* is a classic film that utilizes this.

Ryan (2012) claims that secondary narrativity (without using the term) "is parasitic on the narrativity of the original text, which, most likely, will be known through language" and that this "illustrative function is by far the most common occurrence in non-verbal narration." With the later statement we can only partially agree, since while the narrative scope of single images, statues as well as musical pieces (like Prokofiev's *Peter and the Wolf*) is limited to secondary narrativity, it would be wrong to claim this for all forms of *mimetic* narration.[7] Semiotically speaking, mimetic signs are predominantly based on *iconicity* (similarity) between expressions and their objects, see (4) above, while verbal signs are mostly grounded in *symbolicity* (conventionality). Ryan (2012) remarks that "mimetic narration, interpreted as showing, has become the dominant mode of presentation in multichannel performing arts, such as drama, film, the opera, mime, and ballet. In these last two cases, as well as in silent film, mimetic narration becomes emancipated from language." But such artforms are clearly not limited to secondary narrativity.

Serial, or "polyphase" pictures can also be "emancipated from language" and at the same time engage in primary narrativity. The series in Figure 1 and Figure 2 show two different ways in which they can do so. In the first case, as typical for the genre of wordless comics strips, there is a link of "every image with one moment in a continuous action as if it were a frozen frame in a silent film" (Ryan, 2012). In the second case "narrative content is suggested on the level of the individual images by their reliance on familiar scripts" (Ryan, 2012) and there are considerable temporal gaps between the depicted events. Picture series like 25 *Images of a Man's Passion*, are more dependent on background knowledge (European history, demonstrations, trials, executions), and thus display a larger proportion of secondary narrativity. But once given correct "reading" direction, interpreters can construct relatively consistent ("underlying") stories in both cases. This is so because they can identify participants, like Charlie Brown (Figure 1) or the Man (Figure 2), and "track" them from image to image, imputing coherence relations

---

7. The narratological concepts of mimesis and diegesis, stemming from Plato and Aristotle, are influential, but not used consistently in the literature (Halliwell, 2012). One way to understand these, favored by Brown (this volume), is based on whether the narrator is adopting a protagonist ("egocentric") or external ("allocentric") viewpoint on the events narrated. But another way is to focus on the "showing" nature of the mimetic mode of narration, dominated by iconicity and indexicality, and on the "telling" mode of dietetic narration, dominated by the use of conventional signs, symbols (e.g., Clark, 2004). As pointed out by Ryan (2012), semiotic systems (and the artforms that utilize them) are not neutral in this respect. So, for example, theater lends itself more naturally to mimesis, while (written) language to diegesis. On this take, unlike that of Brown (this volume), the semiotic system of depiction (e.g., drawings) affords predominantly mimetic rather than diegetic narration.

between the depicted events, and leading up to a coherent whole, with a well-defined beginning-middle-end structure.

Figure 1. A wordless comics strip from *Peanuts*, depicting micro-events as in a "silent film" Charles Schulz *Peanuts* Sunday Comic Strip Charlie Brown and Friends Original Art dated 8–9–53 (United Feature Syndicate, 1953)

Silent film can narrate at least as effectively, and even more so when supplemented with music as customary, even without the usual verbal "intertitles" that are for the most part redundant. But what about the semiotic system of gesture, unaided by the technology of film? Ryan (2012, our emphasis) offers an interesting discussion, but is in general skeptical:

> Can body movement tell a story that is new to the spectator without external help? The answer is yes, but the repertory is very limited. ... Narrative is about evolving networks of human relations; and gestures and movement, by varying the distance between bodies, are reasonably good at representing the evolution of interpersonal relations, as long as mental life can be translated into visible body language. But even though gestures add a kinetic element to serial still pictures, this does not result in a significant increase in narrative power. *On the contrary: it is much more difficult to narrate through continuous gestures than it is through discrete pictures frames. The chronological rearrangements ... would be impossible in a pantomime because gestural narration unfolds entirely in the present. It also operates in a simulacrum of real time that largely limits the narrated time to the time of narration.*

Chapter 5. Can pantomime narrate? 123

Figure 2. The final four of the 25 *Images of a Man's Passion* (Masereel, 1918), where each picture represents a stereotypical event, with considerable temporal and causal distance in between

Interestingly, it is exactly the capacity of "chronological rearrangements" of the story in comparison to the underlying Event sequence, see (5) above, that is being highlighted as a defining feature of the capacity not only for primary narrativity – this much is granted! – but for the production of what we can call *complex narratives*, a capacity that Ryan (2012) appeals to arguing for "the primacy of language as narrative medium."

To sum up, we have defined narrative as a three-part structure, consisting of Narration, Story and Event sequence, inheriting these three levels from those of the sign, with its Expression, Object and mediating Content (construal). Narration can take place in language and is then predominantly diegetic, or in other semiotic systems relying on iconicity, and is then predominantly mimetic (see footnote 7). At least some forms of mimetic narrations: serial pictures, silent film and gesture/mime can partake of primary narrativity, where stories unfamiliar to the audience can be narrated, and not only in secondary narrativity, which is more of an "illustrating function," relying prior knowledge of the stories. The question remains if there are any inherent limitations to mimetic narrations in general, and to pantomime in particular. It was suggested that this may have to do with the ability to communicate complex narratives, one of the defining features of which is for the Story not to follow the chronological beginning-middle-end structure. In Sections 4 and 5 we return to this question with the help of the findings of the mentioned empirical study. But prior to that, we must define the nature of the "medium" of pantomime.

3. Pantomime as a prototype-based concept

In everyday contexts, the notion of pantomime is most often associated with "mime": the artform of acting without speaking. In the Western intellectual tradition, its history is dated back to the 5th century BC in Ancient Greece, where mime developed as a theatrical form used to illustrate fragments of myths (see Brown, this volume). Subsequently, it started to become more and more associated with comedic forms and farce (Slater, 1994). In today's theatre, mime is both an independent artform, stabilized as a genre in the 1920s in France (Leabhart, 1997), and a medium used in traditions such as that of "physical theatre" (Lecoq, 2006). In both cases, mime can involve whole-body movements, but also a lot of exaggeration facial expressions and gestures, as well as dance, off- and on-set music, or non-verbal vocalizations. The *polysemiotic* (i.e., involving the use of two or more semiotic systems) expression can also be supported with costumes, props, and sets.

While there is nothing wrong in exploring the narrative potentials of such artforms, this is not the sense of "pantomime" that is most relevant for our title question: Can pantomime narrate? This is so because, in one sense, a positive answer concerning the artform of pantomime has already been given, albeit with questions remaining about the complexity of the narratives that can be expressed, as discussed in Section 2. But more importantly, while we do not situate the present investigation in an explicitly evolutionary context, much of the recent interest in pantomime has been kindled by the hypothesis that it served as a key "missing link" in the evolution of human communication, bridging the gap between animal signals and human languages (Arbib, 2005, this volume; Donald, 2012; Gärdenfors, this volume, Tomasello, 2008; Wacewicz & Żywiczyński, this volume; Zlatev, Żywiczyński & Wacewicz, 2020). And if it is indeed the case that pantomime preceded language in human evolution, the first narratives would presumably have needed to be expressed in pantomime (Boyd, 2017).

Yet, authors differ in their precise understanding of the concept of pantomime, beyond the general agreement that it involves iconic, more or less improvised, bodily reenactments. From our perspective, the nature of pantomime as a human communicative system is best understood in the context of *mimesis theory* (Donald, 1991, 1998, 2013) which proposes that at the dawn of humanity our ancestors thought and communicated literally with their whole bodies, rather than verbally. Since there are different manifestations of mimesis, including those in depiction and speech (see footnote 7), Zlatev (2014: 206) spells out the notion of *bodily mimesis* in terms of three positive and two negative characteristics:

> (1) it involves a *cross-modal mapping* between exteroception (e.g., vision) and proprioception (e.g., kinesthesia); (2) it is *under conscious control* and *is perceived by the subject to be similar to* some other action, object or event, (3) the subject *intends* the act to stand for some action, object or event *for an addressee*, and for the addressee to recognize this intention; (4) it is *not fully conventional and normative*, and (5) it does *not divide (semi)compositionally* into meaningful sub-acts that *systematically relate* to other similar acts, as in grammar.

With respect to the notions discussed in Section 2, we can point out that the first two features imply that mimetic acts consist of *iconic signs*, with bodily expressions that are understood by their users to represent "some action, object or event," and the remaining features imply that combinations of such signs can be used communicatively in an explicit enough manner, without prior agreement (i.e., conventions) on what they mean, and without systematic (syntactic) combinations, as in language. Consistent with this, Żywiczyński, Wacewicz, and Sibierska (2018: 315) have proposed the following influential definition of pantomime in the context of evolutionary studies:

> Pantomime is a non-verbal, mimetic and non-conventionalized means of communication, which is executed primarily in the visual channel by coordinated movements of the whole body, but which may incorporate other semiotic resources, most importantly non-linguistic vocalizations. Pantomimes are acts of improvised communication that holistically refer to a potentially unlimited repertoire of events, or sequences of events, [potentially] displaced from the here and now.

Taken together, these definitions of bodily mimesis and pantomime complement one another. The term "mimetic" in the latter definition can be clarified to imply iconic signs. "Non-conventionalized" and "improvised" should not be taken to mean that there is no degree of social agreement and/or negotiation on what the expressions in question mean, but that this is not the *dominant* semiotic ground for interpretation, which is rather that of iconicity. "Holistically refer" should analogously not be taken to mean completely undifferentiated "strong gestalt" representations, since mimes can represent people, objects, actions, as components of these events. But they do not do so in the rule-based manner of language, and perhaps most relevantly for narrative, there are no signs for causal, temporal, logical or other relations between the events. Finally, while iconic gestures are the core of this communicative system, other semiotic systems such as facial expressions, vocalizations and possibly even the rudiments of depiction – gestures can leave traces on a surface – can be included (cf. Brown, this volume; Mineiro & Moita, this volume; Marentette, this volume). This makes pantomime a (potentially) polysemiotic (in terms of semiotic systems) and multimodal (in terms of sensory modalities) communicative system, a point that is elaborated by Zlatev et al. (2020).

The latter work also addresses the question: what kind of iconic (i.e., resemblance-based) gestures can be considered as definitional of pantomime? On the basis of a review of the literature the authors propose the following four features which are in principle independent of one another: (a) using *more of the whole body* rather than less, (b) performed mostly from a *participant* than observer perspective, (c) denoting actions in *peripersonal* rather than extrapersonal space and (d) employing an *enacting* mode of representation, more than any of the other modes, including the *embodying kind* (Müller, 2016).[8] For example, the gestures shown in Figure 3 are similar in terms of feature (b), but differ in terms of all the others, making gesture B ("House/roof") less pantomimic than gesture A.

This approach has the advantage of defining pantomime in general, and specific pantomimic acts ("pantomimes") in particular, as a *prototype-based* concept: the more of the features that are present, the more pantomimic it will be. At the same time, the definition of bodily mimesis cited above gives clear categorial criteria: if it is no longer iconicity but conventionality that grounds the meaning of the communicative signs, and/or they start to be organized in regular, syntactical patterns, then we have transitioned from pantomime to protolanguage. It is good to keep this in mind as we turn to interpretations of the empirical study described in the following section.

---

8. To some degree the enacting mode corresponds to what the developmental literature classifies as Imaginary Object (IO) gestures and the embodying mode to Body Part as Object (BPO) gestures. While there is some evidence that it is the latter that are acquired earlier by children (see Marentette, this volume), it follows from our definition that the former are more pantomimic than the latter. This could potentially be one of many aspects where phylogeny does not recapitulate ontogeny.

Figure 3. (A) Hammering: whole-body, participant viewpoint, peripersonal space, Enacting mode, (B) House/roof: Part-body, participant viewpoint, extrapersonal space, Embodying mode (reprinted from Figure 1 and Figure 4 in Zlatev et al., 2020)

4. Pantomiming simple and (more) complex narratives

We designed the study, described in detail by Sibierska et al. (2023), inspired by the "referential communication games" used in experimental semiotics. However, we extended this experimental paradigm, as the task was not only to communicate single *concepts* (e.g., Fay, Arbib & Garrod, 2013), or even *events* (Zlatev, Wacewicz, Żywiczyński & van de Weijer, 2017) without the help of language, but of minimal stories, representing three interconnected events, with beginning, middle and end (see Section 2). The second inspiration was *intersemiotic translation* (Jakobson, 1959; Li & Zlatev, 2021), so that each round of the "game" could be seen as consisting of two steps of transfer from one semiotic system to another. In the first step, the Communicator was given a narrative through verbal narration in the form of text on a computer monitor, such as that in (6). The task was to communicate it to the Interpreter by means of "body movements," without using words or vocalizations, in effect translating from language to silent pantomime. In the second step, the Interpreter had to match this pantomime to one of four comic strips, given on their own computer monitor, thus translating from pantomime to serial pictures. Only one of the four strips was the correct answer – for (6) the one given in Figure 4 – while another strip showed the same Event sequence, but in an end-beginning-middle order, as shown in Figure 5. The remaining two strips showed a completely different narrative, in the two different orders. The presentation order of the four strips was randomized on the monitor of the Interpreter. Picking the correct comic strip was thus the way successful communication was operationalized in the study, and both participants received immediate positive or negative feedback on whether they had succeeded or not when the Interpreter had made their choice.

(6) *A man opened the door. He saw a bear. He ran away.*

Figure 4. The correct pictorial Narration corresponding to the Story expressed verbally in (6)

Figure 5. One of the three incorrect pictorial Narrations when (6) was being communicated, corresponding to the same narrative, but in a different Story order: End-beginning-middle

26 pairs of Polish participants were recruited for the study (with 35 females/17 males, mean age 25.5), taking turns to play the role of Communicator and Interpreter in consecutive rounds. They played a total of four games, each comprising 12 rounds. There were 24 stories in total, some of which were repeated in the successive games in a randomized order. The interactions between the participants were video recorded and later analyzed.

As could be surmised by the presentation so far, the main independent variable was the complexity of the mapping between the chronological Event sequence and the presented order, the Story. The intention was precisely to test Ryan's (2012) claim that "chronological rearrangements … would be impossible in a pantomime because gestural narration unfolds entirely in the present" (see Section 2). Thus, in half of all rounds in each game (i.e., 6 of 12, in randomized order), the stories were presented to the Communicator in the beginning-middle-end order, as in (6). In the remaining, they were given in the order of end-beginning-middle, as in (7), which is both conceptually and linguistically more complex than (6).

(7) *A man ran away, because when he opened the door, he saw a bear.*

We formulated two general hypotheses. The first (H1) was that even monosemiotic pantomime (i.e., without vocalizations or props) has the potential for primary narrativity, but is mostly fit for *simple narratives* (e.g., with isomorphic Event sequence-Story mappings, see Figure 7). The second (H2), was that in order to be able to express *complex narratives* (e.g., non-isomorphic Event sequence-Story mappings), pantomime will be enhanced with *markers of event order* (MEOs). Since these would need to be conventionalized by the participants, and possibly even introduce a degree of proto-grammatical structure (i.e., features (4) and (5) in the definition of bodily mimesis in Section 3), this would imply a transition from pantomime to protolanguage.

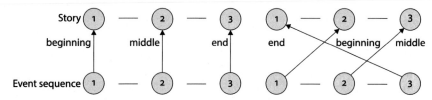

Figure 7. The isomorphic (Left) and non-isomorphic (Right) mappings of Story and Event sequence in the simple and the complex narratives, respectively

We identified and defined the MEOs given in Table 1 on the basis of the recordings of 10 randomly selected participant pairs (from the total of 26 pairs) using the usual first-person (e.g., intuition) and second-person (e.g., intersubjective dialogue) methods of cognitive semiotics (e.g., Devylder & Zlatev, 2020).

Subsequently we trained two coders to identify these markers, who then independently of the main researchers analyzed the video recordings of each round ($N=1248$) for their presence and type. In many cases the difference between E and AA could not be reliably established, for example when the Communicator gestured as shown in Figure 8; hence we allowed the coders to select a neutral E/AA code for such inherently ambiguous expression.

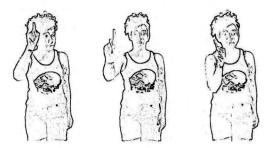

Figure 8. Three examples of an ambiguous Enumeration (E) or Attract Attention (AA) marker of event order, provoking the need for a neutral E/AA code

Table 1. The *markers of event order* (MEOs) identified by the main investigators, and used by the expert coders to analyze the material in the study

Name	Abbreviation	Description
Enacting Non-chronology	EN	Enacting the events in a non-chronological order, end-beginning-middle, but also e.g., beginning-end-middle
Metaphorical	M	Using an EARLIER IS BEFORE gesture to communicate the fact that the event took place earlier in time
Enumeration	E	Using a gesture for enumeration (e.g., equivalents of "1," "2," "3")
Attract Attention	AA	Using a gesture, or a series of gestures, to attract the Interpreter's attention
Timeline	T	Using a gesture, or a series of gestures, to refer to a visual representation of events on a timeline or on a comic strip
Other	O	Any other strategy for communicating events in a non-chronological order than the above, e.g., using a whole-body spin

The two expert coders analyzed the material independently from each other for the presence of a MEO (and obtained a substantial agreement, see Sibierska et al., 2023), as well as the type of a MEO and the number of times ("tokens") it was used in each round. The final version of the coding was created on the basis of negotiation and consensus, with no unsettled disagreement between the coders.

As shown in Figure 9, the results of the study showed unequivocal support for the first hypothesis (H1), namely that simple narratives, with isomorphic Event sequence-Story mappings, will be more easily communicated through pantomime (mean of 94% correct matches) than complex, non-isomorphic ones (34% correct matches), for details, see Sibierska et al., 2023). Interestingly, as can be seen in Figure 9, when no MEOs were used, the participants were equally successful in the simple narrative condition from the start to the end. On the other hand, for the complex narratives, the participants were at floor levels at the start, and improved only when MEOs were used.

Clearly the markers of event order (MEOs) were instrumental for communicative success in the complex narrative condition, thus supporting the second hypothesis (H2). In addition to the findings reported by Sibierska et al. (2023), we enhanced this hypothesis with the prediction that there would be a higher number of MEOs in the complex narrative condition. This hypothesis was also confirmed: markers of event order were much less likely to appear in simple narratives ($M = 0.35$, $SD = 0.93$) than in complex narratives ($M = 1.09$, $SD = 1.55$). Figure 10 shows the estimated numbers of MEOs across the four games in the

Chapter 5. Can pantomime narrate? 131

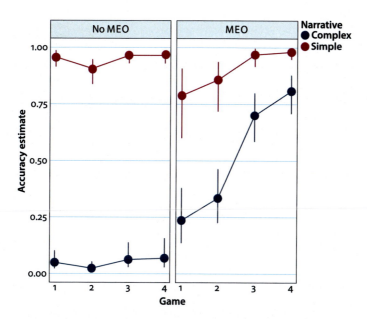

Figure 9. Estimated proportions of correct matches in the two conditions, with and without MEOs (markers of event order) was used. In the complex narrative condition, a clear learning effect can be observed (taken from Sibierska et al., 2023)

two kinds of narrative with 95% confidence intervals. Using a generalized (Poisson) mixed effects regression analysis, we found significant main effects of *narrative complexity* (likelihood ratio test, chi-square = 248.860, $df = 1$, $p = 0.000$) and *game* (likelihood ratio test, chi-square = 126.078, $df = 3$, $p = 0.000$). In other words, there was an increase in the use of MEOs across the four games in both narratives, and the number of MEOs in the complex narratives was significantly higher than that in the simple narratives. All these findings suggest a strong role of MEOs for successful communication of complex (non-isomorphic) narratives, but not for simple narratives.

Qualitative analysis of the coding of the video recordings showed that successful negotiation and conventionalization of the use and meaning of MEOs in the case of complex narratives was possible, but far from trivial. As can be seen in the example from Figure 11, in Games 2 and 3, each participant consistently used their own combination of MEOs, represented by different geometrical shapes. However, in Game 4, participant B (black) decided to pick up on the combination of MEOs proposed by participant A (round 1), while participant A (white) did the opposite and tried the combination of MEOs proposed by participant B (round 4). Eventually, towards the very end of the experiment session, they managed to agree on using the combination originally proposed by participant B. Quite often,

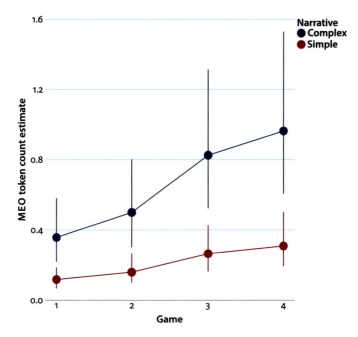

Figure 10. Estimated number of tokens of MEOs in each game in the two conditions

though, the participants did not manage to agree on a combination of MEOs. In Figure 12, we can see a situation where participant A suggests a use of a MEOs in Game 3, but this is not picked up by participant B. Participant A gives up on the use of MEOs up till Game 4, where they introduce a new type of MEO. This, however, is also not picked up by participant B, and, ultimately, no shared system for using MEOs is established. It is worth noting, perhaps, that in this case MEOs are not used as frequently as in the case in Figure 11.

Figure 11. A timeline of Games 2, 3, and 4 (each consisting of 12 rounds) played by one pair of participants. The two shapes correspond to two different combinations of MEOs. The white shapes correspond to participant A, the black shapes correspond to participant B

When comparing the proportions of the different types of MEOs (see Figure 13) it became clear that enacting non-chronological order (EN) was by far the most frequent type of marker, but only for the complex narrative condition. This is a rather remarkable result in itself, showing that pantomime need not

Figure 12. A timeline of Games 2, 3, and 4 (each consisting of 12 rounds) played by another pair of participants. The two shapes correspond to two different uses of MEOs, but, this time, both are used by the same participant

"operate[s] in a simulacrum of real time," but can very well distort this, *pace* the statement by Ryan (2012), cited in Section 2.

With the other markers, however, and especially with M(etaphorical) and E(numeration), the participants were clearly moving beyond pantomime towards protolanguage, since at least some of these markers qualify as predominantly *symbolic* (i.e., dominated by conventionality) rather than iconic signs. The clearest case for this is E(numeration), but to the extent that any of the markers has emerged as a result of conventionalization processes, as in Figure 11, the semiotic ground of symbolicity can be said to play a key role in the communication of complex narratives. The role of conventionality was also visible in another aspect: most of the MEOs were based on already existing communicative and cultural conventions, such as counting, visualizing the passage of time in terms of spatial relations, and as a timeline. In this context, it is interesting to note that M only occurred in the complex narrative condition, as a form of translation of constructions involving grammatical words such as "before," and "because of," very much as we had expected. This was also the case for AA, which served as an indexical expression of a warning: "don't interpret this as normally but as...".

More surprising was the fact that E(numeration) and the ambiguous E/AA marker were about as frequent in the two conditions. But upon inspection, it became clear what the participants were very often "enumerating" were not the beginning, middle and end events (as we had expected), but rather they used it to differentiate between characters (character 1 vs. character 2) or to refer to the types of conditions (simple vs. complex) since distinguishing these (e.g., (6) vs. (7), Figure 4 vs. 5) that was instrumental for success in the game. So the strategy of contrastive marking the two kinds of narratives with ONE (e.g., Figure 6) and TWO gestures was indeed quite common, and accounts for the fact that, as we can see in Figure 10, the overall number of MEOs used in the simple condition also increased in the course of the four games. Likewise, the very infrequent T(imeline) gesture was used in both conditions.

Still, such factors cannot account for the use of MEOs in all simple narrative rounds. For example, the few but notable cases of Enacting Non-chronology (EN) in the simple narrative condition testify to the fact that the participants sometimes introduced "distortions" of the chronological orders spontaneously. For instance, they chose to enact all the events connected with one of the characters in the

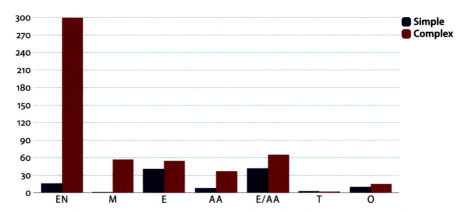

Figure 13. Number of tokens of each type of MEOs in the two conditions: *EN* = Enacting Non-chronology, *M* = Metaphorical, *E* = Enumeration, *AA* = Attract Attention, *T* = Timeline, *O* = Other

story first, then all the events connected with the other character, regardless of their temporal order. Once again, this shows that pantomime need not be a "simulacrum of real time."

5. Summary and conclusions

Experiments such as the one described in the previous section are very important for cognitive semiotics (as well as for language evolution studies), not so much as validations of theoretical models but as "intuition pumps" (e.g., Dennett, 2013) – with the difference that getting one's hands dirty in actual experiments rather than "thought experiments" can give rise to more fine-grained insights. Applying the theoretically defined concepts of *narrative* and *pantomime* as in Sections 2 and 3, respectively, in an empirical study both supported and qualified strong statements concerning the limits of pantomime made in the literature, such as those of Ryan (2012). Indeed, communicating with isomorphic beginning-middle-end narrations was much easier than when the order of events of the story to be communicated was the non-isomorphic end-beginning-middle. At the same time, once the participants in the study realized that they needed to communicate narratives of the latter kind, they started to search for ways to do so, and in many cases were successful. As suggested at the end of the previous section, simply re-enacting the event in a non-chronological order, the most common "marker of event order" in the study, sometimes occurred spontaneously also for simple narratives. In fact, the use of the Enacting Non-chronology marker on its own does not imply that the performances are no longer to be treated as pantomimes. This is so, since the predominant semiotic ground remains iconicity rather than conventionality. Thus, we can draw the conclusion that *pantomime, as a communicative system anchored in the semiotic system of gesture and characterized by highly iconic expression, is fully capable of primary narrativity as long as the stories to be communicated are of "moderate" complexity*: either representing the sequence of events in the same order in which they occurred (in the story world) – most often in the simple narrative condition – or with variations of this that could simply be reenacted in an order that subverted chronology.

At the same time, we could witness (and not just reflect, as in thought experiments) how hard it was for the participants in the study to express temporal and causal relations, leading them to invent and conventionalize markers expressing metaphorical BEFORE or indexical WATCH-OUT. Previously sedimented meanings of such gestures, in combination with local conventionalization, were needed for such complex meanings to be communicated successfully. Hence, considering once again the definition of bodily mimesis in Section 3, our participants can be said to have been induced to undergo one of the many transitions from pantomime (the first three conditions of the definition: cross-modality, differentiation, communicative intent) to *protolanguage* (as we understand this concept, see footnote 4), with a strong degree of conventional normativity.

But once again, one should not extrapolate too boldly from the results of experiments such as those described in Section 4. Not only because it is always doubtful how much they can be projected back into prehistoric time, but also because they always involve compromises with *ecological validity* (how well they correspond to the real-life phenomena) and *translation validity*, "the closeness with which the study's intended meaning of constructs matches their operationalization" (Krathwohl, 2009: 405). For example, we can notice a discrepancy between the construct of primary narrativity – interpreting the narrative by "going" from the narration to the story – and the design of the study. This is so since many of the same stories recurred several times between the first and last games and were thus no longer novel for communicators and interpreters. So at least some of the progress witnessed in the comprehension of complex narratives (see Figure 9), could have been due to secondary narrativity, "going" from the story to the narration. In this respect, the near-ceiling results from the first games concerning the simple narratives were of greater translation validity for the conclusion that pantomime can narrate.

Perhaps an even more serious issue is how comprehension was operationalized – by matching the pantomime to the only "correct" of four comic strips (such as those in Figures 4 and 5 in Section 4). This could be regarded as a fairly artificial way to measure "successful communication," also as testified by the participants themselves. In the case of even successful renditions of non-isomorphic end-beginning-middle stories by the Communicators, the Interpreters often failed to select the "correct" corresponding strip, and in the post-experimental interviews many reported that translating the stories into non-isomorphic strips (e.g., Figure 5) was "unnatural." Indeed they are – since pictorial narrations do not easily subvert chronology either, as pointed out by Ryan (2012).

But problems like these are to be anticipated and are even considered useful for further iterations of the conceptual-empirical loop. We have already studies underway where all narratives in the game are novel, i.e., never repeated by the participants, and where the interpreters express their comprehension by intersemiotically translating the pantomime/protolanguage performances back to language, allowing straightforward comparison between "source" and "target" narrations. But this is the topic for another story.

Funding

This research was in part supported by the Polish National Science Centre (NCN) under grant agreement UMO-2017/27/B/HS2/00642. Additionally, Marta Sibierska was supported by the Polish National Agency for Academic Exchange (NAWA) under the agreement PPN/BEK/2020/1/00319/U/00001.

Acknowledgements

We thank the coders Adam Gutowski and Mariusz Lewandowski, as well as the participants in the empirical study for their time and effort. Johan Blomberg provided helpful comments on a previous version of the paper.

References

Allen, R. J. (2013). Beginning, middle, end of an era: Has technology trumped Aristotle? *Journal of Film and Video*, 65(1–2), 9–29.

Arbib, M. (2005). From monkey-like action recognition to human language: An evolutionary framework for neurolinguistics. *Behavioral and brain sciences*, 28, 105–168.

Aristotle. (1987). *The Poetics of Aristotle*. Translation and Commentary S. Halliwell. The University of North Caroline Press.

Bal, M. (1997). *Narratology: Introduction to the theory of narrative*. University of Toronto Press.

Boyd, B. (2017). The evolution of stories: From mimesis to language, from fact to fiction. *WIREs Cognitive Science*, 9(1), 1444. .

Clark, H. (2004). Variations on a Ranarian theme. In S. Strömqvist & L. Verhoeven (eds). *Relating events in narrative. Typological and contextual perspectives* (pp. 457–476). Lawrence Erlbaum.

Currie, M. (2007). *About time: Narrative, fiction, and the philosophy of time.* Edinburgh University Press.

Dennett, D.C. (2013). *Intuition pumps and other tools for thinking.* W. W. Norton & Company.

Devylder, S., & Zlatev, J. (2020). Cutting and Breaking Metaphors of the Self and the Motivation and Sedimentation Model. In A. Baicchi & G. Radden (Eds.), *Figurative meaning construction in thought and language* (pp. 253–281) Benjamins.

Diget, I.S.K. (2019). *Intersemiotic translation from film to audio description: A cognitive semiotic approach.* (MA Thesis) Lund University.

Donald, M. (1991). *Origins of the modern mind: Three stages in the evolution of human culture.* Harvard University Press.

Donald, M. (1998). Mimesis and the executive suite: Missing links in language evolution. In J.R. Hurford, M. Studdert-Kennedy, & C. Knight (Eds.), *Approaches to the evolution of language: Social and cognitive biases* (pp. 44–67). Cambridge University Press.

Donald, M. (2012). The mimetic origins of language *The Oxford handbook of language evolution* (pp. 180–183). Oxford University Press.

Donald, M. (2013). Mimesis theory re-examined, twenty years after the fact. In G. Hatfield & H. Pittman (Eds.), *Evolution of mind, brain and culture* (pp. 169–192). Philadelphia, PA: University of Pennsylvania.

Fay, N., Arbib, M., & Garrod, D. (2013). How to bootstrap a human communication system. *Cognitive Science*, 37, 1356–1367.

Frege, G. (1948 [1892]). Sense and reference. *The Philosophical Review*, 57(3). 209–230.

Genette, G. (1980). *Narrative discourse: An essay in method.* Cornell University Press.

Halliwell, S. (2012). Diegesis – mimesis. *The living handbook of narratology.* Hamburg University. http://www.lhn.uni-hamburg.de

Hutcheon, L. (2006). *A theory of adaptation.* Routledge.

Hühn, P., Pier, J., Schmid, W. & Schönert, J. (2009). *The living handbook of narratology.* Hamburg. http://www.lhn.uni-hamburg.de.

Jakobson, R. (1959). On linguistic aspects of translation. In *On Translation* (pp. 232–239). Harvard University Press.

Konderak, P. (2018). *Mind, cognition, semiosis: Ways to cognitive semiotics.* UMCS Press.

Krathwohl, D.R. (2009). *Methods of educational and social science research: The logic of methods.* Waveland Press.

Leabhart, T. (1997). *Modern and post-modern mime.* St. Martin's Press.

Lecoq, J. (2006). *Theatre of movement and gesture.* Routledge.

Li, W., & Zlatev, J. (2021). Intersemiotic translation from fairy tale to sculpture: An exploration of secondary narrativity. *Sign Systems Studies*, 1–29.

Masereel, F. (1918) *25 Images de la Passion d'un Homme. Édition de Sablier.*

Möttonen, T. (2016). *Construal in expression: Intersubjective approach to cognitive grammar.* University of Helsinki.

Müller, C. (2016). From mimesis to meaning: A systematics of gestural mimesis for concrete and abstract referential gestures. In J. Zlatev, G. Sonesson & P. Konderak (Eds.), *Meaning, mind and communication: Explorations in cognitive semiotics*, (pp. 211–226). Peter Lang.

Prince, G. (2008). Narrativehood, narrativeness, narrativity, narratability. In: J. Pier, L. García & A. José (Eds.), *Theorizing narrativity* (pp. 19–27). De Gruyter.

Ryan, M.-L. (2007). Toward a definition of narrative. In D. Herman (Ed.), *The Cambridge companion to narrative* (pp. 22–35). Cambridge University Press.

Ryan, M.-L., (2012). Narration in various media. In: Hühn, P., et al.. (Eds.), *The living handbook of narratology*. Hamburg University. http://www.lhn.uni-hamburg.de

Sibierska, M. (2017). Storytelling without telling: The non-linguistic nature of narratives from evolutionary and narratological perspectives. *Language & Communication*, 54, 47–55.

Sibierska, M., Żywiczyński, P, Zlatev, J., van de Weijer, J, Boruta-Żywiczyńska, M. (2023). Contraints on communicating the order of events in stories. *Journal of Language Evolution*, XX: 1–15.

Slater, W. J. (1994). Pantomime riots. *Classical Antiquity*, 13(1), 120–144.

Sokolowski, R. (2000). *Introduction to phenomenology*. New York: Cambridge University Press.

Sonesson, G. (1997). Mute narratives. New issues in the study of pictorial texts. In U.-B. Lagerroth, H. Lund, & E. Hedning (Eds.), *Interart Poetics* (pp. 243–250). Rodophi.

Sonesson, G. (2007). From the meaning of embodiment to the embodiment of meaning: A study in phenomenological semiotics. In T. Ziemke, J. Zlatev, & R. Frank (Eds.), *Body, language and mind. Vol 1: Embodiment* (pp. 85–128). Mouton de Gruyter.

Sonesson, G. (2014). Translation and other acts of meaning: In between cognitive semiotics and semiotics of culture. *Cognitive semiotics*, 7(2), 249–280.

Stampoulidis, G. (2019). Stories of resistance in Greek street art: A cognitive-semiotic approach. *Public Journal of Semiotics*, 8(2), 29–48.

Todorov, T. (1969). Structural analysis of narrative. *NOVEL: A Forum on Fiction*, 3(1), 70–76.

Tomasello, M. (2008). *The origins of human communication*. Cambridge, MA: MIT Press.

Werner, H., & Kaplan, B. (1963). *Symbol formation: An organismic-developmental approach to language and the expression of thought*. Wiley.

Zlatev, J. (2014). Bodily mimesis and the transition to speech. In M. Pina & N. Gontier (Eds.), *The Evolution of Social Communication in Primates* (pp. 165–178). Springer.

Zlatev, J. (2015). Cognitive semiotics. In P. Trifonas (Ed.), *International handbook of semiotics* (pp. 1043–1067). Springer: Dordrecht.

Zlatev, J. (2016). Turning back to experience in Cognitive Linguistics via Phenomenology, *Cognitive Linguistics*, 27 (4): 559–572.

Zlatev, J., Sonesson, G., & Konderak, P. (2016). Introduction: Cognitive semiotics comes of age. In J. Zlatev, G. Sonesson, & P. Konderak (Eds.), *Meaning, Mind and Communication* (pp. 9–28). Peter Lang.

Zlatev, J., Wacewicz, S., Żywiczyński, P., & van de Weijer, J. (2017). Multimodal-first or pantomime-first? Communicating events through pantomime with and without vocalization. *Interaction Studies*, 18(3), 455–479.

Zlatev, J., Żywiczyński, P., & Wacewicz, S. (2020). Pantomime as the original human-specific communicative system. *Journal of Language Evolution*, 1–19.

Żywiczyński, P., Wacewicz, S., & Sibierska, M. (2018). Defining pantomime for language evolution research. *Topoi*, 37(2), 307–318.

CHAPTER 6

The pantomimic origins
of the narrative arts

Steven Brown
McMaster University

The evolutionary study of pantomime provides important insights into the origins of the narrative arts, including visual art, theatre, and narrative forms of dance (e.g., ballet). Drawing, as a motoric activity, shows a strong resemblance to tracing pantomimes. The main difference is that drawing generates an enduring image on a surface, whereas pantomime is "drawing in the air." The theatrical arts – including dramatic acting, mime acting, and narrative forms of dance – take a more egocentric approach to pantomime than drawing, employing full-body mimicry of the expressive actions of a referent person. Overall, iconic gesturing through pantomime provides an evolutionary foundation for all of the narrative arts. On the flip side, a consideration of the narrative arts themselves provides many new avenues for the exploration of pantomime, including shedding light on gestural models of the origins of language.

Keywords: pantomime, arts, narrative, theatre, storytelling, visual art, dance, music

Introduction

While pantomime has been used to account for the origins of language capacity (Arbib, 2012; Armstrong & Wilcox, 2007; Hewes, 1973; Tomasello, 2008), I will present some new proposals in this chapter that pantomime also provides a reasonable foundation for many of the arts, most especially the category known as the narrative arts. I will proceed in this chapter by first talking about the nature and classification of the arts. I will next discuss the nature of pantomime, as based on an account presented in Brown et al. (2019) in which we made a distinction between two categories of pantomime: egocentric and allocentric, where egocentric pantomime is done from a first-person perspective and allocentric pantomime from a third-person perspective (see also Zlatev & Andrén, 2009; and

https://doi.org/10.1075/ais.12.06bro
© 2024 John Benjamins Publishing Company

Zlatev et al., 2020, for a similar use of first-person and third-person). I will then apply this distinction to the narrative arts in accounting for the origins of visual art, theatre, mime theatre, and narrative forms of dance, including the latter's association with music.

The narrative arts

It is interesting to point out that gestural theorists of the origins of language admonish people against conflating the evolutionary notion of pantomime with pantomime's artistic rendering in mime theatre in contemporary culture. However, it is exactly this conflation that I would like to achieve here. We need it in order to understand the "panto" aspect of pantomime. In ancient Greece, the pantomime was someone who performed all (=panto) of the characters in a drama (Hall, 2008, 2013). Hence, the concept of pantomime is about personal mimicry and character portrayal. It is an intrinsically theatrical concept. While this approach to pantomime has not been taken by gestural theorists of language origin, I will argue that they need to adopt it.

In *The Republic* (380BCE/1968), Plato classified narrative communication into the two complementary forms of *diegesis* and *mimesis*, where diegetic forms of narrative are those that are produced from the perspective of the storyteller (e.g., oral storytelling) and mimetic forms are those that proceed through an impersonation of the characters of a story, as seen in theatre (Berger, 2000; Halliwell, 2014). Diegesis involves describing characters using a narrator's voice, whereas mimesis involves describing characters using the characters' own voices, as produced by actors portraying these characters. These two manners of storytelling can be conceived of using the more common terms of *narration* and *acting*, respectively. Gestural theories of language origin have not come to terms with whether the pantomimic precursor that is posited in these models was diegetic or mimetic. Given that pantomime can be produced in both manners (see below), then we need to develop a principled understanding of this dual route to pantomime production. Were the first pantomimes third-person descriptions of objects and people, or were they first-person impersonations of people's actions (and potentially animal actions as well)? Were they perhaps a combination and/ or interleaving of the two formats of pantomiming?

Figure 1 presents a classification scheme for the arts that will serve as a guide for the discussion of the arts in this chapter (Brown, 2019). The scheme is based on a classification of the arts into the two broad functional categories of the *narrative arts* and the *coordinative arts*. The narrative arts are used to tell stories, often to promote social learning through the modeling of prosocial behaviors (Boyd,

2009; Gottschall, 2012; Mar & Oatley, 2008; Scalise Sugiyama, 2017). They are comprised of both diegetic (narrated) and mimetic (acted out) forms of narrative. In contrast to this, the coordinative arts of dance and music are the arts of interpersonal coordination. They function to stimulate collective participation and synchronized action, thereby serving as a reinforcer of group affiliation, a symbol of group unity, and a promoter of social cooperation (Brown, 2000; Launay, Tarr & Dunbar, 2016; Reddish, Fischer & Bulbulia, 2013; Savage et al., 2021). Narrative forms of dance can sit in both categories.

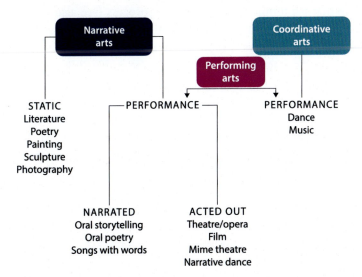

Figure 1. A classification of the arts into the narrative arts and coordinative arts. The performance-related forms of the narrative arts are divided into narrated forms (diegetic) and acted out forms (mimetic). The static forms of the narrative arts (visual art) are all diegetic. This figure is based on Brown (2019)

The nature of pantomime

Pantomime refers to iconic gesturing, typically done in the absence of speech or other forms of linguistic communication. By iconic gesturing, I mean the kind of gesturing that spatially resembles the actions and/or objects being depicted in the pantomime (Arbib, 2012; Perniss & Vigliocco, 2014). As Arbib writes, pantomime is "a performance that resembles an action of some kind and can thus evoke ideas of the action itself, an associated action, object, or event, or a combination thereof" (2012: 217). Pantomime is done for the purposes of narrative communication, most especially when speech is not available. It sits in contrast to other kinds of behaviours, such as instrumental actions (e.g., hammering a nail) and the gesticulations that accompany speaking. Pantomimes also differ from emblems – conventionalized gestures like the "thumbs up" gesture – since they are iconic, rather than being abstract or conventionalized. According to Żywiczyński, Wacewicz, & Sibierska (2018), other salient features of pantomime beyond its iconicity include that it is improvised, non-conventionalized, holistic, and open-ended, thus having a broad semantic potential. It is also referential, or triadic (Arbib, 2012; Zlatev, 2014). While Żywiczyński, Wacewicz, & Sibierska (2018) argue that pantomime is a whole-body process (see also Zlatev, 2014), it is quite easy to think of counter-examples to this, such as when a person uses their index and middle fingers to represent somebody walking. Hence, while pantomime can indeed engage the full body, it can also employ body parts alone.

Pantomime is frequently conceptualized as a behaviour that occurs in the absence of speech (McNeill, 2005). However, nothing precludes pantomime from being done with sounding, and I would contend that much about co-speech gesturing is pantomimic, meaning that it is iconic. So the idea that pantomime and speech are mutually exclusive categories of communication seems inaccurate to me, creating a slippery slope for those gestural models of language origin that divorce vocalizing from gesturing. All that we can really say with certainly is that pantomime *can* be effective in the absence of speech. However, it can also work in combination with speech, as occurs in certain forms of co-speech gesturing. Therefore, I strongly agree with Żywiczyński et al. (2018) and Zlatev, Żywiczyński, & Wacewicz (2020) that vocalization can and should be part of the behavioural suite of pantomime.

Various classifications have been put forth to account for the forms of pantomime (Boyatzis & Watson, 1993; Overton & Jackson, 1973). My colleagues and I argued for a five-category typology in Brown et al. (2019), with a primary split between what we called "egocentric" and "allocentric" forms, as shown in Figure 2. In an egocentric pantomime, the parts of the body that are used in pantomime production preserve their identity. What is absent is the object being manipulated in a transitive action. This is typically referred to as an "imaginary object" (IO) pantomime (Boyatzis & Watson, 1993; Dick, Overton & Kovacs, 2005; Suddendorf, Fletcher-Flinn & Johnston, 1999), and is typified by the pantomiming of a tennis serve in which the dominant hand grasps an imaginary tennis racquet, and the non-dominant hand holds an imaginary tennis ball. Egocentric pantomimes, almost by definition, are *empty-handed* gestures; they symbolically convey transitivity without the presence of the manipulated object. Because egocentric pantomimes preserve the identity of the body parts that are used in the action (e.g., the hands are hands), their gesturing occurs in peripersonal space. The extreme version of an egocentric pantomime is a full-body pantomime, especially of an intransitive action, such as a pantomime of walking or swimming.

Chapter 6. The pantomimic origins of the narrative arts

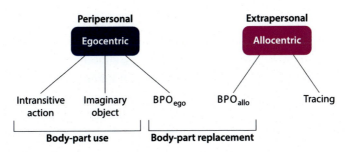

Figure 2. A classification scheme for pantomime proposed in Brown et al. (2019). Five categories of pantomime are shown, divided into egocentric and allocentric varieties. Body-part use pantomimes are egocentric, whereas body-part replacement pantomimes can be either egocentric or allocentric, depending on the space being depicted (peripersonal for BPOego and extrapersonal for BPOallo). Abbreviations: allo, allocentric; BPO, body-part-as-object; ego, egocentric

In an allocentric pantomime, the parts of the body that are used for the pantomiming change their identity and come to symbolically represent an object other than the body part itself. This is generally referred to as a "body-part-as-object" (BPO) pantomime (Boyatzis & Watson, 1993; Dick et al., 2005; Suddendorf et al., 1999), and is typified in adults by the "call me" pantomime, in which a person's hand gets formed into the shape of a telephone receiver and essentially becomes a telephone receiver from the standpoint of communication. Allocentric pantomime is thus characterized by a process of body-part *replacement*. As such, it generally occurs in extrapersonal space, rather than peripersonal space. For example, hitting the two fists together to represent two cars crashing into one another indicates an event that is far removed from peripersonal space. The exception to this is the unusual category that we called BPO_{ego}, such as running one's fingers through one's hair to represent a comb, hence a BPO in peripersonal space.

In Brown et al. (2019), we provided a detailed account of the various manners of performing egocentric and allocentric pantomimes with the two hands. For two-handed IO's and BPO's, a pantomime is said to be "double" if the two hands represent two different objects (e.g., a tennis racquet serving a tennis ball [double IO]; a pen writing on a pad [double BPO_{ego}]). A pantomime is referred to as "joint" if the two hands represent or contribute to a single object (e.g., lifting a large box [joint IO]; rain falling [joint BPO_{allo}]). Combinations of different types of pantomimes by the two hands are referred to "intra-category mixes" if both hands perform either egocentric pantomimes alone or allocentric pantomimes alone (e.g., ladling soup into a bowl [IO/BPO_{ego}, where both are egocentric]). Combinations of different categories of pantomimes by the two hands are referred to as "inter-category mixes" if one hand performs an egocentric pantomime while the other hand performs an allocentric pantomime (e.g., pressing a launch button [IO, egocentric] to make a rocket take off [BPO$_{allo}$, allocentric]).

Gestural theories of language origin have not come to terms with *whether pantomime originated as an egocentric or allocentric form of gesturing at its origin.* This is an important point that needs to be clarified. In Brown et al. (2019), we proposed two contrasting evolutionary models in which either egocentric or allocentric pantomime holds evolutionary priority. In the People First model, the original pantomimes were egocentric depictions of people's actions, including their tool-use gestures. By contrast, in the Environment First model, precedence is given to the allocentric representation of scenes and objects. I can now see that the People First model of egocentric pantomiming is mimetic, while the Environment First model of allocentric pantomiming is diegetic, although this point was not made in the original publication. As mentioned above, there are also mixed egocentric/allocentric pantomimes. In addition, a mimer can alternate between egocentric and allocentric formats in a sequential fashion. There is thus a great diversity of manners in which pantomimes can be carried out, and gestural models of language origin need to take this diversity into account.

The principal objective of the current chapter is to look beyond theories of pantomiming per se, and to apply these ideas to evolutionary theories of the arts. Figure 3 integrates the thinking of the last two sections by presenting *a pantomimic model of the origin of the narrative arts*, which will occupy the rest of this chapter. The central plank of this model is that the diegetic arts evolved from a pre-existing capacity for allocentric pantomime, whereas the mimetic arts evolved from a pre-existing capacity for egocentric pantomime. The mimetic arts themselves are broken down into formats that incorporate vocalization (dramatic theatre) and formats that tend to be mute (mime theatre and narrative dance). I use the term mute here, rather than silent, to indicate that vocalization is actively suppressed in such contexts. The remainder of the chapter will explore the origin of these various narrative artforms from a pantomimic perspective.

Diegesis: The gestural origins of visual art

Let us begin our exploration of the narrative arts from the side of diegesis. In the realm of pantomime, this would correspond with allocentric pantomiming. I want to propose that the capacity for allocentric pantomiming provided the representational basis for drawing as a human-specific activity. In order to ground this idea, I first need to describe a concept that I call "emanation." While viewers of action-based art have to suffice with the *implicit* motion contained in still images,

Chapter 6. The pantomimic origins of the narrative arts

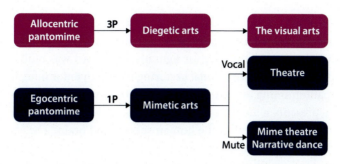

Figure 3. The pantomimic origins of the narrative arts. 1P, first-person; 3P, third-person

artists perceive *actual* motion during the creation of these artworks in terms of the unfolding of a visual image on the canvas during the course of drawing. In other words, the production of an image on a canvas creates optic flow that is perceived as visual motion by the brain of the artist (Yuan & Brown, 2014). I refer to this phenomenon of optic flow during the process of drawing as the "emanation" of an image (Brown, 2022; Yuan & Brown, 2014), since the image essentially emanates from an initially blank canvas. This is intimately related to the visual feedback that the artist receives during drawing. Although the end result of the creation of a drawing is a static product, the motoric act of drawing itself is a dynamic process, both in the sense that it requires ongoing coordination of the eyes, hands, and body, and more uniquely in that it involves the emanation of an image, in other words the progressive expansion of visible trail on a drawing surface as the motor action takes place.

Emanation is critically connected with pantomime, most especially allocentric pantomime. To think about this, imagine yourself pantomiming a rectangle by tracing out a rectangular shape in the air with your index finger. Now imagine grasping a drawing tool in your hand and drawing a rectangle on a surface. From a kinematic standpoint, these are nearly identical motor actions. However, the act of drawing lays down a trail on a surface in the form of the image of a rectangle in a way that a pantomime does not. Looking at this in reverse, pantomime is drawing without the drawing tool; it is drawing in the air. As a result, it is a type of proto-drawing or what Zlatev et al. call proto-depiction, "which given time and appropriate context could have evolved into depiction proper" (2020: 164). Ekman and Friesen (1969) refer to the pantomimes of objects as "pictographs," referencing their implicit pictorial nature. Despite this name, there are no actual pictures generated during pantomiming, since no emanation occurs. Therefore, while both drawing and pantomime are forms of re-creation, pantomime achieves this without leaving a lasting physical trace, while drawing achieves this by leaving a trail behind as the emanated image unfolds on the drawing surface. As Arnheim pointed out, "[t]he hand that traces the shape of an animal in the air during a conversation is not far from fixating this trace in the sand or on a wall" (1974: 172). I suggest that the human capacity for figurative visual art was built upon a pre-existing capacity for representational gesturing through pantomime, in particular allocentric pantomiming as a third-person diegetic device.

Figure 4 presents a neuro-evolutionary model from Brown (2022) of how visual art may have emerged in the human species and brain. The starting point of the model is the general ability to perceive complex visual forms, a capacity mediated by the ventral visual stream of the brain (the "what" pathway). The next step in the model is the transition from the general ability to use tools to the specific ability to use tools to fashion intentional marks on object surfaces, leading ultimately to visual art as we know it. I contend that the evolutionary emergence of mark-making as a novel human skill required neural changes to the motor-sensory system for emanation, including its connectivity to the motor system, such that the optic flow coming from emanation could now be used in a voluntary and intentional manner to guide drawing, serving as both a source of visual feedback during mark-making and as an indicator of the success of the intended drawing. I argue that this is the pivotal change that underlies visual art as an evolved human activity. The end result of this process for ancient humans is the realization that tool-use gestures can leave stable traces on a surface, and ultimately that these traces can become narratively and communicatively meaningful and can thus serve as images whose content can be shared with others as *static social displays*.

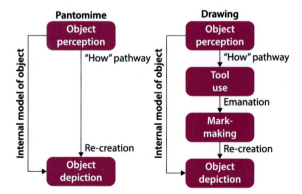

Figure 4. A gestural model of drawing origin. Drawing is seen as an evolutionary offshoot of the representational capacity of pantomime. Drawing adds the processes of tool use and marking-making through emanation onto the object-depiction capacity of pantomime. This figure is taken from Brown (2022)

The initial step in the evolution of mark-making, preceding the de novo creation of dedicated artworks, would have been *the modification of existing objects*, such as through the incising of marks onto the surface of stones and other objects (Beaumont & Bednarik, 2013; Bednarik, 2003; Morriss-Kay, 2010). The archaeological record is inconclusive with regards to the antiquity of this practice, with reports of the earliest modifications of existing objects occurring anywhere from 100,000 years ago (Henshilwood et al., 2011) to 500,000 years ago (Bednarik, 2003). The mark-making stage of visual art's evolution established drawing as an indexical activity by marking the recipient object as distinct or special, whether this be an environmental object or a human body. The last stage, then, is the transition from index to icon and then to symbol. This involves the emergence of *figurative* representations in visual art through the generation of iconic re-creations of environmental objects or living beings. This is clearly a late appearance in the evolution of visual art. Geometric and abstract mark-making predate figurative images/objects by tens if not hundreds of thousands of years.

Arnheim (1969) referred to iconic gestures as the "forerunners of line drawing" (p. 117). I propose that the human capacity to create figurative visual art was built upon a pre-existing capacity for representational gesturing through pantomime, and that the new ability to work with visual emanation transformed this from a pantomime system into a novel drawing system during human evolution. This idea forms the foundation of my *gestural model of drawing origin* (Brown, 2022). In thinking about a pantomimic origin of drawing, it is important to consider that both pantomime and drawing can be done in three different manners: through copying of a present model (i.e., imitation), through tracing, and from memory. This provides three distinct but related routes by which figurative drawing may have evolved out of pantomimic gesturing during human evolution.

What does this analysis of visual art add to existing pantomime theories of human communication? Figure 5 is a summary figure that applies to the remainder of the chapter. Part A summarizes the contributions of visual art to a theory of pantomime. First, visual art adds the evolved human capacity for tool use (dating back 2.4 million years) and the related capacities for praxis, demonstration, teaching, and creative production that are extensively discussed in the human evolution literature (Gärdenfors, 2017; Osiurak & Reynaud, 2020; Wynn & Coolidge, 2014). Second, the emanative nature of drawing leads to a product that can endure over time, namely the generated image. Such images have the capacity to be not only private symbols, but public symbols with shared meanings. Hence, drawing leads to the origins of visual symbols, which themselves can be transmitted across generations and cultures through cultural evolution. The earliest form of figurative image in 2D dates back to 45,000 years ago (Brumm et al., 2021), as of this writing. However, pantomime, as a communication system, is no doubt far more ancient than this. It is important to note that while pantomime is obligatorily figurative, drawn images can be abstract as well, hence devoid of explicit iconicity, for example through the use of geometric marks (Hodgson, 2006; Lewis-Williams & Dowson, 1988; Malotki & Dissanayake, 2018).

Figure 5. A summary of what the narrative arts contribute to an understanding of the nature and social functions of pantomime

A. Visual art (allocentric)
- Tool use
- Praxis, demonstration, teaching
- Creativity
- Emanation (mark-making) to generate images
- Images as enduring social displays
- Cultural evolution of visual symbols

B. Theatre (egocentric)
- Personal mimicry: proto-acting in human life
- Theatrical acting
- Multimodal communication: vocalization and gesture combined
- A unification of vocal and gestural imitation
- The origins of fictionality and pretense

C. Dance (egocentric)
- Theatricalization of pantomime
- Ritualization of pantomimic gestures
- Interpersonal coordination in group rituals
- A coupling of pantomime with music and rhythm

Mimesis I: The theatrical arts

Having discussed the diegetic route to narrative production in visual art, I will spend the rest of the chapter discussing the mimetic arts and their proposed origin in egocentric pantomime. I will divide this into two parts. In the current section, I will discuss the theatrical arts, whereas in the next one, I will discuss mime theatre and narrative dance. This distinction is basically one between vocal (theatre) and mute (mime, dance) forms of the mimetic arts (see Figure 3). A key argument that I will make in this section is that nothing necessitates that a pantomimic theory of language origin be non-vocal and thus mute. To my mind, gestural theories of language origin have created a false dichotomy between pure gesturing and pure vocalizing, as if one process had to preclude the other. Abandoning a commitment to muteness greatly enriches the scope of gestural theories.

Chapter 6. The pantomimic origins of the narrative arts   149

In the mimetic arts, a narrative can be communicated not only in the third-person by a narrator, but also in the first-person by an actor portraying a character, whether that character be real or fictional. An actor tells a story about a character by *being* that character, not by describing the character in words the way that a narrator does in folk tales and novels, or by depicting that character graphically the way that visual artists do. The gestures produced by an actor are not their own personal gestures, but instead those of the character being portrayed in the story. In Brown (2017), I proposed a new concept that I called "proto-acting" as an intermediate process between the role playing of everyday life and that of dramatic acting. Proto-acting is similar to dramatic acting, and different from everyday role playing, in that it involves character portrayal. However, such portrayal can occur in everyday contexts, as well as in stage performances. In fact, the contexts for proto-acting are quite diverse. Proto-acting is, first and foremost, a process of *personal mimicry*, often carried out in a multimodal manner using the voice, face, body posture, and body movement. It is a means of re-creating a person through an imitation of their superficial gestures and/or manner of speaking. From the standpoint of communication, it is a means of "staging" the scene being depicted in a story (Clark, 2016). While dramatic acting focuses on literary characters, proto-acting generally involves a mimicry of familiar people, such as members of one's social circle or contemporary celebrities, such as media figures and politicians.

In the Brown et al. (2019) article about the classification and evolution of pantomime, we talked about a fundamental conundrum about the performance of egocentric pantomimes: how does a viewer know if I am miming my own actions or those of another person (or even those of an animal)?[1] In other words, how do I communicate to my recipient that I am representing my own actions vs. engaging in a process of personal mimicry through proto-acting? How do I distinguish between "I killed the bear," "John killed the bear," and even "The bear killed John," since all of them can involve highly similar gestures? While there is no simple

---

1. Another fundamental problem about personal mimicry that was brought up in Brown et al. (2019) is about how to characterize mimicry from a pantomime perspective. At an intuitive level, mimicry seems to be a form of full-body egocentric pantomime. However, if allocentric pantomime is defined as a process of body-part replacement, then the act of impersonating another person or an animal is actually a process of full-body replacement. If I do an impersonation of a friend, then no part of my body is my own, hence violating the stipulations of an egocentric pantomime. The same is true if I impersonate a bird by flapping my arms the way that a bird would flap its wings. This is another example of full-body replacement, in this case a cross-species replacement. Zlatev et al. (2020) refer to this as a "first-person embodying" mode of pantomime, but I do not think it gets around the contradiction of how a gesture can be first-person and, at the same time, be an embodiment of some non-self entity.

solution to this self/other conundrum for egocentric pantomime, I contend that adding vocalization to the process of gesturing provides an important means of disambiguating these gestures. For example, "the bear killed John" would almost certainly be accompanied by different vocalizations than "John killed the bear."

It is thus far better to theorize that pantomime evolved in a *multimodal* manner (Zlatev et al., 2020; Żywiczyński et al., 2018) than it is to propose that it evolved in a manner that obligatorily excluded vocalization (see also Kendon, 2014, for a perspective outside of a pantomime context). The latter does not offer any theoretical advantages, even if the motivation is to argue that pantomiming preceded full-fledged speech. As Zlatev, Wacewicz, Żywiczyński, & van de Weijer have argued: "[i]n assuming that early hominins, who had already parted evolutionary paths with (the ancestors of) chimpanzees, first communicated with whole-body pantomime, there is no reason to suppose that this would have been fully 'silent'" (2017: 471). There are numerous ways to incorporate vocalization into the gesturing that do not require full-fledged lexico-syntactic speech. The vocalizations need only be acoustic pantomimes (e.g., the growl of a bear) or emotive vocalizations (e.g., John's cry of terror upon being attacked) to achieve a sense of multimodality in the communication process. Clark's (2016) staging theory provides a rich repertoire of "sound effects" that can accompany communicative gesturing that do not require speech. Overall, I believe that making the primordial pantomime system multimodal, rather than mute, aids recipients in identifying if an egocentric mime is a depiction of the mimer's own actions or those of another person (or animal). While the game of Charades imposes specific rules about muteness onto its players, human evolution requires no such constraints.

While a muteness requirement offers no theoretical advantage to a pantomime theory of language origin, a multimodal theory does provide a key advantage. It permits a unification of the two novel human-specific means of producing imitation, namely vocal imitation and gestural imitation. These capacities are discussed in completely separate literatures, and yet the phenomenon of personal mimicry through proto-acting provides a means of unifying these two imitative capacities into a single newly-evolved behaviour. I argued in Brown (2017) that the personal mimicry of proto-acting was underlain evolutionarily by the capacity for full-body (egocentric) pantomime, but that it supplemented this with vocal mimicry as well.

The mimetic arts not only shed light on the nature of pantomime, but provide additional insight into the origins of pretense and fictionality in the human species. Personal mimicry through proto-acting serves as the most fundamental mechanism of someone pretending to be a person who they are not, as seen universally in the pretend play of children, another important form of proto-acting. In fact, one could not imagine the emergence of theatre in human cultures without the pretend play of children. The phenomenon of pretense reflects the unlimited ability of people's imaginations to produce simulations of possible scenarios and characters. Importantly, the pretense of the theatrical arts is a socially sanctioned form of impersonation. Viewers appreciate the skilfulness that actors bring to their portrayal of fictional characters. However, there are also non-sanctioned forms of character portrayal that involve deception and false impersonation, such as when people act as imposters of others (Goffman, 1959).

Figure 5B summarizes what theatre contributes to the study of pantomime. This includes the basic egocentric process of personal mimicry through proto-acting. It also includes the human cultural phenomenon of theatre. Compared to mute gestural models of language origin, theatre adds a multimodal component to communication by combining vocalization and gesturing into a single communicative behaviour. This provides an important unification of vocal and gestural imitation as the two novel imitative capacities that evolved in humans. In addition, we see the origin of human-specific cognitive functions like pretense and fictionality. As a final point, I would say that our capacity for personal mimicry is not restricted to explicit acts of communication through proto-acting, but also to our implicit ability to imitate the actions of others around us. Cultural evolutionists point out that humans have a strong "conformist bias" (Boyd & Henrich, 1998; Boyd & Richerson, 1985; Legare & Nielsen, 2015; Mesoudi & Lycett, 2009; Sternberg & Lubart, 1995) and that this is underlain by our ability to imitate the actions of the majority and to follow the pack.

Mimesis II: Mime theatre and narrative dance

In addition to mimetic artforms that are vocal, there are those that are mute by convention. Mime theatre is a clear example of this. The artform of pantomime dates back to the ancient Greeks. The word pantomime contains two roots. The "mime" part refers to the well-known process of personal mimicry, or what I have called proto-acting. However, the "panto" part of pantomime is far less familiar to most people. The root "panto," like "pan," refers to the concept of all or every. The pantomime got its name from the fact that they portrayed *all of the characters* in a story, rather than just one (Hall, 2008, 2013), effected through the use of multiple masks. Ancient Greek theatre had its origins in the performances of single actors, typically interacting with a chorus (Storm, 2016). The great playwright Aeschylus is credited with the innovation of adding a second actor to the cast, where each actor performed a different character. The pantomime, by contrast, was someone who performed all of the characters, rather than just one. I mentioned earlier in the chapter that gestural theorists of language origin admonish people against confusing pantomime with mime theatre, but it is important to recognize that mime theatre is a *theatricalization* of pantomime, and that it serves as a unique form of the narrative arts. In fact, the ancient pantomime's craft was truly a "total work of art," integrating storytelling, poetry, theatre, dance, music (both sung and instrumental), and visual implements such as costumes, make-up, and masks.

Pantomime in the modern sense is characterized as being not just a mute form of gesturing, but an *empty-handed* form as well, most especially in the performance of transitive actions. In order to pantomime a tennis serve, one holds an imaginary tennis racquet in one hand and an imaginary ball in the other. If one held an actual tennis racquet and ball in one's hands in order to demonstrate a serve to someone, then this would not be called a pantomime. Mime theatre abides by the joint requirements for muteness and empty-handedness. Performances typically take place as a series of vignettes. The actions are a combination of transitive actions (e.g., holding imaginary objects) and intransitive actions (e.g., walking, climbing). Mime theatre is susceptible to the same self/other conundrum about pantomime mentioned in the previous section. It is not always clear who the mime actor is portraying. The mime has his/her mime persona – complete with the traditional white-face make-up and costumes of a mime actor – but it is not always easy to tell when the mimer is departing from this persona to depict another person.

Let us now consider the other major form of mute pantomiming, namely the kind that occurs in narrative forms of dance, such as ballet. The history of the ancient pantomime is strongly linked with dance, as the pantomime was considered to be first and foremost a dancer (Hall, 2013; Żywiczyński et al., 2018). It needs to be stated upfront that many forms of dance are not narrative, but are instead comprised of abstract movement patterns. In addition, many of the movements performed by a narrative dancer are not pantomimic, but are either expressive or are part of the conventionalized "language" of the dance, for example ballet's lexicon of 200 or so basic movement patterns (Foster, 1986). Iconic gesturing of the pantomimic type is only one type of movement and gesturing that a narrative dancer performs. While narrative dances are similar to mime theatre in being a theatricalization of pantomime, they show far more similarities to standard theatre than they do to mime theatre, since they tend to have ensemble casts, dramatic scenarios, costumes, and props. The ballet *Romeo and Juliet* has just as large a cast as the theatrical version. A sword fight in the ballet uses swords, whereas a sword fight in a mime vignette would only ever be empty-handed, and might only depict one of the two duellers. So, dance dramas really are danced dramas. They substitute the speaking with expressive and often times pantomimic gesturing, accompanied by a musical score congruent with the emotions depicted in the drama.

One important feature that narrative dance adds to a theory of pantomime is *ritualization*.[2] If one looks at the narrative dances of indigenous cultures, one sees that the movements are often times ritualizations of everyday instrumental actions. For example, in some forms of traditional West African dancing, the wrist gestures of the dancers are choreographic representations of the hand actions that are used to spread seeds onto the ground in everyday agricultural behaviours. These actions tend to be repeated in a rhythmic manner. This rhythmicity allows the gestures to be performed by multiple dancers in a coordinated manner, since many indigenous dances are group dances. Dissanayake (2009, 2013, 2018a, 2018b) devised the term "artification" to refer to this transformation of ordinary behaviours into an artistic and aesthetic form. Narrative dances in many traditional cultures are indeed artifications of everyday instrumental behaviours that become ritualized and performed in a rhythmic manner. This applies not only to human actions but to those of animals as well, as animal dances are quite prevalent throughout the world (Sachs, 1937). For example, the Huli people of the Southern Highland region of Papua New Guinea perform a group dance that is mimetic of a local bird of paradise (Knauft, 1985). The dancers – donned in regalia and body paint that make them resemble the bird – engage in pantomimic dance movements that iconically resemble the bird's movement style. Moreover, they vocalize musically like the featured bird while dancing, and coordinate their vocalizations into a synchronous chorus, one that is perfectly matched to the rhythm of the dance movements. This is yet another example of pantomimic gesturing that is accompanied by non-linguistic vocalizing in an integrated communicative behaviour.

This discussion of rhythm in dance highlights another unique feature of dance as an expression of pantomime, namely the inclusion of music. The relationship between dance and music – i.e., the choreomusical relationship – is a highly complex one (Hanna, 1982; Hodgins, 1992; Jordan, 2011; Mason, 2012). Historical accounts tell us that music was an intrinsic part of the performance of pantomimes in ancient Greece (Hall, 2008, 2013). However, while the pantomime's performance was accompanied by music, it is not clear if the mime's movements were done *to* the music. This contrasts with traditional African dancing and modern-day ballet, where the movements of the dancers are typically entrained to the beat of the music. When Romeo and Tybalt engage in a sword fight in the ballet version of *Romeo and Juliet*, the clank of their swords is choreographed to occur according to the beats in Prokofiev's musical score for the ballet. The music, separate from its rhythmic properties alone, is generally a critical ingredient in the narrative of the dance drama, one that works to amplify the emotions conveyed in the story.

---

2. The discussion of ritualization in this section might have relevance to Arbib's (2012) notion of "ontogenetic ritualization" for the evolution of gestural symbols.

The killing of Tybalt by Romeo is manifested not only by the dancer's pantomimic depiction of Tybalt dying, but by the tragic emotional music that Prokofiev composed to accompany this scene. Space limitations prevent me from getting into a discussion of the origins of music itself (see Brown, 2022; as well as Filippi, 2016; Fitch, 2013; and Mithen, 2005). However, I simply point out here that a consideration of narrative dance adds music and rhythmicity to the overall picture of pantomimic gesturing.

Figure 5C summarizes what mime theatre and narrative dance contribute to a theory of pantomime. This includes both a theatricalization and ritualization of pantomimic gestures, a sense of interpersonal coordination in group dances, and a coupling of pantomimic gesturing to music, where music enhances the narrative features of the gestural depiction in an emotionally-congruent manner, thereby creating an audiovisual intensification of the conveyed emotions.

Conclusions

I have argued in this chapter that the ancestral human capacity for pantomimic gesturing provides a reasonable foundation for the narrative arts, both their diegetic and mimetic formats. I proposed that the diegetic-*vs.*-mimetic contrast for narrative communication maps onto the contrast between allocentric and egocentric pantomime, respectively. Gestural models of language origin have not broached the issue of whether the ancestral state of pantomime was diegetic (third-person) or mimetic (first-person). However, one thing that many gestural models assume is that pantomime originated as a mute activity, since gestural models are presented as counterproposals to vocal models of the origins of language. I have taken issue with this muteness assumption by proposing that proto-acting was a joint vocal/gestural precursor state of egocentric pantomime. This proposal not only makes the behaviour more naturalistic from an ecological perspective, but also provides a basis for coupling the emergences of vocal imitation and gestural imitation into a joint communicative behaviour during human evolution.

With regard to the mimetic arts, I distinguished the vocal form of theatrical acting from mute forms, such as mime theatre. The latter category includes narrative forms of dance, which themselves are quite pantomimic. Many forms of narrative dance in indigenous cultures are pantomimes of everyday instrumental actions (such as agricultural behaviours) or animal movement patterns. Hence, dance provides a view of pantomime that is ritualized in addition to being theatricalized. A consideration of the evolutionary origins of dance allows for a coupling of pantomime with music. Music becomes an extra-pantomimic acoustic factor that reinforces the narrative signification of the gesture, not least its emotional meaning. Figure 5 provided an overall summary of what the arts – most especially the narrative arts – contribute to an understanding of pantomime. The list is quite extensive. I believe that a consideration of the narrative arts can open up many new directions of inquiry into the nature and social functions of pantomime, not least to gestural models of the origins of language. But in some sense, this is nothing more than history repeating itself, as the pantomime theatre of the ancient Greeks and Romans was a highly integrative activity, combining all of the branches of the arts into a single performance ritual.

Funding

Work on this chapter was supported by a grant from the Natural Sciences and Engineering Research Council (NSERC) of Canada.

References

Arbib, M.A. (2012). *How the brain got language: The mirror system hypothesis.* Oxford: Oxford University Press.

Armstrong, D. F., & Wilcox, S. E. (2007). *The gestural origins of language.* Oxford University Press.

Arnheim, R. (1969). *Visual thinking.* University of California Press.

Arnheim, R. (1974). *Art and visual perception: A psychology of the creative eye.* University of California Press.

Beaumont, P. B., & Bednarik, R. G. (2013). Tracing the emergence of palaeoart in sub-Saharan Africa. *Rock Art Research* 30, 33–54.

Bednarik, R. G. (2003). The earliest evidence of palaeoart. *Rock Art Research* 20, 89–135.

Berger, K. (2000). *A theory of art.* Oxford University Press.

Boyatzis, C. J., & Watson, M. W. (1993). Preschool children's symbolic representation of objects through gestures. *Child Development* 64(3), 729–735.

Boyd, B. (2009). *On the origin of stories: Evolution, cognition, and fiction.* Harvard University Press.

Boyd, R., & Henrich, J. (1998). The evolution of conformist transmission and the emergence of between-group differences. *Evolution and Human Behavior* 19, 215–241.

Boyd, Robert, & Richerson, P. J. (1985). *Culture and the evolutionary process.* University of Chicago Press.

Brown, S. (2000). Evolutionary models of music: From sexual selection to group selection. In F. Tonneau & N. S. Thompson (Eds.), *Perspectives in ethology. 13: Behavior, evolution and culture* (pp. 231–281). Plenum Publishers.

Brown, S. (2017). Proto-acting as a new concept: Personal mimicry and the origins of role playing. *Humanities* 6, 43.

Brown, S. (2019). A unifying model of the arts: The narration/coordination model. *Empirical Studies of the Arts*, 37 172–196.

Brown, S. (2022). *The unification of the arts: A framework for understanding what the arts share and why.* Oxford University Press.

Brown, S., Mittermaier, E., Kher, T., & Arnold, P. (2019). How pantomime works: Implications for theories of language origin. *Frontiers in Communication* 4, 9.

Brumm, A., Oktaviana, A. A., Burhan, B., Hakim, B., Lebe, R., Zhao, J.X., … Aubert, M. (2021). Oldest cave art found in Sulawesi. *Science Advances* 7(3), eabd4648. 10.1126/sciadv .abd4648.

Clark, H. H. (2016). Depicting as a method of communication. *Psychological Review* 123, 324–347.

Dick, A. S., Overton, W. F., & Kovacs, S. L. (2005). The development of symbolic coordination: Representation of imagined objects, executive function, and theory of mind. *Journal of Cognitive Neuroscience* 6, 133–161.

Dissanayake, E. (2009). The ratification hypothesis and its relevance to cognitive science, evolutionary aesthetics, and neuroaesthetics. *Cognitive Semiotics* 9, 136–158.

Dissanayake, E. (2013). Genesis and development of "making special": Is the concept relevant to aesthetic philosophy? *Rivista Di Estetica*, 54, 83–98.

Dissanayake, E. (2018a). From play and ritualisation to ritual and its arts: Sources of Upper Pleistocene ritual practices in Lower Middle Pleistocene ritualised and play behaviours in ancestral hominins. In C. Renfrew, I. Morley, & M. Boyd (Eds.), *Ritual, play and belief, in evolution and early human societies* (pp. 87–98). Cambridge University Press.

Dissanayake, E. (2018b). The concept of artification. In E. Malotki & E. Dissanayake (Eds.), *Early rock art in the American west: The geometric enigma* (pp. 23–45). University of Washington Press.

Ekman, P., & Friesen, W. V. (1969). The repertoire of nonverbal behavior: Categories, origins, usage, and coding. *Semiotica* 1, 49–98.

Filippi, P. (2016). Emotional and interactional prosody across animal communication systems: A comparative approach to the emergence of language. *Frontiers in Psychology* 7, 1393.

Fitch, W. T. (2013). Musical protolanguage: Darwin's theory of language evolution revisited. In J. J. Bolhuis & M. Everaert (Eds.), *Birdsong, speech, and language: Exploring the evolution of mind and brain* (pp. 489–503). MIT Press.

Foster, S. L. (1986). *Reading dancing: Bodies and subjects in contemporary American dance.* University of California Press.

Gärdenfors, P. (2017). Demonstration and pantomime in the evolution of teaching. *Frontiers in Psychology* 8, 415.

Goffman, E. (1959). *The presentation of self in everyday life.* Anchor Books.

Gottschall, J. (2012). *The storytelling animal: How stories make us human.* Houghton Mifflin Harcourt.

Hall, E. (2008). Introduction: Pantomime, a lost chord of ancient culture. In E. Hall & R. Wyles (Eds.), *New directions in ancient pantomime* (pp. 1–40). Oxford University Press.

Hall, E. (2013). Pantomime: Visualising myth in the Roman empire. In G. W. M. Harrison & V. Liapis (Eds.), *Performance in Greek and Roman theatre* (pp. 451–473). Brill.

Chapter 6. The pantomimic origins of the narrative arts **157**

Halliwell, S. (2014). Diegesis – mimesis. In P. Huehn (Ed.), *The living handbook of narratology* (pp. 129–137). de Gruyter.

Hanna, J. L. (1982). Is dance music? Resemblances and relationships. *The World of Music* 24, 57–71.

Henshilwood, C. S., D'Errico, F., Van Niekerk, K. L., Coquinot, Y., Jacobs, Z., Lauritzen, S. E., ... García-Moreno, R. (2011). A 100,000-year-old ochre-processing workshop at Blombos Cave, South Africa. *Science* 334, 219–222.

Hewes, G. W. (1973). Primate communication and the gestural origin of language. *Current Anthropology*, 14(1/2) 5–24.

Hodgins, P. (1992). *Relationships between score and choreography in twentieth-century dance: Music, movement and metaphor.* Edwin Mellen Press.

Hodgson, D. (2006). Understanding the origins of paleoart: The neurovisual resonance theory and brain functioning. *Paleoanthropology* 54–67.

Jordan, S. (2011). Choreomusical conversations: Facing a double challenge. *Dance Research Journal* 43(1), 43–64.

Kendon, A. (2014). Semiotic diversity in utterance production and the concept of "language." *Philosophical Transactions of the Royal Society B: Biological Sciences* 369, 20130293.

Knauft, B. M. (1985). Ritual form and permutation in New Guinea: Implications of symbolic process for socio-political evolution. *American Ethnologist* 12, 321–340.

Launay, J., Tarr, B., & Dunbar, R. I. M. (2016). Synchrony as an adaptive mechanism for large-scale human social bonding. *Ethology* 122, 779–789.

Legare, C. H., & Nielsen, M. (2015). Imitation and innovation: The dual engines of cultural learning. *Trends in Cognitive Sciences* 19, 688–699.

Lewis-Williams, J. D., & Dowson, T. A. (1988). The signs of all times: Entoptic phenomena in Upper Palaeolithic Art. *Current Anthropology* 29, 201–245.

Malotki, E., & Dissanayake, E. (2018). *Early rock art in the American west: The geometric enigma.* University of Washington Press.

Mar, R. A., & Oatley, K. (2008). The function of fiction is the abstraction and simulation of social experience. *Perspectives on Psychological Science* 3, 173–192.

Mason, P. H. (2012). Music, dance and the total art work: Choreomusicology in theory and practice. *Research in Dance Education*, 13 5–24.

McNeill, D. (2005). *Gesture and thought.* University of Chicago Press.

Mesoudi, A., & Lycett, S. J. (2009). Random copying, frequency-dependent copying and culture change. *Evolution and Human Behavior* 30, 41–48.

Mithen, S. (2005). *The singing Neanderthals: The origins of music, language, mind and body.* Weidenfeld & Nicolson.

Morriss-Kay, G. M. (2010). The evolution of human artistic creativity. *Journal of Anatomy* 216, 158–176.

Osiurak, F., & Reynaud, E. (2020). The elephant in the room: What matters cognitively in cumulative technological culture. *Behavioral and Brain Sciences* 43, e156.

Overton, W. F., & Jackson, J. P. (1973). The representation of imagined objects in action sequences: A developmental study. *Child Development* 44(2), 309–314.

Perniss, P., & Vigliocco, G. (2014). The bridge of iconicity: From a world of experience to the experience of language. *Philosophical Transactions of the Royal Society B: Biological Sciences*, 369, 20130300.

Plato. (380BCE/1968). *The republic*. New York: Basic Books.

Reddish, P., Fischer, R., & Bulbulia, J. (2013). Let's dance together: Synchrony, shared intentionality and cooperation. *PloS ONE* 8, e71182.

Sachs, C. (1937). *World history of the dance*. W.W. Norton & Company.

Savage, P.E., Loui, P., Tarr, B., Schachner, A., Glowacki, L., Mithen, S., & Fitch, W.T. (2021). Music as a coevolved system for social bonding. *Behavioral and Brain Sciences*. .

Scalise Sugiyama, M. (2017). Oral storytelling as evidence of pedagogy in forager societies. *Frontiers in Psychology*, 8 471.

Sternberg, R.J., & Lubart, T.I. (1995). *Defying the crowd: Cultivating creativity in a culture of conformity*. Free Press.

Storm, W. (2016). *Dramaturgy and dramatic character: A long view*. Cambridge University Press.

Suddendorf, T., Fletcher-Flinn, C., & Johnston, L. (1999). Pantomime and theory of mind. *Journal of Genetic Psychology*, 160 31–45.

Tomasello, M. (2008). *Origins of communication*. MIT Press.

Wynn, T., & Coolidge, F.L. (2014). Technical cognition, working memory and creativity. *Pragmatics & Cognition*, 22 45–63.

Yuan, Y., & Brown, S. (2014). The neural basis of mark making: A functional MRI study of drawing. *PloS ONE* 9, e108628.

Zlatev, J. (2014). Human uniqueness, bodily mimesis and the evolution of language. *Mente Journal of Philosophical Studies* 27, 197–219.

Zlatev, J., & Andrén, M. (2009). Stages and transitions in children's semiotic development. In J. Zlatev, M. Andrén, M. Johansson-Falck, & C. Lundmark (Eds.), *Studies in language and cognition* (pp. 380–401). Cambridge University Press.

Zlatev, J., Wacewicz, S., Żywiczyński, P., & van de Weijer, J. (2017). Multimodal-first or pantomime-first? *Interaction Studies* 18, 465–488.

Zlatev, J., Żywiczyński, P., & Wacewicz, S. (2020). Pantomime as the original human-specific communicative system. *Journal of Language Evolution* 5(2), 156–174.

Żywiczyński, P., Wacewicz, S., & Sibierska, M. (2018). Defining pantomime for language evolution research. *Topoi* 37, 307–318.

CHAPTER 7

The pantomime roots of Sao Tome and Principe Sign Language

Ana Mineiro[1] & Mara Moita[1,2]
[1] Universidade Católica Portuguesa | [2] NOVA University Lisbon

Pantomime is a unique semiotic resource for human communication despite its non-linguistic character because it allows a wide spectrum of meanings (Zlatev et al., 2020). In our view, gestures and vocalizations are interconnected from the beginning of the emergence of language in human beings (Corballis, 2014). Recent studies in a newborn language showed a boost of linguistic systematicity (Mineiro et al., 2021; Abreu et al., 2022), which included a reduction in the use of pantomime, amplitude of signs, and an increase in articulation economy within a social interaction process. We claim this process constitutes a continuum and not a cut-off system. The evolution of a newborn sign language seems to follow the same phases of psychomotor development and to be linked to efficient use of energy while enhancing cognition, allowing for the accomplishment of social communication enabled by sign language.

Keywords: pantomime, sign language, newborn language, language evolution

1. Brief notes on language genesis

Many studies on the genesis of language point to the emergence of communicative conventions as the key to the debut of language (Vieira, 1995). Żywiczyński and colleagues (2021) suggest that the first communication system was sign-based, based on bodily mimesis as a cognitive mechanism and primary iconicity as a semiotic principle (Zlatev et al., 2020). Motivated signs can be iconic, easily interpretable outside the discursive context, and comprehensible when they occur in isolation (for example, the iconic sign formed by the hand grabbing a glass and bringing it to the mouth to express DRINK).

Bodily mimesis engenders non-linguistic communication by using the body as a tool for intentionally transferring referential-propositional information. It

https://doi.org/10.1075/ais.12.07min
© 2024 John Benjamins Publishing Company

employs motivated signs to establish a connection between their non-pre-established meaning and their expressions (Żywiczyński et al., 2021; Zlatev et al., this volume). Bodily mimesis fits with the Mirror Neuron Hypothesis (Arbib, 2012; Rizzolatti & Arbib, 1998; Arbib, this volume), which argues that the roots of speech are integrated into a unique communicative system composed of sounds, facial expressions, and manual gestures. Arbib's evolutionary scenario (2012) includes: mirror system > simple imitation > complex imitation > pantomime > proto-sign and proto-speech > language-ready brain. This scenario was observed in the emergence of the Sao Tome and Principe Sign Language (LGSTP), in which pantomimic gestures were produced to communicate in the absence of speech, resourcing bodily mimesis for communication. As the acts of communication become frequent, LGSTP reveals restrictions on using body and spatial parts, culminating later in structural patterns with linguistic specificities (the language-ready brain). The data that we describe in this chapter supports pantomimic scenarios of language origin (Arbib, this volume) by showing that pantomime is an effective means of bootstrapping the new language.

However, Sandler (2013) has identified "kinks" within this chain, possibly disrupting Arbib's scenario. One argument is that each modality (sign and speech) relies on a different articulatory motor system. This is true from an exclusively linguistic perspective regarding input and output modality. Nevertheless, as neurolinguistic studies have overwhelmingly shown (Bellugi et al., 1988; Emmorey et al., 2007), language in the broad sense, which comprises both vocal and manual modalities, is processed in the same left-sided sections of the neocortex. In addition, recovery symptoms of brain damage support a "motor-gestural history of speech and language evolution" (e.g., Code, 2021). Furthermore, it is observed that deaf infants exhibit early vocal and manual babbling as also hearing babies exposed to sign language produce manual babbling along with vocal babbling, revealing that the babbling phenomenon, which is the babies' first step toward building a developed linguistic system during language acquisition, is amodal (Petitto et al., 2004; Petitto & Marentette, 1991). Regarding this evidence, it makes sense that both modality systems (manual and vocal) co-evolved together and seem coordinated in our species (Mineiro, 2020; Mineiro et al., 2021).

Another of Sandler's (2013) arguments points to the basic distinction between pantomime and symbolic signs, as it suggests that sign language has an abundance of iconically motivated signs, which can lead to the false supposition that they are conventionalized pantomime. Based on an analysis of the Al-Sayyid Bedouin Sign Language (ABSL), Sandler (2012, 2013) defines pantomime as a different non-linguistic form of expression that reenacts an event by recruiting body parts imitating certain body actions and which can go along with symbolic signs. Representation of an action or an object of any other kind using body parts is defined as symbolic signs, distinguished by symbolically representing a meaning without reenacting it. Sandler proposes that this symbolic representation moves away from the iconic and mimetic nature of the new gestures. It is essential to notice that Sandler's (2013) distinction between pantomimic gestures and symbolic signs follows the observation that in ABSL, these symbolic signs occurred mainly in storytelling without the involvement of other body parts. However, as we will see in the analyzed data of LGSTP, the involvement of body parts other than the hand in gesture elicitations and conversation context was observed, revealing the linguistic nature of the body parts as elements in the first phases of this language emergence.

Sandler's argument follows from the distinctive definition of pantomime. Following gestural theories of language evolution (Arbib, 2012; Perniss & Vigliocco, 2014; Żywiczyński et al., 2018; Sibierska et al., 2022), pantomime is defined as iconic gesturing where there is no speech or no established sign language, although it can be accompanied by non-linguistic vocalization (Zlatev et al., 2017; Brown, this volume) that engages whole-body or body parts alone and can depict both objects and actions. In this context, pantomime occurs for communicative purposes, referring to entities that are and are not present in time (Gärdenfors, 2021, 2022). However, it is essential to recognize that both perspectives consider pantomimic gestures as non-linguistic signs (Arbib, this volume; Gärdenfors, this volume; Zlatev, this volume).

The beginning of human language may have been triggered by the necessity to communicate cooperatively via pantomimic gestures and non-pantomimic manual gestures (Tomasello, 2008) or by the neurocognitive adaptation to tool production and handling (e.g., Osiurak et al., 2021). This communication phenomenon can evolve into bodily mimesis with language communication functions (Wacewicz & Żywiczyński, this volume). When there is no settled language in common, even in modern humans, bodily mimesis and its core component – pantomime – are used. In this sense, we might consider pantomime the original system from which language developed and which is still used by modern humans as a communicative resource when no linguistic system is available (Żywiczyński et al., 2018; Mineiro et al., 2021). In this sense, there is evidence to assume that when there is no common language, modern humans communicate via bodily mimesis and use pantomime:

a. in language loss or impairment, humans rely on pantomime to communicate (Code, 2021; Göksun et al., 2015);
b. when there is no language in common (signed or vocal), humans communicate via pantomime;
c. pantomime gestures are used in the first stage of sign language emergence (Mineiro et al., 2021).

In order to contribute to the discussion of language evolution scenarios and consider pantomime as a communication system up until language emergence in modern humans, we gather some findings from our research on emergent LGSTP. In the first stage of LGSTP emergence, we found a pantomimic stage that arose before the emergence of linguistic complexity. These findings were not present in Sandler's research (2013), which found that the first generation of ABSL signers use only the hands to convey words, with the rest of the body uninvolved linguistically, and only occasionally use whole-body pantomimic expressions (for dramatic purposes).

Tracing language evolution from pantomimic gestures to conventional language supporting the existing pantomimic scenarios of language origins, the next section will summarize the route of a newborn language from pantomime to proto-signs.[1] We will detail the roots and aspects of language emergence in LGSTP, using the key-findings from five recent studies (Abreu et al., this volume; Mineiro, 2022; Mineiro et al., 2017, 2021; Moita et al., 2023).

2. Background information on the LGSTP studies

Sao Tome and Principe (STP) are volcanic islands located in equatorial Africa, off the northwest coast of Gabon. The socio-economic development is relatively low; STP is currently considered an "underdeveloped" or non-industrialized country. The official language is Portuguese, though inhabitants also use diverse island creoles. In this country, around 5000 people (or roughly 3% of the population) have been identified as deaf or hard of hearing and the causes of hearing loss were studied by Caroça (2017).

Due to social deprivation and a lack of communication opportunities, deaf children in STP have been excluded from schooling. The project Sem Barreiras, involving local governmental structures such as the Education and Cultural Min-

---

1. As proto signs, we understand the first gestures that exhibit preferences for manual configurations, movements, locations and other non-manual elements to represent specific semantic features of the referent.

ister of Sao Tome e Principe, was thus undertaken to promote the emergence of a sign language among the deaf people and to provide the deaf community with a language to access education.

This project aimed at creating a community by bringing deeply isolated people together through everyday linguistic immersion. It began in February 2013 and finished in February 2015, gathering deaf and hard-of-hearing people from all regions of the islands of STP in a shared space. Their names were listed from oto-laryngology missions in STP, and also from intensive television and radio advertising campaigns.

2.1 Participants

From February 2013 until February 2015, approximately 100 individuals were enrolled in the project. The deaf participants were aged 4 to 25; 80% were female, and 20% were male. All participants enrolled in the project were deaf or hard-of-hearing children and young adults with hearing loss ranging from severe to profound. These descriptions were based on information obtained through interviews with the participants' families. Recruitment was implemented with ethical authorization, and all the families of the deaf underage participants and deaf adult participants signed informed consent forms to be enrolled in the project. The project transported them to a previously-defined common space where the participants would meet.

2.2 Procedures

Respect for cultural differences led the team leader not to use Portuguese Sign Language (LGP) signs. Instead, gestures, mimes, and other visual representations were used to communicate with participants while potential signs were identified and evaluated. Thus, the political choice of not "teaching LGP" was adopted and the goal was to support the emergence of a natural language.

Along with the various activities that promoted communication between deaf participants, the deaf researchers of our team elicited signs through cards with drawings or pictures of simple objects (animals, everyday items) in different phases of the project. The cards were drawn by local artists so that the participants could easily identify the cultural traits and that the drawing would help recognition of the items presented. As the deaf researcher showed the cards, the participants produced pantomimic gestures That gradually evolved into new iconic signs with manual patterns that may exhibit initial linguistic features.

As time went by, the task became more complex, and instead of simple objects, the researcher showed cards with drawings of more complex and abstract referents (concepts, emotions) and also short stories reproduced in drawings that the participants could sign to each other. This was to promote more extensive utterances and begins dialogues outside the classroom. For communication to flow in a less formal context between the deaf participants, the deaf researcher announced weekend programs, tours, meals, and trips to the beach and the market, so the participants would get used to meeting each other, creating signs naturally and communicating with each other in this modality. As a result of these sessions, the deaf people of STP bootstrapped their language.

The sessions were all video-recorded, totaling about 400 videos of about 60 minutes each. The corpus collected was partially annotated with ELAN and served five different studies.

In the first three studies presented here (Abreu et al., 2022; Mineiro, in press; Mineiro et al., 2021), we divided the corpus into four phases according to the characteristics of the gestures and their evolution across time.

Phase 1: February 2013 to July 2013;
Phase 2: September 2013 to February 2014;
Phase 3: March 2014 to July 2014;
Phase 4: September 2014 to February 2015.

3. From pantomime to proto and early sign

In observing an emerging sign language, it was possible to analyze the trajectory of the emergence of the new linguistic elements and structures, revealing a continuum route from pantomime > proto-signs > early signs in a new sign language, the LGSTP.

In general, in the first phases of LGSTP emergence, communicative acts were grounded in gestures involving whole body parts or body elements from a participant perspective, employing an enacting mode of representation. These gestures mirror the definition of pantomimic gestures (Zlatev et al., 2017, this volume; Brown, this volume). Over time, the pantomimic gestures lost non-manual articulators and decreased in mimetic features turning into the first phonological structures of early signs. The new syntactic and morphological patterns and the emergence of articulation were routed.

3.1 From pantomime to early signs

To discover the emergence of lexical items in LGSTP, we observed 1000 produced items (pantomimic gestures and signs) over the four stages of data collection of LGSTP (Mineiro et al., 2021). From these produced items, only 759 of these were conventionalised signs (signs and classifiers), occurring systematically in the LGSTP corpus. These signs show trends of emergent phonology and morphology and combinatory and recursive characteristics revealed in the produced sentences, displaying iconicity in their formation (Mineiro et al., 2017).

In the early phase (phase 1) of our data collection, the data consisted of 70.1% pantomimic gestures and 29.9% signs and classifiers. In the intermediate phase (phase 2), pantomimic gestures comprised 62.7 % of the data, and 37.3% comprised early signs and classifiers. In the pre-final phase (phase 3), we found that 32.2% of the data consisted of pantomimic gestures and 67,8% consisted of early signs and classifiers, which turned into 24.1% of pantomimic gestures, and 75,9% for early signs and classifiers in the final phase (phase 4). Overall, over two years of data collection, the proportion of pantomime decreased, and signs and classifiers increased, as the following two graphs show (Figure 1).

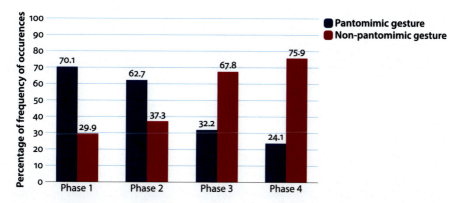

Figure 1. The evolution of LGSTP

In order to verify possible differences in the prevalence of pantomimic gestures between each pair of the phases analyzed, we applied the Mcnemar test (Table 1), which revealed significant differences (p-value<0.001) in the number of pantomime gesture occurrences between all phases. From phase 1 to phase 2, there was a 7.4% reduction in the occurrence of pantomimic gestures. Compared to the drop in occurrence between phases 2 and 3, pantomimic gesture occurrence dropped by 30.5%, and from phase 3 to phase 4 fell by 8.1%. Overall, pantomime decreased significantly along the 4 phases, and over the two years of linguistic immersion, the incidence of pantomime almost disappeared while signs emerged.

Table 1. Comparison of phase pairs based on the number of occurrences of pantomimic gestures and signs or classifiers in the 1 000 items analyzed, using the McNemar Test

	Phase 1 vs. Phase 2	Phase 2 vs. Phase 3	Phase 3 vs. Phase 4
Nb of pantomimic gestures that occurred in both phases	701 (70.1%)	627 (62.7%)	322 (32.2%)
Nb of signs or classifiers that occurred in both phases	299 (29.9%)	373 (37.3 %)	678 (67.8%)
Nb of pantomimic gestures that became signs or **classifiers** from one phase to the next	74 (7.4%)	305 (30.5%)	81 (8.1%)
Total Nb of items	1000	1000	1000
Test McNemar	$p < 0.001$	$p < 0.001$	$p < 0.001$

Over time, particularly in phases 2 and 3, there is a process of change in the way gestures are performed and in the body articulators they recruit.

3.1.1 *What did the evolution from pantomime to signs look like?*

In general, we noted that along the four phases of LGSTP emergence, the signing spaces become smaller, and the production of LGSTP gestures involves less and less effort (Mineiro et al., 2021).

In particular, there was a loss of non-manual articulators (such as *trunk* and *legs* (as shown in the examples in Table 2) and a decrease in two-handed gestures. There was a demand for comfort in the production and articulation economy. This kind of path – in terms of a growing economy of articulation – occurred in almost all of the 1 000 items analyzed.

As we can see, a continuum exists between pantomime and proto-signs in a new sign language. It is a simple matter of time how the communicative system absorbs the rules and begins systematically recombining fractionation processes (Arbib, 2022) to seed the first set of conventional and combinatorial signs.

During phase 3 (Table 2), we saw the emergence of proto-signs which then consolidated themselves as first signs six months later (phase 4). Recently, these signs were analyzed and compared with more recent LGSTP data (Moita et al., 2023), which also contributes to the view that pantomimic gestures evolve into proto-signs and then into signs.

Since the pantomimic gesture evolves and gains constraints, such as space and movement change, how do bodily movements change from pantomimic gestures to proto-signs and early signs?

Chapter 7. The pantomime roots of Sao Tome and Principe Sign Language   167

Table 2. Examples of LGSTP gestures and signs across 4 phases (Mineiro et al., 2021)

	Phase 1	Phase 2	Phase 3	Phase 4
AIRPLANE				
BICYCLE				
FISH				
GOAT				
FOOTBALL				
TO SWIM				
TO BEAT				

3.2 Evolution of movement and articulatory properties

Pantomime can be described as a whole-body process that engages body parts to represent objects and actions (Żywiczyński et al., 2018). When engaging the body, pantomime involves movement and body articulators. Throughout the development of the new sign language, we investigated how movement and body articulators – beyond hands – evolved in LGSTP (Żywiczyński et al., 2021; Abreu et al., 2022).

For this purpose, we focused on the first 100 sketch cards of the original 280 sketch cards (examples in Table 3) presented to the participants over the two-year project timeline. We analyzed the video-recordings registered during the implementation of the project and systematically observed how the gestures produced for the 100 cards evolved across four phases with regard to (i) signing space, (ii) body movement, and (iii) the involvement of hands and other body articulators. This resulted in 100 analyzable signs and gestures based on the highest frequency in the corpus per phase.

In this chapter, we will only report the body movement and involvement of the other body articulators as the main results found (for an in-depth analysis of all the phenomena of gestural evolution analyzed, see (Abreu et al., 2022)).

3.2.1 *Body movement*

As has already been described, as the pantomimic gesture evolves and gains systematic patterns, it decreases the gesturing space. Consequently, it changes the way the movement is performed. Thus, when investigating the approximation to more abstract forms of communication with the appropriation of a new sign language, the type of bodily movements seen in a group can be very informative.

Analyzing the major movements performed in the four phases, in Figure 2, we observe a substantial decrease in the frequency of gestures of the "arched oblique" type and the "oblique in circle" type throughout the four phases of the project. In the same set of analyzed data, the prevalence of linear movements increased slightly.

Observing the prevalence of different minor movements over the specific phases (Figure 3), we found that minor movements also decreased across time, except for the hook-type movement that increased steadily across the phases.

In this study, we could not conclude that the transition from major movements to minor ones showed efficient signing in terms of articulatory economy. However, the number of gestures generally decreased. We could not conclude that the transition from major movements to minor ones showed efficient signing in the articulatory economy. It can be argued that the decrease in gestures needed to represent the same sketches itself indicates a reduction in articulatory effort.

Chapter 7. The pantomime roots of Sao Tome and Principe Sign Language **169**

Table 3. Examples of sketch cards used to elicit LGSTP gestures or signs (in Abreu et al., 2022)

Sketch cards	Meaning
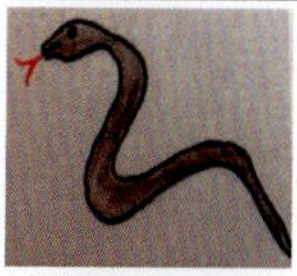	snake
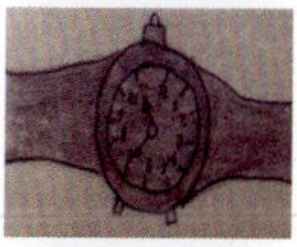	time
	butterfly
	fish
	sadness

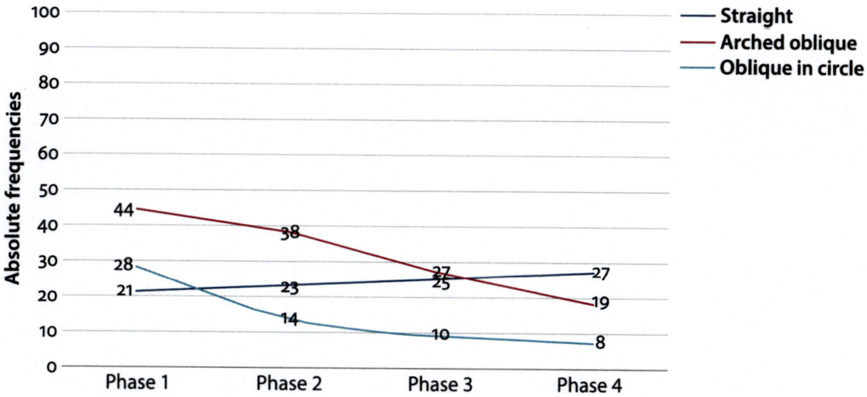

Figure 2. Variation of the prevalence of major movements across the four phases of the project

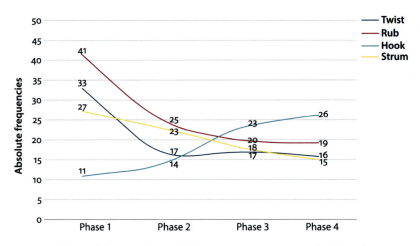

Figure 3. Variation of the prevalence of minor movements across the four phases of the project

3.2.2 *The involvement of body articulators (non-manual articulators)*

From our observations, it seems that the 100 sketches selected elicited pantomime gestures in phases 1 and 2. However, in phases 3 (a year and a half from the beginning of the project) and 4 (two years after the beginning), there was a transition from using the whole body to using restricted, conventional and combinatorial signs.

Analyzing the bimanual involvement and non-manual involvement in the gestures and signs produced across the four phases of the project (Figure 4), we see a decrease in bimanual gesturing.

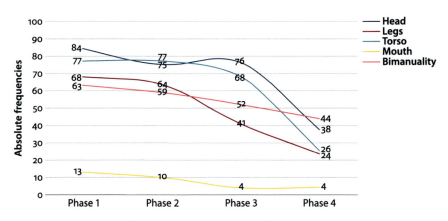

Figure 4. Variation of the prevalence of bimanual and non-manual gestures across four project phases

Overall, bimanual gesturing decreased across time; however, the steepest decreases were observed in non-manual areas of the body, such as the legs, torso, and head, indicating a transition from pantomime to proto-sign and early sign. A slight decrease also occurred in the frequency of mouth use over time. Together, the data shows that the number of manual and non-manual gestures decreases with time, indicating that gestures become more efficient and physically economical.

We hold that there is a strong iconic motivation in creating signs from pantomime (Zlatev et al., this volume). To explore the iconic motivation of emergent signs and their evolution, we explore the role of iconicity in LGSTP evolution.

3.3 The role of iconicity in the emerging phonological system

The visual nature of gestures results in large networks and connections between form and meaning (Perniss et al., 2010). The most recent sign languages, especially the emerging ones, establish their gestures' genesis through metonymy or synecdoche, which testifies to their iconic nature (e.g., Mineiro, 2016; Sandler, 2009).

Iconicity and arbitrariness co-exist in some signed linguistic forms (Gasser, 2004). For instance, iconic signs have phonological features in established sign languages (e.g., Brentari, 2019; Cuxac & Sallandre, 2007; Kooij & van der Kooij, 2002)

In newer sign languages, we see a strong iconic motivation in creating signs from pantomime (Zlatev et al., this volume). New signers use their whole-body, parts of the body, facial expressions, and first-person perspective to enact and express concepts (e.g., instrumentality and humanness) (Mineiro et al., 2021; Senghas & Coppola, 2001).

In order to explore how iconicity might influence the emergence of a phonological system during the evolution of an emerging sign language, we analysed the iconicity and phonological structure of 200 signs collected in two distinct moments of the LGSTP emergence: at T1 (phase 4 (end of 2014)) and at T2 (8 years later (2021)). It is important to remember that in phase 4 (T1), the signs present some systematic patterns (Mineiro et al., 2021), which suggests they should be classified as proto-signs and early signs.

3.3.1 Iconic signs in the evolution of a new sign language

To analyse the iconicity of the signs, we coded all the collected signs of T1 and T2 according to their iconic strategy ground: handling strategy (gestures/ signs represent human handling the referent), instrument strategy (gesture/ sign represents how the referent is used) and object strategy (gesture/ sign does not represent the referent but its shape, properties, or movement). In doing so, we followed Padden's research (Padden et al., 2013, 2015), which analyzes iconicity patterns of lexicon regarding body involvement in sign articulation – *handling, instrument,* and *object*. In addition, we identified the signs that were not iconic. The coding of the internal structure and iconic nature of the signs was performed by one researcher and reviewed by a second researcher. The third researcher was consulted in contexts where there was no coding agreement.

In both moments, we observed the dominance of iconic signs: 194 signs (97%) were iconic in the first moment (T1) and 174 signs (87%) were still iconic in the second moment (T2) (Table 4). To investigate a putative association between the two moments of elicitation (T1 and T2) and iconicity, we performed a Chi-Square test (two-tailed) on 200 items selected from the total item pool. We found an association between iconicity and the elicitation phase ($X^2_{(1)} = 13.587$, $p < 0.001$), observing a decrease in the number of iconic signs from T1 to T2.

Table 4. Iconic and non-iconic signs in the two moments of lexical elicitation in LGSTP emergence (in Moita et al., 2023)

	T1		T2	
	Nb	%	Nb	%
iconic signs	194/200	97%	174/200	87%
non-iconic signs	6/200	3%	26/200	13%

3.3.2 *Internal structure emergence in iconic signs in the evolution of a new sign language*

Regarding the internal structure of LGSTP emerging iconic signs in the two moments, we identified the manual articulators and the internal structure of signs based on sign language phonological parameters – handshapes, location, movement, palm orientation, and non-manual expression (Klima & Bellugi, 1979; Stokoe, 1980; Wilbur, 2000). We then coded (i) the signs that in T2 underwent a total change in their internal structure; and (ii) the gestures and signs that underwent a partial change in the internal structure – excluding the index signs. The analysis of the internal structure of iconic signs was based on identifying the manual articulators and the internal structure of signs (handshapes, location, movement, palm orientation, and non-manual expression).

Hence, we considered 178 items from the 200-item pool. Thus, considering all iconic signs, we observe that the structural changes (partial change (30%) and total change (33%)) tend to be similar to the proportion of signs with no structural changes (31%) (Table 5).

Analyzing the partial change cases, we observe that handshape is the internal element that underwent the most changes, changing in 77% of the iconic signs

Chapter 7. The pantomime roots of Sao Tome and Principe Sign Language 173

Table 5. Internal structure changes in iconic signs from T1 to T2 in LGSTP emergence

	Internal structure changes	
	Nb	%
No change	55/178	31%
Partial change	54/178	30%
Total change	59/178	33%

and, together with location, in 5% of the iconic signs. The other internal elements' changes were residual (for an in-depth analysis, see Moita and colleagues (2023)).

In addition, we assessed a possible association between changes in internal structure (from T1 to T2) and changes in iconic strategy (from T1 to T2). The iconic signs were coded as total or partial changes in phonology from T1 to T2 as (1) and no change in phonology as (0). Moreover, we coded any alteration from simple to iconic composite strategies (with one iconic strategy to two iconic strategies) or alteration in iconic strategy (1) and no alteration in iconic strategy as (0). We eliminated missing values and index strategies because we aimed to focus only on iconic strategies in the emergence of language. Hence, we considered 165 items from the 200-item pool. In addition, we performed a Chi-Square test (two-tailed).

In this analysis, we did not find a statistically significant association between an alteration in phonology and an alteration in strategy, with 93 items (81.6%) with a total or partial change in their internal structure not having an alteration in iconic strategy and only 21 items (18.4%) had a total or partial change in their internal structure, showing an alteration in iconic strategy, given that strategy is essentially maintained from T1 to T2 (Figure 12). Moreover, we found 42 items (82.4%) without a change in their internal structure, not an iconic alteration, and nine items (17.6%) showing a change in their iconic strategy. Thus, no association was found between alteration in phonology and alteration in strategy ($X2(1) = 0.014, p > 0.05$).

This study made us realize that LGSTP is still at an early stage since there seems to be a balance between iconic signs that have not shown a change in their internal structure, iconic signs that have undergone partial changes in their internal structures, and iconic signs that have undergone total changes. Thus, iconic strategies remain stable across time and are independent of the internal structure change. In addition, regarding the internal structural changes, we observed that handshape is the phonological parameter that has undergone the most changes in the iconic signs analyzed (Moita et al., 2023), as reported in conventionalization and emerging processes of other sign languages (Israel & Sandler, 2011; Moita et al., 2018; Sandler, 2014).

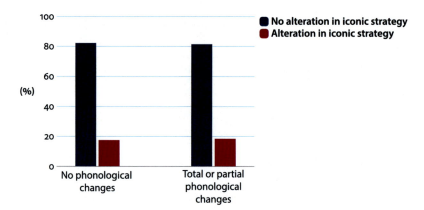

Figure 5. Internal structures change in iconic signs along with iconic strategy alteration between the first and second collection moments in LGSTP emergence

After eight years, the linguistic elements and structures of LGSTP are still developing. This finding supports the observation that a phonological system takes longer to be defined, as proposed by Sandler and colleagues (2014; 2017) concerning ABSL's internal structure emergence, where there were no phonological constraints or phonological processes in co-articulation contexts. Thus, we may conclude that we are still witnessing the linguistic emergence of LGSTP, which is still in the phase of evolution from proto-signs to early signs.

In addition to pantomimic gestures' evolution to proto-signs and early signs and their iconic motivation, the emergence of the basic order of the utterances may also indicate the first conventionalizations of word order structures.

3.4 The evolution of basic order

Research on language evolution has also focused on the issue of natural word order, that is, word order in the phylogenetic and cognitive sense (Gell-Mann & Ruhlen, 2011; Pagel, 2009). Sign language and gesture studies have inspired this discussion in the literature, with particular emphasis on the influence of language on our "linguistic" behavior concerning basic word order (Goldin-Meadow et al., 2008). The starting hypothesis was that if a structural pattern of basic word order for speaking were used in the native language, the production of the same message via non-verbal cues (by gestures) would reflect the same pattern found in the spoken language. Goldin-Meadow and colleagues (2008) found the SVO order for intransitive events much more often than any other order while finding the SOV order for transitive actions when analyzing utterances with intransitive and transitive verbs. The results of this study also revealed that participants tended to produce SVO and SOV word order regardless of the syntax of their native language.

Chapter 7. The pantomime roots of Sao Tome and Principe Sign Language   175

Following this study, new evidence emerged from the work of Gibson and colleagues (2013), who used a new paradigm to investigate word order by using verbs with non-reversible argumental structure (for example, *the man kicks the ball*; **the ball kicks the man*) and reversible argumental structure (for example, *the woman hugs the man*; *the man hugs the woman*). The results from this study indicated that when participants had to pantomime events with irreversible argumental structure, they preferred the SOV word order. However, when participants had to do pantomime events with reversible argumental structure, SOV preference disappeared, giving rise to the SVO word order. Thus, the basic word order preferences were independent of the native language. These data suggest that we communicate events with reversible argumental structure using the SVO order to ensure the message is easily decoded.

A hypothesis is raised in the literature that SOV is the standard word order in events with irreversible argumental structure at an early stage of linguistic communication, which later evolves into the SVO order in events with reversible argumental structure. To address this hypothesis, we explored whether or not there was a dominant basic word order in the linguistic emergence of LGSTP in events with reversible and irreversible argumental structures. For this purpose, we compared ten utterances from phase 1 (a phase previously described as pantomimic) with ten utterances from phase 4 (a phase previously described as one of the proto and early signs) (Mineiro et al., 2021; Abreu et al., 2022). The 20 utterances from each phase were transcribed in gloss[2] (Tables 6 and 7).

Table 6. The 20 LGSTP utterances analyzed from phase 1

Utterances LGSTP from Phase 1	
Utterances with reversible argumental structures	Utterances with non-reversible argumental structures
BREAD MOTHER GIVES BOY	FISH I SELL
MOTHER GIVE SISTER BOX	TREE I CLLMB
DOG HOG BIT	BANANA EAT I
EMBRACE MOTHER ME	DEAF SCHOOL I LIKE
FRIEND BRAIDS ME	DISHES I WASH
RABBIT RUNS BOAR	HAVE FRIENDS FEW
GIFT GRANDMOTHER GAVE ME	LIKE CAJAMANGA
MARILIA LIKES RICARDO	COOK MOTHER (WITH) PALM OIL
GRANDMOTHER HUGGED BROTHER	BATH I (TAKE) RIVER
MOTHER LOOKED (AT) ME	DRAWING (I) LIKE (IN) SCHOOL

---

2. Gloss annotation is an annotation method that represents and describes sequences of gestural/ signed sequences based on oral language words.

Table 7. The 20 LGSTP utterances analyzed from phase 4

Utterances LGSTP from Phase 4	
Utterances with reversible argumental structures	**Utterances with non-reversible argumental structures**
TOMÉ DOG PLAYS	TOMÉ GLASSES HAS
CANDY (GAVE) DOCTOR NEIGHBOR	KEY I LOST
GOAT FIGHTED PIG	NEIGHBOR ATE BREAD FRUIT
CRAB BEACH PLAYS EDGAR	RUBBER ERASE DRAWING
CAT PLAYS DOG	NAME I WRITE
SHE PULLS BRAIDES MARIBEL	SERPENT ATTACK BROTHER
FRIEND CELSO KICKED	DAD MONEY SPEND DRINK
PARROT SPEAKS FATHER	SAFU TASTE SWEET
AMARILDO JULIETA GAVE SNACK	GRANDMA PURCHASED SALT BAG
AMARILDO KISS JULIET	HOT PAN BURNED MOTHER

The results indicated that, in the first phase, the LGSTP is taking shape and communication emerges from pantomime. There is some degree of freedom in the order of gestures in the utterance; however, there was a trend towards the use of the SVO order (60%) for events with reversible argumental structure, and towards the use of the OSV order (60%) in events with non-reversible argumental structure. Other orders coexisted, such as the VSO order in reversible events and OVS in irreversible events (Table 8).

Table 8. The number of occurrences and percentage of word order in 20 utterances from LGSTP during phase 1

	SVO	OSV	VSO	OVS
Events with reversible argumental structure	6 (60%)	3 (30%)	1 (10%)	0 (0%)
Events with non-reversible argumental structure	2 (20%)	6 (60%)	1 (10%)	1 (10%)

In the last phase of data collection (phase 4), in which pantomimic gestures decreased and gave way to signs that, although iconic, were not pantomimic, the data showed that the occurrence of the less frequent orders seemed to decrease, leaving room for the predominant use of the SVO order both in reversible events (50% of occurrences) and in the irreversible events (80% of occurrences) (Table 9).

As indicated above, we had initially hypothesized that, in an initial pantomimic communication phase, the order for events with a non-reversible argu-

Table 9. The number of occurrences and percentage of word order in 20 utterances from LGSTP during phase 4

	SOV	SVO	OSV
Events with reversible argumental structure	2 (20%)	5 (50%)	3 (30%)
Events with non-reversible argumental structure	0 (0%)	8 (80%)	2 (20%)

mental structure would be the SOV order and that, in the case of events with a reversible argumental structure, the order would be SVO. However, we found that the SOV order only appeared in the last phase (phase 4) for events with reversible argumental structure, not occurring in our corpus in the first phase (phase 1) for either type of event. Therefore, we may conclude that SOV order seems to be recurrent in emerging sign language, as our data suggest.

In phase 1, there was a trend towards using the SVO order (60%) in events with reversible argumental structure. The overall percentage of SVO order occurrences decreased in phase 4 to 50%, but still retained predominance over the other orders. This trend is described in the literature and is confirmed in the data collected, possibly indicating a natural order in our case.

In the case of events with a non-reversible argumental structure, phase 1 showed predominant use of the OSV order (60%); however, the percentage of OSV order use dropped to 20% by phase 4, with the SVO order taking precedence (80%) in this phase. The word order observed does not seem to agree with previous studies; future work based on a higher number of data points is needed to deepen our understanding of the predominant word orders which occur during the evolution of emerging sign languages.

3.5 The emergence of linguistic complexity

Linguistic complexity in LGSTP began to grow when the deaf signers started to name objects, feelings, and actions together, negotiating the best proto-sign for representing the referent shown in the cards (Carmo et al., 2014; Mineiro et al., 2021). If the first expression of their communication was pantomimic, gradually but quickly, the pantomimic component decreased, making space for repeatedly-used signs with high lexical frequency to name the referents. Linguistic structure arose within two years with some main trends, namely phonological characteristics – still visible after eight years of language emergence – an emergent morphology and word order.

3.5.1 *The articulatory and phonological characteristics of emerging signs*

The proto-signs in LGSTP follow the same phonological parameters of manual handshape, orientation, finger selection, movement, location, and the use of manual articulators – with either the dominant hand or both hands – like in the signs of other sign languages. No handshape and no location were observed to be particularly prevalent, and many signs were performed with both hands as articulators.

During the evolution of LGSTP, the location was articulated with no limited area; the signs could be performed anywhere in the space area around the signer's body, and some of the signs were anchored to certain body parts, such as the legs, stomach, and above the head. Then, as studies 1 and 2 demonstrated, the whole-body commitment dropped off, and a more economical, two-handed linguistic system emerged.

Numerous facial expressions are also visible in many of the signs collected and might become a parameter of distinguishing phonological features. This may be because, in the early stages of emergence, some concepts that had no sign were expressed by pantomime; for example, the concept ASK was articulated through the facial expression of wondering, similarly to what has been reported in the Israeli Sign Language (Meir et al., 2010).

The first productions also demonstrated a substantial articulatory involvement of other body elements, such as arms, shoulders, back, legs, stomach, and face (Mineiro et al., 2021; Moita et al., 2023). This pattern was similarly found in the first stages of ISL emergence (Meir & Sandler, 2008). For example, the word football was articulated through the leg movement of KICKING A BALL.

3.5.2 *Trends in emergent morphology*

At the level at which the first signs (proto-signs) appear, we lack any evidence; thus, we hypothesize that there might exist a tendency for certain types of compounding, as in the case of BANANA TREE = TREE + BANANA or GIRL = WOMAN + CHILD. In emerging sign languages, such as ABSL, compounding has been reported as prevailing over the derivational process (Aronoff et al., 2003), which also seems to be the case of LGSTP.

There were no compound signs in the sample analyzed in the first 30 videos representing the early data collection stage. In the second stage, we observed 21 compound signs in different contexts, for example: FRUITS (CAJAMANGA = CANJAMANGA + EAT); HUMANS (BOY = MAN + CHILD); and NATURE (SUNRISE = SUN + BORN). These compounds consistently appear in our corpus. In the final stage of data collection, more compounds were found regarding house divisions such as BEDROOM = ROOM + SLEEP, LIVING ROOM = ROOM + SEAT, KITCHEN = ROOM + PAN, and BATHROOM = ROOM + WASH. The total of compounds found at this final stage was 37.

Inflectional morphology in LGSTP is still nonexistent, no different than in other emergent sign languages (Meir et al., 2010), which is not surprising given that it is still a fundamental and developing language.

Nevertheless, we detected a systematic use of personal pronouns as subject and object within phrases. Interestingly, the LGSTP signers do not make any distinction in the videos analyzed between the pronouns I or WE in the position of subject or object. For example, in sentences like WE LIKE BEACH AND TEACHER LIKE US, the pronoun WE and US are signed similarly. This is also the case for the other personal pronouns.

The use of personal pronouns is one of the first steps in language acquisition in deaf children, which they acquire very early (Carmo et al., 2014). Thus, we can compare this initial use of pronouns with the first stages of sign language acquisition in deaf children from other sign languages. Another interesting finding is that the personal pronouns in LGSTP have a baseline of pointing just like in other sign languages (Petitto, 1987).

4. Signs do not emerge ex-nihilo

Signs or words do not emerge ex-nihilo. Within the studies on the origins of language, three main streams of thought regarding the role of gestures and other visually perceived body movements (Corballis, 2003; Tomasello, 2008; Zlatev, 2008) in the emergence of speech can be delineated: the gesture-first (Corballis, 2009; Hewes et al., 1973; Arbib, 2012, this volume), the multimodal, or equal partners, hypotheses (Kendon, 2004; McNeill 2012) and mimesis theory (Zlatev et al., this volume). If we consider Corballis' and Kendon's points of view, they differ only in the evolutionary timing and manner in which gesture was incorporated into language (Corballis, 2014).

We will agree with the statement that gestures and vocalizations are intertwined from the beginning of language emergence in human beings. This point of view is supported by the following evidence: both modalities of language, oral and visuospatial, are closely linked; in sign language, language involves not only manual articulation but also some vocalizations and movements of the face and hands, while spoken language is predominantly accompanied by manual co-speech gestures (Kendon, 1980; McNeill, 1992). Gesture research suggests that speech and gesture have the same underlying conceptual system (Kendon, 2004). In terms of human evolution, it makes sense that those systems (manual and vocal) co-evolved together and are intertwined with each other.

The five studies presented in the previous section led us to the following conclusions: signing in the absence of speech begins in pantomimic gestures to communicate, and the first resource for communication in the absence of a structured linguistic system is bodily mimesis through pantomime.

The analysis of the evolution from pantomime to early signs showed how a community communicated through pantomime before having a structured linguistic system. This communication lasted for two years and was substantially reduced after one year when agreed-upon proto-signs began to appear in the community, solving the communication needs more economically in terms of articulation and time efficiency. There is no disruption between pantomime and proto-signs, and they fell onto a continuum during the emergence of the language (Table 2).

The analysis of the evolution of the movement and the articulatory properties showed us how the range of gestures, as well as the use of the hands, face, and body parts required by pantomime are reduced over time on account of neural efficiency. Regarding communication, when a more structured linguistic system appears, pantomime begins to become residual or a language fossil.

Analyzing the iconicity motivation of new sign emergence may reveal that iconicity motivates the emergence of signs' forms. However, this analysis does not provide evidence that iconic nature might influence phonological patterns since, at this linguistic phase of LGSTP, it is impossible to identify phonological patterns, constraints, and phenomena involved. Considering that iconicity might influence phonological patterns observed in spoken languages (Auracher et al., 2019), the strong presence of iconic strategies in new signs narrows the gap between the nature of the sign and spoken language, supporting that iconicity is a universal mechanism of language. This corroborates the hypothesis that pantomime can be considered a fossil of this new language.

The grammatical characteristics of the first type of communication amongst this population are also altered when the use of pantomime decreases. The analysis of basic word order showed us that in the first phase of sign language emergence, which is primarily comprised of pantomime, the order of reversible and irreversible events is communicated with great syntactic freedom regarding the order of the constituents; the same is not confirmed by the fourth phase of sign language emergence when linguistic characteristics begin to appear. In this last phase, syntax becomes more rigid with regard to the order of constituents. Again, pantomimic communication in an early phase of language emergence can be considered a fossil of this new language.

LGSTP's evolution showed mainly articulatory and morphological tendencies of the first signs that are in a phase of insertion into the linguistic system and exhibit characteristics inherent to it, namely the articulatory concentration in the manual articulators, the visible fall of the M2, as well as the progressive loss of the non-manual articulators (trunk, head, legs). In morphological terms, there is a trend toward the composition of gestures based on existing gestures. These proto-sign trends remind us of a path that began in pantomime and was born from it.

Therefore, is pantomime a communicative fossil of language? Żywiczyński and colleagues (2021) argue that it is, although Marentette´s developmental study shows a different trajectory (see Marententte, this volume). The arguments presented in the introduction are convincing. First of all, pantomime is used when, because of pathology, there is a language impairment in the case of apraxia (Whiteside et al., 2015) or aphasia (Code, 2021; Dronkers et al., 1998). Secondly, pantomime is used to communicate when there is no common language, indicated by (i) the evidence from travelogues from the period of Great Exploration during the 15th to 17th centuries (Żywiczyński & Wacewicz, 2021), (ii) charades when the rules temporarily block the use of language blocked (Żywiczyński & Wacewicz, 2021), and (iii) situations when people who do not share a language try to communicate. Finally, pantomime seems to be a stage that precedes the proto-sign in a new sign language (Arbib, this volume; Gärdernfors, this volume).

Regarding this argument, Sandler's (2013) paper rejects this view by describing a lack of pantomime in ABSL as a precursor to signs and presenting the recordings of the origin of this language (a single video) showing the deaf signer using his hands and not his whole body. However, it is essential to place these findings in time. The example of LGSTP shows that it took less than a year for proto-signs to appear that are no longer pantomime. Thus, it is possible that there was a stage before the emergence of proto-signs or first signs in ABSL that was not recorded, possibly because the pantomime phase did not consist of signs, and linguists focused their work on signs. Another issue with these findings is that one informant – a single signer – cannot fully understand language emergence.

We thus hypothesise that language emergence starts with the stage of pantomimic communication, which at a later stage of language development becomes an evolutionary fossil, following the proposal from Żywiczyński and colleagues (2021).

This theory complements those of Emmorey and colleagues (2011), who found that the production of pantomime and language relies on only partially distinct neural systems in the brain (Arbib, this volume). Their research also revealed that pantomime production engages the superior parietal cortex bilaterally for deaf signers, while sign language production (verbs in ASL) engages the left inferior frontal cortex. Pantomime production does not engage the left inferior parietal cortex for hearing non-signers. Intriguingly, this study also reported that the neural networks for pantomime generation were not identical for the deaf and hearing groups, as deaf signers employ more extensive regions within the superior parietal cortex, and hearing non-signers employ neural regions associated with episodic memory retrieval.

In evolutionary terms, manual and vocal systems co-evolved. They have been neurobiologically sophisticated from the beginning, allowing a man to take food into his mouth without biting his fingers (Mineiro, 2020).

In our view, gestures and vocalizations are intertwined from the very beginning of language emergence in human beings. Our primate heritage has endowed us with hands that can provide a natural signaling system that is more natural than the vocal system. Language did evolve from manual gestures and shifted from a manual to a vocal mode (Corballis, 2000), so speech is also gestural. Sign language consists of vocalizations and movements of the face and hands. Manual gestures accompany spoken language.

In brief, Arbib's evolutionary chain (2012) of a Mirror System > simple imitation > complex imitation > pantomime > proto-sign and proto-speech > language-ready brain is a possible scenario for language emergence in humans, but it does not endorse a polymodal origin of language. Our studies permit us to place pantomime as an effective means of bootstrapping a new language. This scenario of language origin is also proposed by Arbib (this volume), who highlights the expanding spiral of language in line with cultural and narrative evolution. Interestingly, Gärdenfors (this volume) insists that the evolution of casual cognition and event representation are essential to transition phenomena when pantomime is exapted in communicative contexts.

5.   End note

We believe that the studies described above – from pantomime to proto- or early sign – lead us to understand the evolutionary process of a newly-born language. This process allows us to extrapolate these findings to the genesis of language in modern humans, thereby shedding light on the roots of language emergence and evolution.

Acknowledgments

This paper is partially based on interesting talks presented by the author and others at the Workshop "Perspectives on Pantomime" (Toruń, 18–19.11.2021). We dearly thank Sławomir Wacewicz and Przemysław Żywiczyński for inviting us to take part, to Monika Boruta-Żywiczyńska and Przemysław Żywiczyński for their hospitality in Toruń, and Przemysław Żywiczyński and Johan Blomberg for their insightful comments on an earlier version of this paper. Further thanks to Jordan Zlatev, Michael Arbib, Paula Marentette, Przemysław Żywiczyński and Sławomir Wacewicz, for discussions on issues related to their talks.

References

Abreu, A.M., Mineiro, A., Ribeiro da Silva, C. & Castro-Caldas, A. (2022). Space, movement and articulation in a newly emergent sign language: Contributions for neural and sociocognitive efficiency. *International Journal of Psychology and Neuroscience* 8(1), 1–18.

Arbib, M.A. (2024). Pantomime within and beyond the evolution of language. In P. Żywiczyński, J. Blomberg & M. Boruta-Żywiczyńska (Eds). *Perspectives on pantomime* (pp. 16–57). Benjamins.

Arbib, M.A. (2012). How the brain Got language: The mirror system hypothesis. In *How the brain Got language*. Oxford University Press.

Aronoff, M., Meir, I., Padden, C., & Sandler, W. (2003). Classifier constructions and morphology in two sign languages. In K. Emmorey (Ed.), *Perspectives on classifier constructions in sign languages* (pp. 53–84). Lawrence Erlbaum Associates Publishers.

Bellugi, U., Klima, E.S., & Poizner, H. (1988). Sign language and the brain. *Research Publications – Association for Research in Nervous and Mental Disease, 66*, 39–56.

Brentari, D. (2019). *Sign language phonology*. Cambridge University Press.

Brown, S. (2024). The pantomimic origins of the narrative arts. In P. Żywiczyński, J. Blomberg & M. Boruta-Żywiczyńska (Eds). *Perspectives on pantomime.* (pp. 141–160). Amsterdam: Benjamins.

Carmo, P., Oliveira, R., & Mineiro, A. (2014). *Dicionário da Língua Gestual de São Tomé e Príncipe – Dicionário oficial da República de São Tomé e Príncipe*. UCEditora.

Caroça, C. (2017). *Contribution to the study of epidemiological factors associated with neurosensorial hearing loss in the population of Sao Tome and Principe*. [Phd]. Universidade NOVA.

Code, C. (2021). The prehistory of speech and language is revealed in brain damage. *Philosophical Transactions of the Royal Society B: Biological Sciences, 376*(1824), rstb.2020.0191, 20200191.

Corballis, M.C. (2003). From hand to mouth: The gestural origins of language. In *Language evolution*. Oxford University Press.

Corballis, M.C. (2009). The evolution of language. *Annals of the New York Academy of Sciences, 1156*(1), 19–43.

Corballis, M.C. (2014). The word according to Adam. The role of gesture in language evolution. In M. Seyfeddinipur & M. Gullberg (Eds.), *From gesture in conversation to visible action as utterance* (pp. 177–198). John Benjamins Publishing Company.

Cuxac, C., & Sallandre, M.-A. (2007). Iconicity and arbitrariness in French Sign Language (LSF): Highly iconic structures, degenerated iconicity and diagrammatic iconicity. In E. Pizzuto, P. Pietrandrea, & R. Simone (Eds.), *Verbal and signed languages: Comparing structures, constructs and methodologies* (pp. 13–33). De Gruyter Mouton. https://www.degruyter.com/view/title/19037

Dronkers, N.F., Ludy, C.A., & Redfern, B.B. (1998). Pragmatics in the absence of verbal language: Descriptions of a severe aphasic and a language-deprived adult. *Journal of Neurolinguistics, 11*(1–2), 179–190.

Emmorey, K., McCullough, S., Mehta, S., Ponto, L.L.B., & Grabowski, T.J. (2011). Sign language and pantomime production differentially engage frontal and parietal cortices. *Language and Cognitive Processes*, 26(7), 878–901.

Emmorey, K., Mehta, S., & Grabowski, T.J. (2007). The neural correlates of sign versus word production. *NeuroImage*, 36(1), 202–208.

Gärdenfors, P. (2024). The relations of demonstration and pantomime to causal reasoning and event cognition. In P. Żywiczyński, J. Blomberg & M. Boruta-Żywiczyńska (Eds). *Perspectives on pantomime*. (pp. 58–78). Benjamins.

Gärdenfors, P. (2021). Demonstration and pantomime in the evolution of teaching and communication. *Language and Communication*, 80, 71–79.

Gasser, M. (2004). The prigins of arbitrariness in language. *Proceedings of the Annual Meeting of the Cognitive Science Society*, 26(26). https://escholarship.org/uc/item/34g8355v

Gell-Mann, M., & Ruhlen, M. (2011). The origin and evolution of word order. *Proceedings of the National Academy of Sciences of the United States of America*, 108(42), 17290–17295.

Gibson, E., Piantadosi, S.T., Brink, K., Bergen, L., Lim, E., & Saxe, R. (2013). A noisy-channel account of crosslinguistic word-order variation. *Psychological Science*, 24(7), 1079–1088.

Göksun, T., Lehet, M., Malykhina, K., & Chatterjee, A. (2015). Spontaneous gesture and spatial language: Evidence from focal brain injury. *Brain and Language*, 150, 1–13.

Goldin-Meadow, S., So, W., Özyürek, A., & Mylander, C. (2008). The natural order of events: How speakers of different languages represent events nonverbally. *Proceedings of the national academy of sciences*.

Hewes, G.W., Andrew, R.J., Carini, L., Choe, H., Gardner, R.A., Kortlandt, A., Krantz, G.S., McBride, G., Nottebohm, F., Pfeiffer, J., Rumbaugh, D.G., Steklis, H.D., Raliegh, M.J., Stopa, R., Suzuki, A., Washburn, S.L., & Wescott, R.W. (1973). Primate communication and the gestural origin of language [and comments and reply]. *Current Anthropology*, 14(1/2), 5–24.

Israel, A., & Sandler, W. (2011). Phonological category resolution in a new sign language: A comparative study of handshapes. In *Formational units in sign languages* (pp. 177–202). De Gruyter Mouton. https://www.degruyter.com/document/doi/10.1515/9781614510680.177/html

Kendon, A. (1980). Gesture and speech: Two aspects of the process of utterance. In M.R. Key (Ed.), *Nonverbal communication and language*. Mouton.

Kendon, A. (2004). *Gesture: Visible action as utterance*. Cambridge University Press.

Klima, E.S., & Bellugi, U. (1979). *The signs of language*. Harvard University Press.

Kooij, van der, E. (2002). Phonological categories in sign language of the Netherlands: The role of phonetic implementation and iconicity. Utrecht: LOT.

Marentette, P., Inaba, C., & Petrie, R. (2024). Symbolic distancing in three-year-old children's pantomime. In P. Żywiczyński, J. Blomberg & M. Boruta-Żywiczyńska (Eds) *Perspectives on pantomime*. (pp. 190–218). Benjamins.

McNeill, D. (1992). *Hand and mind: What gestures reveal about thought*. University of Chicago Press.

McNeill, D. (2012). *How language began: Gesture and speech in human evolution*. Cambridge: Cambridge University Press.

Chapter 7. The pantomime roots of Sao Tome and Principe Sign Language 185

Meir, I., & Sandler, W. (2008). *A language in space: The story of Israeli Sign Language* (1st ed.). Psychology Press.

Meir, I., Sandler, W., Padden, C., & Aronoff, M. (2010). Emerging sign languages. In M. Marschark & P.E. Spencer (Eds.), *The Oxford handbook of deaf studies, language, and education*, Vol. 2 (pp. 267–280). Oxford University Press.

Mineiro, A. (2016). Língua gestual de São Tomé e Príncipe: Retrato dos primeiros gestos. In *Revista de estudos linguísticos da Universidade do Porto* (Faculdade de Letras da Universidade do Porto e Centro de Linguística da Universidade do Porto, Vol. 11, p. 22).

Mineiro, A. (2020). *Ensaio sobre génese e evolução da linguagem na espécie humana: Entre o gesto, a fala e a escrita*. Novas Edições Acadêmicas.

Mineiro, A. (2022). *Evolução da linguagem e ordem natural de Palavras: Os verbos reversíveis e não reversíveis na gestual de São Tomé e Príncipe num estudo piloto.*

Mineiro, A., Báez-Montero, I.C., Moita, M., Galhano-Rodrigues, I., & Castro-Caldas, A. (2021). Disentangling pantomime from early sign in a new sign language: Window into language evolution research. *Frontiers in Psychology*, 12, 1130.

Mineiro, A., Carmo, P., Caroça, C., Moita, M., Carvalho, S., Paço, J., & Zaky, A. (2017). Emerging linguistic features of Sao Tome and Principe Sign Language. *Sign Language & Linguistics*, 20(1), 109–128.

Moita, M., Abreu, A.M., & Mineiro, A. (2023). Iconicity in the emergence of a phonological system?. *Journal of Language Evolution*, 8(1), 1–17.

Moita, M., Gonçalves, E., Medeiros, C., & Mineiro, A. (2018). A phonological diachronic study on Portuguese Sign Language of the Azores. *Sign Language Studies*, 19(1), 138–162.

Osiurak, F., Crétel, C., Uomini, N., Bryche, C., Lesourd, M., & Reynaud, E. (2021). On the neurocognitive co-evolution of tool behavior and language: Insights from the massive redeployment framework. *Topics in Cognitive Science*, 13(4), 684–707.

Padden, C.A., Meir, I., Hwang, S.-O., Lepic, R., Seegers, S., & Sampson, T. (2013). Patterned iconicity in sign language lexicons. *Gesture*, 13(3), 287–308.

Padden, C., Hwang, S.-O., Lepic, R., & Seegers, S. (2015). Tools for Language: Patterned Iconicity in Sign Language Nouns and Verbs. *Topics in Cognitive Science*, 7(1), 81–94.

Pagel, M. (2009). Human language as a culturally transmitted replicator. *Nature Reviews Genetics*, 10(6), 405–415.

Perniss, P., Thompson, R., & Vigliocco, G. (2010). Iconicity as a general property of language: Evidence from spoken and signed Languages. *Frontiers in Psychology*, 1.

Perniss, P., & Vigliocco, G. (2014). The bridge of iconicity: From a world of experience to the experience of language. *Philosophical Transactions of the Royal Society B: Biological Sciences*, 369(1651), 20130300.

Petitto, L.A. (1987). On the autonomy of language and gesture: Evidence from the acquisition of personal pronouns in American Sign Language. *Cognition*, 27(1), 1–52.

Petitto, L.A., Holowka, S., Sergio, L.E., Levy, B., & Ostry, D.J. (2004). Baby hands that move to the rhythm of language: Hearing babies acquiring sign languages babble silently on the hands. *Cognition*, 93(1), 43–73.

Petitto, L.A., & Marentette, P.F. (1991). Babbling in the Manual Mode: Evidence for the Ontogeny of Language. *Science*, 251(5000), 1493–1496.

Rizzolatti, G., & Arbib, M.A. (1998). Language within our grasp. *Trends in Neurosciences*, 21(5), 188–194.

Sandler, W. (2009). *Symbiotic symbolization by hand and mouth in sign language*. https://www.ncbi.nlm.nih.gov/pmc/articles/PMC2863338/

Sandler, W. (2012). Dedicated gestures and the emergence of sign language. *Gesture*, 12(3), 265–307.

Sandler, W. (2013). Vive la différence: Sign language and spoken language in language evolution. *Language and Cognition*, 5(2–3), 189–203.

Sandler, W. (2014). The emergence of the phonetic and phonological features in sign language. *Nordlyd*, 41(2), 183–212.

Sandler, W. (2017). The challenge of sign language phonology. *Annual Review of Linguistics*, 3(1), 43–63.

Sandler, W., Aronoff, M., Padden, C., & Meir, I. (2014). Language emergence: Al-Sayyid Bedouin Sign Language. In J. Sidnell, N.J. Enfield, & P. Kockelman (Eds.), *The Cambridge handbook of linguistic anthropology* (pp. 250–284). Cambridge University Press.

Senghas, A., & Coppola, M. (2001). Children creating language: How Nicaraguan sign language acquired a spatial grammar. *Psychological Science*, 12(4), 323–328.

Stokoe, W.C. (1980). Sign language structure. *Annual Review of Anthropology*, 9(1), 365–390.

Sibirska, M., Boruta-Żywiczyńska, M., Żywiczyński, P., & Wacewicz, S. (2022). What's in a mime? An exploratory analysis of predictors of communicative success of pantomime. In M. Couto, S. Chandra, E. Yadollahi and V. Charisi (Eds). *Interactions studies*, 23(2) (pp. 289–321).

Tomasello, M. (2008). *Origins of human communication*. The MIT Press. https://mitpress.mit.edu/books/origins-human-communication.

Vieira, A.B. (1995). *Ensaios sobre a evolução do homem e da linguagem*. Fim de Século.

Wacewicz, S., & Żywiczyński P. (2024). Two types of bodily-mimetic communication: Distinct design specifications and evolutionary trajectories. In P. Żywiczyński, J. Blomberg & M. Boruta-Żywiczyńska (Eds). *Perspectives on Pantomime* (pp. 101–115). Amsterdam: Benjamins.

Whiteside, S.P., Dyson, L., Cowell, P.E., & Varley, R.A. (2015). The relationship between apraxia of speech and oral apraxia: Association or dissociation? *Archives of Clinical Neuropsychology*, 30(7), 670–682.

Wilbur, R.B. (2000). Phonological and prosodic layering of nonmanuals in American Sign Language. In K. Emmorey & H. Lane (Eds.), *The signs of language revisited: An anthology to honor Ursula Bellugi and Edward Klima* (pp. 215–244). Lawrence Erlbaum Associates Publishers.

Zlatev, J. (2008). The co-evolution of intersubjectivity and bodily mimesis. In J. Zlatev, T. Racine, C. Sinha, & E. Itkonen (Eds.), *The shared mind: Perspectives on intersubjectivity* (pp. 215–224). John Benjamins Publishing.

Zlatev, J., Wacewiz, S., Żywiczyński, P. & deWeijer, J. (2017). Multimodal-first or panomime-first? Communicating events through pantomime with and without vocalization. In S. Hartmann, M. Pleyer, J. Winters and J. Zlatev (Eds.) *Interaction in the evolution of language* (pp. 465-488). John Benjamin Publishing.

Chapter 7. The pantomime roots of Sao Tome and Principe Sign Language 187

Zlatev, J., Sibierska, M., Żywiczyński, P., van de Weijer, & Boruta-Żywiczyńska, M. (2024). Can pantomime narrate? A cognitive semiotic approach. In P. Żywiczyński, J. Blomberg & M. Boruta-Żywiczyńska (Eds). *Perspectives on Pantomime.* (pp. 116–140.) Amsterdam: Benjamins.

Zlatev, J., Żywiczyński, P., & Wacewicz, S. (2020). Pantomime as the original human-specific communicative system. *Journal of Language Evolution*, 5(2), 156–174.

Żywiczyński, P., Sibierska, M., Wacewicz, S., van de Weijer, J., Ferretti, F., Adornetti, I., Chiera, A., & Deriu, V. (2021). Evolution of conventional communication. A cross-cultural study of pantomimic re-enactments of transitive events. *Language & Communication*, 80, 191–203.

Żywiczyński, P., Wacewicz, S., & Lister, C. (2021). Pantomimic fossils in modern human communication. *Philosophical Transactions of the Royal Society B: Biological Sciences*, 376(1824), 20200204.

Żywiczyński, P., Wacewicz, S., & Sibierska, M. (2018). Defining Pantomime for Language Evolution Research. *Topoi*, 37(2), 307–318.

CHAPTER 8

Symbolic distancing in three-year-old children's object-use pantomime

Paula Marentette, Chelsea Inaba & Rebecca Petrie
University of Alberta

Children's early pantomime of how to use objects is thought to demonstrate "symbolic distancing," ostensibly providing an opportunity to observe the development of symbolic reference between the ages of three- and six-years. This chapter argues, in contrast, that the modes of representation used by three-year-olds may be better explained by item, task, and communicative factors revealing children's functional knowledge of objects and social knowledge of communicative conventions rather than symbolic development. Detailed analysis of the children's manual mode of representation in conjunction with their speech challenges assumptions about which forms are viewed as more or less pantomimic. Interpretation of iconicity may be a function of human adult convention; we discuss the implications for our understanding of the role of iconic gestures depicting object-use in communicative situations.

Keywords: symbolic distancing, pantomime, representational gesture, iconicity, modes of representation

Symbolic distancing in three-year-old children's pantomime

Children are thought to be capable of demonstrating symbolic representation (defined further below) across several formats at quite young ages: words (by 1.5 years, Tomasello, Striano & Rochat, 1999), pictures (by 2.5 years, Deloache, 1991), video (by 2.5 years, Troseth & DeLoache, 1988), play and objects (by 3 years; Elder & Pederson, 1978; Striano, Tomasello & Rochat, 2001). Indeed, very young children have been shown to accept a range of signs as names for things (Namy, 2001). In contrast, pantomimes of object use have been interpreted as revealing a lack of symbolic capacity in three-year-old children (Boyatzis & Watson, 1993; Kaplan, 1968; Mitchell & Clark, 2015; O'Reilly, 1995; Overton & Jackson, 1973; Weidinger, Lindner, Hogrefe, Ziegler & Goldenberg, 2017). This conclusion arises from an

https://doi.org/10.1075/ais.12.08mar
© 2024 John Benjamins Publishing Company

Chapter 8. Symbolic distancing in three-year-old children's object-use Pantomime **189**

observed difference in the form of children's and adults' pantomime for object use that is "resolved" around 6- to 8-years of age (see Mitchell & Clark, 2015).

In this chapter we specifically examine the formational difference in gestured representations of object use between children and adults, and explore its significance for symbolic development. We examine two key questions: (a) whether these gestures can be accurately described as pantomime, and (b) whether or not the process of symbolic development can be demonstrated by these gestures. In particular, our examination of symbolic development is grounded in the idea of *symbolic distancing*, as proposed by Werner and Kaplan (1963). Symbolic distancing describes a gradual developmental process relying on iconicity as a support on the road to representational insight. We will argue that gestures of object use may not be well described by the term pantomime, and that they demonstrate the same kind of symbolic representation as those of adults. That is, we argue that there is no difference in symbolic status between the forms of children and adults. As explanation for why children's object-use representations differ from those of adults, we consider the role of primary and secondary iconicity as well as the communicative context in which children produce these gestures.

"Pantomiming" how to use an object

In this chapter we examine a particular task, in which three-year-old children pretend to use familiar objects (e.g., brushing their teeth, cutting with scissors, drinking from a cup, etc.) with cues that may be solely verbal, include objects, or include pictures of objects. This task is typically used with children three-years-of-age and older, as it is thought to be difficult to elicit pantomime from children younger than three-years-old (Overton & Jackson, 1973; but see Marentette, Pettenati, Bello & Volterra, 2016, for spontaneous object-use gestures with two-year-olds). The resulting gestures are categorized into two types: (a) use of hand(s) to represent the form and action of the object, for example, extending the index finger and middle finger in a V while opening and closing them to depict cutting with scissors (see Figure 1a), or b) the use of hand(s) to represent grasping the object and performing the action, for example, using a fist to enact holding a pair of scissors while pretending to open and close the fist (see Figure 1b).

Labels for these two types of gesture vary widely by field. In this paper we will call the use of the hands to represent the object (and frequently its action), **body-part-as-object** (BPO). We choose this label because the literature (reviewed below) that most directly evaluates the idea of symbolic distancing uses this nomenclature. Other areas of research use different labels for this same kind of representation: as-if being an object (Müller, this volume), object handshapes

(Brentari et al., 2012; Miniero & Moita, this volume); hand-as-object (Marentette, Pettenati, Bello & Volterra, 2016). Brown et al. 2019 (also Brown, this volume) uses the term BPO but further subdivides this term to indicate whether the use is egocentric or allocentric. In the task discussed in this paper, all BPO are egocentric. The use of the hands to depict grasping an object while showing how to use it are here called **imaginary-object** (IO, see literature below as well as Brown et al. 2019; Brown, this volume). Other labels for this type of depiction include: as-if action (Müller, this volume), handling (Brentari et al., 2012; Miniero & Moita, this volume), and hand-as-hand (Marentette et al., 2016).

Between the ages of 3- and approximately 6-years, children produce BPO forms more frequently than adults who primarily produce IO forms in similar tasks (*inter alia*, Boyatzis & Watson, 1993; Kaplan, 1968; Mitchell & Clark, 2015; O'Reilly, 1995; Overton & Jackson, 1973). This task is often described as an elicited pantomime task.

a. Body-part-as-object (BPO): Hand as object

b. Imagined-object (IO): Hand as hand

Figure 1. Examples of gesture types for the representation of "using scissors."
Note: Video clips viewable at https://ualberta.aviaryplatform.com/r/8s4jm24d8r

Is this pantomime?

Our first question with respect to this task, is whether the gestures produced during the "elicited pantomime task" are indeed pantomime. There are at least three groups of researchers that use the term pantomime in related but slightly varying ways. In studies of cognitive development in three-year-olds, *pretending to use an object* (regardless of specific form) equals pantomime (e.g., Mitchell & Clark, 2015; Weidinger et al., 2017). This assumption applies generally to the research reported on BPO and IO use in children. To date, no attention has been paid to whether or not the children's manual responses are accompanied by speech.

A second use of the term pantomime contrasts with that approach with respect to the relevance of speech. For gesture researchers, pantomime has a more specific definition: it is the depiction of action *that occurs in the absence of speech* (McNeill, 1992; though see Gullberg, 1998, for a more graded approach). From McNeill's ontogenetic perspective, pantomime precedes co-speech gesture (McNeill, 2016). Levy and McNeill (2015) argue that gesture-speech integration begins to displace pantomime around age three. In McNeill's view, the absence of speech is a defining and semiotic difference between gesture and pantomime. In his view, the relationship between gesture and speech arises out of the *growth point*, which describes the linked relationship between speech and gesture, a dual semiotic that permits the tightly synchronized production of a single message across two modalities (McNeill, 2016, Chapter 2). For McNeill at least, the use of whole body enactment decreases in production with the increase of synchronized co-speech manual gestures.

In adulthood, the term pantomime, also known as silent gesture, emphasizes the disconnect between speech and gesture and focusses on the resulting formational and combinatorial differences that occur when gesture is the sole mode of communication (Goldin-Meadow et al., 1996; Ortega & Özyürek, 2019; Schouwstra, Swart & Thompson, 2019). Typically for adults, pantomime is most likely to occur when language use is not permitted or not possible (see Żywiczyński et al., 2021). Müller (this volume) rejects the focus on the presence of speech as relevant to gesture analysis. She persuasively argues for a continuum of "mimetic expressive movement" whose forms are differentiated based on their spontaneous through conventionalized gesture. In this analysis, the stability of a gestured form varies regardless of the presence of speech. Given the historical understanding of pantomime as occurring in the absence of speech (following McNeill, 1992), Müller argues that the term pantomime be limited to artistic performances, and not used by gesture researchers.

A third approach to pantomime arises in cognitive semiotics with the discussion of the origins of language in our species. Zlatev, Żywiczyński, and Wacewicz

(2020) propose a set of clines that define pantomime and its role as "the original human-specific communicative system." Necessarily occurring in a non-linguistic environment, core components of early pantomime include *primary iconicity* and *the use of enacting as a representational form*. Note here that the use of a specific form is indicated: the use of enactment. Żywiczyński, Wacewicz, and Lister (2021) further argue that pantomime precedes the development of symbolic reference: from an evolutionary perspective, a referential form must show primary iconicity to provide displaced reference in the absence of an existing system (see Sonesson, 2010, re primary iconicity). The description of pantomime as a transitional form in the establishment of the Sao Tome and Principe Sign Language (LGSTP, Mineiro & Moita, this volume; Mineiro et al., 2021) supports the claim that pantomime is central in the initial stages of development of a communicative system. Zlatev et al. (2020) explicitly refer to the idea of symbolic distancing as supporting pantomime as a transitional phase of language evolution.

Do these multiple definitions of pantomime describe the same phenomenon? Do they accurately describe the manual responses of three-year-olds in this task? These are questions we will explore in this analysis. Next, however, we turn to symbolic representation, and the proposal of Werner and Kaplan that its development is achieved by a process of symbolic distancing.

Symbol development and symbolic distancing

Heinz Werner & Bernard Kaplan argued for a process of symbolic distancing as a mechanism for the development of symbolic reference in language. They assumed that ontogeny recapitulates phylogeny, not morphologically, but in the cognitive development of symbol capacity. Werner and Kaplan (1963: 18) argued that symbols arise from an internal shift from objects as "things of action to things of contemplation." One way this shift is described is through a multi-faceted process of differentiation (Piaget, 1962; also McNeill, 2016: 36 with respect to growth points). In this chapter, we focus on the differentiation of the symbolic vehicle and the referent: the process called symbolic distancing.

For Werner and Kaplan (1963: 15), a symbol requires an **arbitrary pattern**, used **intentionally**, with a form that has a **dual** nature. Duality is, of course, central to both signs and symbols. Sonesson (2010: 32, italics in original) argues that "signs have to do with something which is *something else* than what it stands for." For a symbol, the child's awareness that the symbol and its referent are two distinct things adds an extra dimension, the feature of intentionality. DeLoache (2004: 66, italics added) argues that "a symbol is something that *someone intends* to represent something other than itself." Finally, note the absence of a require-

Chapter 8. Symbolic distancing in three-year-old children's object-use Pantomime **193**

ment of arbitrariness in DeLoache's definition. Arbitrary form was considered uncontroversial at the time of Werner and Kaplan's writing (e.g., Hockett, 1958:577). We highlight this point because we argue the insistence of Werner and Kaplan on arbitrary form has influenced, and continues to influence, thought about the role of iconicity and the symbolic status of representational gestures, specifically pantomime, in children.

Werner and Kaplan (1963:45–48) propose a three-stage progression of sound to symbol, from bodily mimesis of an object, gradually increasing the "distance" through the use of a multi-modal form of mimesis (still based on sound, but here, for example, using sound to represent shape), to a symbolic form that is both arbitrary and conventionalized:

> ... here the external forms of vehicle and referent have lost most, if not all, of their surface similarity. Thus there is a progressive distancing – a decrease in tangible 'likeness' – between the external forms of vehicle and referent.
>
> (Werner & Kaplan, 1963:48)

What then, of manual representation? Can iconic gestures be symbolic? We focus here on symbolic reference to the exclusion of indexical reference, demonstrated most notably in pointing. We also ignore conventional and emblematic gestures, as these are often not iconic, and are clearly already conventional, therefore not the type of gestures typically discussed in the context of symbolic distancing. According to Werner and Kaplan, true symbols are arbitrary and conventional, and therefore, verbal. They describe gestures as "natural symbols" (1963:89): forms that *present* rather than *represent*. Manual forms are claimed to "lack intention" because they are too close in form to the pragmatic action. At best, iconic gestures are depictive rather than symbolic (1963:90). Werner and Kaplan appear to argue that *iconicity bars intentionality*:

> The fully autonomous medium of representation is one that is clearly differentiated from the events represented by it: the vehicles which constitute such a medium are distinct in form and context of execution from the contents such vehicles serve to depict. Now, as has been suggested, bodily gestures rarely, if ever, attain a level of full autonomy ... Perhaps the most important factor working against the full-fledged development of an autonomous gestural medium is the development of the medium of speech: the linguistic medium is 'free' from direct involvement in pragmatic action and can be formed to depict and describe contents with much greater precisions than can gestures.
>
> (Werner & Kaplan, 1963:92)

With the advent of sign language studies and sign linguistics, among other developments, we have fundamentally shifted our understanding of symbolic form and symbol systems away from an insistence on arbitrary form (Perniss et al., 2010; Stokoe, 1960; Wacewicz & Żywiczyński, 2015). This shift is further supported by the recognition and reinterpretation of sound symbolism in adult language (e.g., Edmiston, Perlman, & Lupyan, 2018; note that Werner and Kaplan, 1963: 107, discuss sound symbolism in children as transitional forms on the path to "denaturalization of the vocal symbol"). Recently there is increased discussion of the presence and role of iconicity in both spoken and sign language (Dingemanse et al., 2015; Perniss et al., 2010).

The useful terms primary and secondary iconicity (Sonesson, 2007; 2010) capture aspects of the distinction in form that may reframe Werner and Kaplan's concerns while enabling us to recognize the persistent presence of iconicity in languages. A child whose referential vehicle shows "no distance" is using *primary iconicity*: a form that reveals its meaning due to perceptual similarity with the referent. *Secondary iconicity*, in contrast, describes a form that has lost the "surface similarity" between vehicle and referent. The meaning of a form showing secondary iconicity is opaque rather than transparent (terms borrowed from sign linguistics, Klima & Bellugi, 1979: 22–24). In secondary iconicity, the connection between vehicle and referent must be established *before* the iconicity can be discovered in the form of the vehicle. This opacity may be framed as movement toward arbitrariness. Increasing arbitrariness, in combination with conventionalization of the vehicle, is the process described as symbolic distance. The greater the "distance" between the vehicle and the referent, the closer the child is toward symbolic representation. This is the central aspect of Werner and Kaplan's claim.

Werner and Kaplan's ideas about iconicity and symbolic reference underlie assumptions that continue to be made in the research literature. Although Werner & Kaplan's work is less frequently cited in recent papers, we argue that this is a result of general acceptance of their position on symbolic development. This view of gesture and its role in symbolic development exerts an ongoing influence on research.

We see this in several areas of developmental and cognitive developmental research. Most notably, McNeill's perspective on pantomime and the development of gesture (McNeill, 1992: 296–300; McNeill, 2016) is strongly influenced by Werner and Kaplan. The idea of symbolic distancing is also central to the study of "symbolic gesture" (Acredolo & Goodwyn, 1988; Goodwyn & Acredolo, 1993; Goodwyn, Acredolo, & Brown, 2000; Vallotton & Ayoub, 2010; Vallotton, 2011) in which the claim is made that gestures, *because* they are iconic, are easier for children to produce, enabling earlier access to communication than is possible with words. This leads directly to the baby sign industry (for critical reviews of baby sign, see Johnston, Durieux-Smith & Bloom, 2005; Kirk, Howlett, Pine & Fletcher, 2013). The idea of symbolic distancing strongly influenced early and influential papers examining symbolic play (Elder & Pederson, 1978; Jackowitz & Watson, 1980) and distinction between form and function of the substitute object is still critical in this field (*inter alia* Bigham & Bourcher-Sutton, 2007; Hopkins et al., 2016). Finally, symbolic distancing is also used as an explanation of the "less is more" task devised to test executive functioning (Carlson et al., 2005; Labuschagne et al., 2017).

This paper explores the implications of this set of assumptions first tested with the elicited pantomime task. We turn now to examine the combination of assumptions about iconicity and symbolic form in the context of the pantomime of object use.

Symbolic status of pantomime forms

The attribution of symbolic status to manual gestures is challenging due to overlap in form between action and gesture (see Bates et al., 1979). The earliest iconic gestures of one-year-old children, those that occur when they are likely to be sorting out communicative systems and symbolic reference, are treated as pantomime (Acredolo & Goodwyn, 1988; McNeill, 1992). In these cases, pantomime is used to refer to manual gestures that use the hands (and body) to replicate an action of the body and that are not accompanied by speech. These early gestures are thought to be enactments of familiar actions or imitations of adult productions (Behne et al., 2014; Bellagamba & Tomasello, 1999; Caselli et al., 2012; see Capirci et al., 2022 for a detailed review of the links between action, gesture, and word in early language).

Familiar with Werner and B. Kaplan's contemporary work, Goodglass and E. Kaplan (1963) used an enacted pantomime task with familiar tools and objects to explore the connections between apraxia and aphasia. Their study compared men with aphasia to age- and intelligence-matched men with non-aphasic brain-injury and found that those with aphasia used a higher portion of pantomimes in which the hands were used to represent the object. They argued that BPO was less symbolic than IO because the hands provide a concrete representation of the object *as well as* its action. The more arbitrary IO form, only representing the action, was therefore more symbolic. Goodglass and Kaplan interpreted their results as follows:

> One may say both of the child and of the brain-injured, dyspraxic patient that BPO permits them to avoid an impaired (or, for the children, undeveloped) function. (Goodglass & E. Kaplan, 1963:718)

Work with children has continued since the 1960s and consistently supports this finding: children at age three-years show a dominant use of BPO. The BPO form is said to reveal a lack of symbolic distancing because the child must rely on their hand(s) or body to "represent" the object; they require the perceptually available form to support the function of symbolic reference (E. Kaplan, 1968; Overton & Jackson, 1973; O'Reilly, 1995). Furthermore, the use of BPO shows that they cannot "differentiate between the agent (actor) and the implement (the tool)" (E. Kaplan, 1968:70). In contrast, IO gestures show "increased symbolic distance" because the tool is imagined and the hand represents only how the agent would interact with the object (Overton & Jackson, 1973). IO is therefore interpreted as a symbolically mediated representation (Boyatzis & Watson, 1993; O'Reilly, 1995).

By age 8, children perform much like adults in this task (see Figure 1 in Mitchell & Clark, 2015, which summarizes the results of elicited pantomime research (*inter alia*, Boyatzis & Watson, 1993; Kaplan, 1968; Mitchell & Clark, 2015; O'Reilly, 1995; Overton & Jackson, 1973). This finding has been replicated and is resistant to factors such as training, the choice of cue, use of familiar objects. It appears in comprehension as well as production (O'Reilly, 1995). Explanations for the preference of BPO over IO forms include the formal nature of the task (Overton & Jackson, 1973), the familiarity with the function of the objects (Mizuguchi & Sugai, 2002; O'Reilly, 1995), the features of the objects themselves (England & Nicoladis, 2018; O'Reilly, 1995).

Unfortunately, the distinction between BPO and IO is not straightforward in application. There are several issues: first, although BPO dominates, data from all studies demonstrate that children from the youngest ages produce both BPO and IO forms of representation; second, the interpretation of a particular form as more or less representational is problematic. Bigham and Bourchier-Sutton (2007) found that the representation of form and function is not consistently controlled for or interpreted in the literature. In their exploration of object substitution, they report that 4- and 5-year-olds showed no difference in their comprehension of BPO and IO pantomimes. That is, representation of form (generally agreed to be BPO) was not easier for the child to interpret than representation of function (generally agreed to be IO).

The example of gestural forms for *scissors* is instructive (see Figure 1). This is one object for which adults often produce the BPO (more "concrete") form, using the index and middle fingers to represent the blades of the scissors. Werner and Kaplan argue that representative gestures are less pragmatic and therefore more symbolic. In practice, it is not clear which form is more representative. In the scissors example below, Werner and Kaplan carefully lay out a predicted developmental sequence: from anticipatory to representational. In the end, they argue that the BPO form (elsewhere assumed to be more pragmatic and concrete, therefore **less** symbolic) is the **more** representative and symbolic form. This example illustrates the challenge of determining which form is more symbolic. Werner and

Kaplan's explanation conflicts with their own interpretation of symbolic distancing and that of subsequent research findings.

> It is important to note that the transition from anticipatory behavior to representative gesture is often marked by a change in form of the activity: movements which derive from pragmatic actions but which have become depictive gestures are in subtle ways distinct in pattern of execution from anticipatory responses. A good example of this is the difference observable between anticipatory movements in cutting with scissors and representative gestures of cutting with scissors. In the first instance, the individual sets thumb and forefinger in a way to fit the handles of the scissors [typically coded as IO, and in subsequent literature, considered the more abstract form]. When, however, one exploits the pragmatic action for representation, there is a change in the selection of fingers and in the manner in which they are held. The movements do not correspond with those of actual cutting; instead, the express the dynamic activity of 'scissors-cutting' by imitating the movements of the instrument [typically coded as BPO and, in subsequent literature, considered the concrete or primary form].
>
> (Werner & Kaplan, 1963: 94,
> parenthetic comments added for ease of interpretation)

Mitchell and Clark (2015) discuss this confusion with respect to applying symbolic distancing to transition from anticipatory (and therefore pragmatic, interpreted as BPO) gestures to representational (and therefore more symbolic, interpreted as IO) gestures.

> But it is important to note that where the BPO pantomime is highly similar to the object, the IO pantomime is highly similar to the "anticipatory movements" (Werner & Kaplan, 1963: 94, quoted above) exhibited just prior to using an object and to one's actions when using the object and thus shows less distinctiveness or distancing from this action than does the BPO pantomime. In other words, either the IO or BPO pantomime could be viewed as exhibiting more distancing than the other, depending on which aspect of distancing or distinctiveness is examined in the representation: The IO gesture is usually distinct in form from the *object*, but the BPO gesture is usually distinct in form from the *action* one uses when handling the object. (Mitchell & Clark 2015: 705–706, italics in original)

As observed by Bigham and Bourchier-Sutton (2007), we see that application of symbolic distancing to specific objects can be challenging. Indeed, Boyatzis & Watson (1993) earlier emphasized that BPO gestures typically include information about *both* form *and* function. That is, in comparison to IO, BPO is more accurately described as *over*representing. Capirci et al. (2011) provide another argument for complexity in BPO forms: these require a dual representation of the hand, first as a hand, and second as a tool of representation.

Finally, although all studies consider the manual forms produced by children in the elicited pantomime task to be pantomime, whether or not these forms fit the definition of pantomime has been assumed. This volume explores different approaches to pantomime. In this chapter we ask a more basic question: is it appropriate to label these gestures as pantomime?

Indeed, children must "enact" the action of the object to respond to the question posed in the present task. Whether or not children are producing these forms in the absence of speech is, as yet, undocumented. In this study we compare children's responses to two different instruction cues: *show* and *tell* which should elicit either manual or spoken responses.[1] We further document whether or not the child spoke or gestured when producing their response, regardless of cue. If the cues are attended to by children, then they might produce more gestured responses to the *show* cue and more spoken responses to the *tell* cue. In addition, one might assume that the show cue will be associated with fewer co-speech gestures. As the literature assumes this task produces pantomime, there are no clear predictions whether these variables (cue, associated speech) will be associated with BPO or IO production. McNeill (2012, Chapter 5; 2016, Chapter 7) argues that pantomime in young children is less developed than co-speech gesture. If so, we might assume that BPO (the more "concrete" form) will occur more frequently in the *show* condition or without accompanying speech. It is possible that the forms of children's gestures will not differ based on the accompaniment of speech, for example, Marentette, Furman, Suvanto, and Nicoladis (2020) found no distinction in mimetic form between pantomime and co-speech gesture for children aged 8–11 years in a narrative task.

In sum, we explore whether BPO and IO are equally representational, rather than distinct steps in symbolic development. Such a finding may more accurately reflect the results of the literature. Furthermore, exploration of the multimodal nature of modern children's gestures production will clarify the assertion that these forms are indeed pantomime. Such clarity could enhance our definition and understanding of the role of "primary iconicity" and pantomime in language development.

In this study we examined three-year-olds' production of manual gestures to explore whether there are representational differences in children's use of BPO and IO. We used a puppet task that provide a motivating context for the generation of representational gestures. Within that task, we conducted a between-samples comparison of two cues: *tell* Sammy (the puppet) how to use this object vs. *show* Sammy how to use this object. This allows us to explore compare non-

---

1. The use of the terms "show" and "tell" evokes the language of Gärdenfors (this volume). We use the terms without the theoretical distinctions Gärdenfors makes. While we claim the task is broadly communicative, we are agnostic about whether the children assume the task is didactic.

Chapter 8. Symbolic distancing in three-year-old children's object-use Pantomime   199

co-speech gesture or "pantomime" and co-speech gesture. The literature assumes that what the child has produced is pantomime as it reflects the request: *show* me how to use this tool. It is as yet untested whether or not gestures accompanied by speech are different in their representation from pantomime. Finally we used 20 objects, a larger number of objects than observed in other studies (typically 8). This enables us to explore whether the variation observed in gesture form can be specific to particular objects.

Method

Participants

Forty three-year old children participated in this study ($M = 42.0$ months, $SD = 3.6$ months; 25 female). Monolingual children were recruited from small rural towns in Western Canada. Reflecting the population makeup of the area of recruitment, the parents of 32 children were white. The remaining families identified themselves as of African, Arabic, Indigenous, or mixed ethnicities. All mothers had a high school diploma with a mode of some postsecondary education. All but 3 fathers had a high school diploma with a mode of some postsecondary education. Families were recruited through a local Facebook group, posters in the local library and university, and word of mouth. We received ethics approval for this study (University of Alberta Research Ethics Board Pro00018088) and all parents/guardians provided written consent for their child's participation.

Procedure

Sammy's birthday task

The children participated in a gesture production task called Sammy's Birthday. The task involves a puppet sloth named Sammy, a large box wrapped in birthday paper with a central hole in the top, and 20 objects presented in gift bags as Sammy's "presents." The experimenter used the following script:

> This is my friend Sammy and it's their birthday, so they have a bunch of birthday presents to open. But Sammy is a sloth and has to sleep all the time, so they need your help to open them!

While Sammy was "sleeping," the children chose gift bags (each in their own order) and opened them. The child was asked what the object was and they were given the opportunity to interact with the object. They were then instructed to put the object in Sammy's birthday box. When the object dropped into the box it made a noise, causing Sammy to wake up. Dropping each object in a large box after the children examined it ensured the object was not in their hands or in sight during the gesture. Children were asked to either *show* or *tell* Sammy how to use the birthday present: as a sloth, Sammy did not know what to do with the presents. Two practice items (soap, swim goggles) were used; experimenters demonstrated gestures for these two objects. Note that the practice item gestures (rubbing hands together, producing a swimming stroke) do not involve the representation of objects or actions with objects. The procedure was recorded on a video camera.

A between sample design was used: children were placed into one of two groups (*show/tell*). Children were alternately assigned to the groups; this allocation was made when the parent was scheduling their visit to the lab.

The twenty objects selected included familiar household objects, see Figure 1. Children were able to name almost all of the objects ($Mode = 18$ of 20 objects; $M = 14.9$. $SD = 5.8$). The unfamiliar objects included the drill ($n = 3$ children named accurately, several others called it a screwdriver) and the round pizza cutter ($n = 6$, red handle, white plastic blade in Figure 1). Approximately half of the children were able to name the flyswatter ($n = 17$), the door handle, (lever style, $n = 20$), and the hairdryer ($n = 22$). All children readily named the rotary phone and knew how to use it. A Wilcoxon signed rank test showed that there was no difference in familiarity of objects between children in the show and tell conditions, $W = 211.5$, $p = .77$.

Figure 2. Objects used in Sammy's birthday task

Coding

A total of 796 cues were given. Due to experimenter error, the flyswatter was not presented to 4 of the children. Responses were coded for each object. Some children produced multiple response types for each object. Repetitions of the same gesture type were not included in the analysis.

All responses were coded as one of the following: (a) **body-part-as-object** (BPO), the hands physically represented the object, for example, a hand resting on top of the head depicts a hat; (b) **imagined object** (IO), the hand forms a grasp and appears to be holding the imagined object while producing the appropriate action, for example, holding an imaginary whisk and stirring; (c) **simultaneous** (SIM) use of both BPO and IO, for example for PHONE, holding the right hand to the right ear (BPO as receiver), with the left hand holding the right hand (IO as hand), these were infrequent ($n=9$); (d) **other**, a gesture was produced that did not fit into any of the 3 above categories: deictic gestures or a representational gesture that was unrelated to the object; and (e) **no gesture.**

A standard coding guide was developed by groups of coders over several iterations of coding. When in doubt, coders were encouraged to designate a gesture as "other" which was preferred over BPO which was preferred over IO; this was considered the most conservative approach given the claims we are investigating about children's ability to produce IO. Reliability was calculated on eight randomly selected participants (20% of dataset). Coders agreed on 87% (150/173 responses), $\kappa=0.78$.

Results

Gesture type by child, cue and speech

Children produced a total of 812 responses of which 452 (56%) included representational gestures: these include 257 (32%) instances of BPO, 9 (1%) instances of gestures with features of both BPO and IO (conservatively grouped here with BPO for analysis), 186 (23%) instances of IO. Figure 3 shows the percent of responses by type by cue. The remaining responses did not include a representational gesture (44%). A box plot was chosen to demonstrate the individual variability that exists across response types.

Children's dominant response was NOT to respond with a representational gesture. Indeed there were 8 children in the study (5 in the *tell* condition, 3 in the *show* condition) who did not produce any gestured responses at all, a known finding in English-speaking preschoolers (Iverson et al., 2008; Marentette et al., 2016).

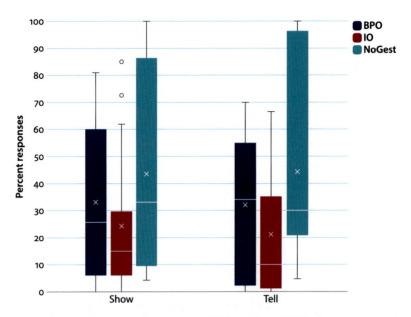

Figure 3. Responses by type and cue across children. *Note:* Middle bar represents the median, × marks the mean. ° indicates an outlier. There are 20 children in each condition

Among the remaining 32 children, all but 1 child produced at least one example each of both IO and BPO. That child produced only 1 BPO gesture (for *flyswatter*). Thirteen children produced BPO gestures for more than half of the objects. Six children produced IO gestures for more than half of the objects. There were 9 children in the study who produced more IO forms than BPO forms. These data demonstrate that, although as a group these three-year-olds preferred BPO forms, the majority of children produced IO gestures, some with great regularity, and a few as a preferred option over BPO. With the exception of 4 instances (<1%), all gestures produced were manual rather than full-body enactments.

The children responded to a direct question with speech even if they did not gesture ($n = 334$), producing few responses in which they neither gestured nor spoke ($n = 26$). The remaining analyses in this section use only the responses from the 32 children who produced gestures.

Speech accompanied slightly more than half of the children's gestured responses (57%). Figure 4 shows the distribution of children's gestured responses by cue and speech accompaniment. Across both *show* and *tell* conditions, children produce more BPO than IO forms. Children did respond differentially to the show/tell cues: they produced more co-speech responses with *tell* (59.3%) and more non-co-speech responses with *show* (65.5%), $\chi^2(1, N = 452) = 27.19$, $p < .001$. In the *show* condition, the means and medians are similar for both BPO and IO forms for co-speech and non-co-speech responses. This differs in the *tell* condition. Here we see a preference for co-speech accompanying BPO forms. This difference in not replicated for the non-co-speech productions. Statistical analysis is challenging given the number of variables, the use of repeated measures, and the smallish *n* (20 per condition). A repeated measures ANOVA shows that the interaction of cue × speech × gesture type may be significant, $F(1,38) = 6.02$, $p = .02$, $\omega^2 = .04$, a small effect. Post hoc tests suggests that the possible interactions are between BPO responses with co-speech and without co-speech in the *tell* condition, $t = 3.4$, $p_{bonf} = .03$, but note the more conservative $p_{sheffé} = .14$. There is also a possible difference in the *tell* condition between BPO and IO responses with co-speech, $t = 3.3$, $p_{bonf} = .05$, $p_{sheffé} = .18$. Replication of this finding, ideally with a more highly powered dataset that would permit regression analysis, will be needed to clarify the strength and size of this potential effect.

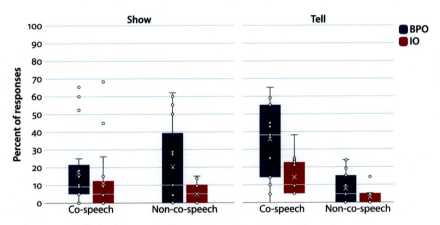

Figure 4. Gesture types and speech accompaniment across children by cue.
Note: Middle bar represents the median, × marks the mean. ° indicates data points. Children who gestured in the *show* condition: $n = 17$; in the *tell* condition, $n = 15$

Gesture type by object

Gesture types were collapsed across cue to show the preferred gesture type by object, see Figure 5. These data indicate that there were 5 objects for which most gestured responses were IO (from left to right: *door handle, screwdriver, rolling pin, scissors, hairdryer*). This includes *scissors*, an object that is often produced as BPO by adults. Although the dataset is not large enough to perform a meaningful statistical analysis, it is clear that, in this dataset, response type varies by object as well as by child. This extends the variability observed in datasets the examined fewer objects.

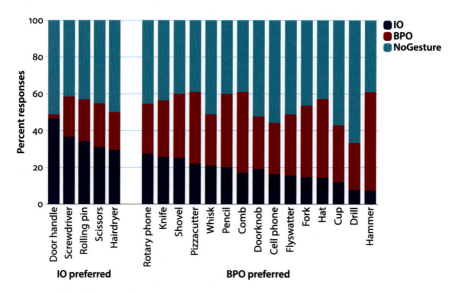

Figure 5. Distribution of response types by object. *Note:* The objects in this figure are presented in decreasing frequency of use of IO as a representational gesture. Starting at *rotary phone* and continuing to the right, the remaining objects show an equal likelihood through to a strong propensity to prefer BPO over IO. *Door handle* is a lever handle; *doorknob* is a round knob

Discussion

In this study, three-year-old children demonstrated three results that help us frame conversations about symbolic distancing in pantomime. First, while these results reaffirm the observation that 3-year-olds tend to produce more BPO forms than IO forms, they also highlight the finding that children regularly produce IO forms. All but one child who gestured produced both IO and BPO forms. Second, while children recognize the distinction between *show* and *tell* cues in their use of speech, these cues are not strongly associated with different forms of gesture representation. There was no clear association between use of speech and mode of representation: BPO forms in the *tell* condition may show an (unexpected) effect of speech accompaniment whereas this effect is not observed for either response type in the *show* condition. Third, at least some objects appear to be associated with specific modes of representation, demonstrating a possible role of item effects and affordances.

These results have bearing on the issues that are the focus of this chapter. First, should these manual responses be considered pantomime? Second, is there a link between the mode of gesture representation used and mastery of symbolic

Chapter 8. Symbolic distancing in three-year-old children's object-use Pantomime   205

reference? Both of these questions have implications for understanding the role of pantomime in children's development of multimodal communication.

Pantomime? The effects of cue and speech

Our results suggest mixed effects with respect to the role of cue and speech accompaniment in iconic representation of object use. Children's **spoken** responses reveal attention to cue with respect to use of speech: *show* is associated with less speech, *tell* is associated with more speech. **Gestured** responses, on the other hand, are not clearly associated with either cue or spoken accompaniment. IO occurred equally often across the cues *show* and *tell*, with and without co-speech. In this study, BPO showed a frequency spike in the *tell* condition with co-speech gesture. That is an unexpected constellation of features. If replicated, it warrants further examination and explanation. Minimally we can say there is no strong pattern of association between manual modes of representation and either cue or associated speech. Although children produce both modes of representation (BPO and IO), the forms are not differentiated by the categories of co-speech and non-co-speech representational gesture.

The traditional analysis of this object-use task labels all forms as pantomime, regardless of form or speech. McNeill's definition (McNeill, 1992, 2016) suggests that pantomime is a whole-body action that does **not** occur with speech: "gesture-orchestrated speech *cannot* descend from pragmatic action." McNeill is influenced here by Werner & Kaplan (1963), who label any form that has a pragmatic base as non-symbolic, and thus clearly outside of speech-gesture integration, or in McNeill's language, the growth point.

Using the cognitive semiotic definition of pantomime, which places a higher focus on enactment using the whole-body, few of the forms produced by children in this study would clearly be labelled pantomime. That is, the IO forms produced by children are enactment, but in this study are manual depictions rather than whole-body. The BPO forms are object descriptions, with some enactment (though 4 instances do use non-manual articulators). Using the characteristics of pantomime presented by Zlatev et al. (2020:166) we would suggest that both the IO and BPO forms examined here are "less" pantomimic, perhaps typical of secondary iconicity (a point to which we will return below).

The challenge presented by these data is that there is no evidence based on children's production of object-use forms for a clear determination of pantomime status. Children use primarily manual representation for both IO and BPO forms. These forms are used interchangeably, with and without speech.

Although grounded in enactment and object depiction, IO and BPO forms are used for a clearly communicative rather than pragmatic purpose.

Müller (this volume) proposes a multimodal approach to "as-if" gesture: gesture that uses mimesis to depict an action or an object. Here Müller argues against a distinction based on speech accompaniment in favour of a continuum based on the stability of form and meaning. Although all of the gestures produced in this task are "singular" gestures, the least stable form generated in the moment of communication, our results support Müller's argument that mimetic expressive movements are a key aspect of multimodal communication, regardless of the presence of speech.

The earliest gestures of the previously isolated deaf young adults of São Tomé and Príncipe provide relevant comparison about the nature of pantomime in the development of systematic communication. Mineiro & Moita (this volume) observed this group through their first opportunities to gather with other deaf individuals. In this context, communication is the goal: these gestures are not primarily pragmatic. The majority of early gestures are iconic and involved non-manual articulators. Based on these (and other) characteristics, Mineiro and Moita claim that these early forms are pantomime and serve a transitional role as the community develops a conventionalized communicative system.

In comparison, the three-year olds in the study reported here use almost exclusively manual articulators in their communicative gesture. Taken together, examination of children's (i) response to the distinct cues of *show/tell*, (ii) use of speech to accompany their gesture, and (iii) predominant use of manual articulators over non-manual articulators, raise questions about object-use gestures can meaningfully be considered pantomime. This decision may depend on the definitional priorities of researcher. The evidence presented here suggests that children do not distinguish what they are doing with their hands from what they are doing with their mouths. Given that three-year-olds are already embedded in a social context that is rich in communicative intent and interpretation, it is possible that their manual gesture is just that: gesture, rather than pantomime interpreted as a kind of interim step toward fully arbitrary communication. This claim reframes the relevance of these types of object-use depictions with respect to our understanding of children's cognitive and symbolic development: it raises doubts about the distinctive status of the forms. We proceed to examine more closely the mode of representation produced in these object-use gestures.

Mode of representation and primary vs. secondary iconicity

The term "primary iconicity" identifies signifiers for which iconicity is readily perceivable without previous knowledge of the referent. Secondary iconicity requires knowledge of the signifier's referent before the iconicity of the signifier can be perceived. As indicated in the introductory sections of this chapter, these terms may be connected to Werner and Kaplan's idea of symbolic distancing. Roughly stated, if IO is more symbolically distant, more abstract (since the object itself is not made concrete), then it might be expected to demonstrate secondary iconicity. If accepted, this point highlights the challenge of Werner & Kaplan's approach in comparison with other views of pantomime. It also conflicts with the account of Zlatev et al. (2020).

Extending Sonesson's idea of primary vs. secondary iconicity, Zlatev et al. follow Müller (2014) in distinguishing enactment and embodiment. Zlatev et al. define *enactment* as hands and body used to depict manual activities: in the language of this paper, IO. The hand is depicted holding or using an imagined object. In contrast, *embodiment* occurs when the hands are used to depict the object itself, here called BPO. Zlatev et al. argue that enactment (IO) is the more pantomimic form and embodiment (BPO) is less pantomimic. These comparisons are laid out clearly in Table 3 (Zlatev et al., 2020:166). Müller (2014) does not so distinguish the modes except as offering alternative modes of representation. Zlatev et al. argue that pantomimic gestures should have the least symbolic distance: they have iconic ground rather than symbolic ground. We interpret this to mean that a mode that is less pantomimic would be expected to show greater symbolic distance (we return to this idea below). From this perspective on pantomime, IO forms should occur prior to BPO forms. This is the opposite conclusion reached by Werner & Kaplan.

As we have demonstrated, children do not show either path of development clearly. In this and previous studies, younger children produce more BPO forms than IO. When we examine the pantomimes of the "new communicators" reported on here by Mineiro and Moita, we note that they use a variety of representational strategies. It is worthwhile to directly compare the representational strategies of the two groups. Moita et al. (2022) found the dominant mode of representation use by the young adults of STP was "object depiction" (45% of representations; elsewhere called *tracing*, an allocentric representation, e.g., Brown et al., 2019; Brown, this volume). This form of depiction was not observed at all in three-year-old children completing the object-use task reported here: these children restricted themselves to egocentric depictions. The next most frequent form observed by Moita et al. was handling (37%, here called IO) and a small portion of gestured representation using instrument depiction (10%, here called BPO, or BPO_E, Brown et al., 2019).

This distribution profile is no doubt influenced by the particular set of picture cues the children of STP received. If one restricts the strategy to the depiction of actions, then there is an increase in BPO (to ~40%) and a decrease in tracing (to ~15%). The amount of IO remains fairly stable (~40%). This distinction reveals a point that has been made repeatedly in the sign language literature: representational strategy is strongly associated with semantic category (e.g., Brentari et al., 2015; Hwang et al, 2017; Ortega & Özyürek, 2020; Padden et al., 2013).

The comparison of representational strategy between new communicators and three-year-olds reveals that there is not a common representational strategy that occurs early in the development of communicative systems in modern humans: neither in children, nor in young adults newly exposed to a conversational community. Werner & Kaplan's prediction that symbolic distancing will describe these early communications does not hold in either group. Neither does the expectation that primary iconicity will appear first. Both groups used BPO and IO modes. The young adults of STP used a third strategy, tracing, that was not observed at all in the children. Tracing is considered less pantomimic (Zlatev et al., 2020); we agree and would further argue, it is the least pantomimic of the three representational modes discussed here.

The distinction between primary and secondary iconicity, and Werner & Kaplan's use of the term symbolic distancing, are intuitively sensible: iconicity surely serves an important role in the development of reference and symbolic status. Arbitrary reference surely arrives later. While these ideas *may* effectively describe the work of the receiver of pantomime (Bigham & Bourchier-Sutton, 2007; O'Reilly, 1995) our research suggests that these distinctions do not matter to gesture producers, particularly not to young children.

Most importantly, our assumptions as adult researchers about which forms are "more iconic" do not appear to match the assumptions of young children. This observation could explain three key findings: the adult preference for an IO representational strategy for object use, Werner and Kaplan's confusion about how to apply their own theory (discussed earlier), and the mixed production of these forms throughout the developmental time scale.

We argue here that iconic gestural representation is more complex than arbitrary spoken representation. We need to scrutinize claims that iconicity supports the development of symbolic representation in children: the data from three-year-olds shows a much more sophisticated relationship between symbolic understanding and representation. Children of this age readily use words (a completely arbitrary form, one that Werner and Kaplan consider to be the most complex form of symbol). They do not show the adult form of representational mode: primary iconicity (IO). Instead they prefer a form that might be described as showing secondary iconicity (BPO) that, some (Zlatev et al., 2020, but see also Capirci et al., 2011) consider more complex. Not until 6- to 8-years of age do children's iconic forms resemble those of adults. The question that must be addressed is what motivates children's use of varied types of gestural representation?

Alternatives to symbolic distancing

Let us turn now to the question of what the object-use task does demonstrate about children's development. Developmental researchers have frequently cited and been influenced by Werner and Kaplan's (1963) argument that children develop symbolic knowledge through a process that moves from action in the world to an interiorized representation that is a distinct entity from the object itself (duality) and is produced with communicative (rather than pragmatic) intent. The referent gradually becomes more distant from the object represented.

It is the case that detection of dual representation is more challenging when the referent is iconic than when it is arbitrary. This may be what has made the distinction between IO and BPO forms originally attractive to researchers interested in cognitive development and symbolic play: these referential modes provide a tool that made overt the act of symbolic processing in children. In adults with apraxia, the distinction between IO and BPO is used to examine neural representations of tool use and imitation of actions (e.g., Buxbaum et al., 2014).

If the choice of mode of representation is primarily a function of the child's mastery of symbolic reference, then we should not find individual variation both within and across children but we do. In addition, we should not find variation across objects in children within a tight age range, yet we do. Of course, children's representational gestures can be influenced by multiple factors. We argue here that an alternative explanation consistent with the data could explain children's shift from primarily BPO to primarily IO forms. This explanation arises from consideration of contexts and details of the task. We explore three linked elements of context: item effects, conventionalization, and the broader communicative task.

Item effects on representational mode are observed across studies with children and adults. Items are reported for which children show IO use early (e.g., unlock a door, stir batter), and adults show continued BPO use for certain items (e.g., scissors; O'Reilly, 1995). Van Nispen et al. (2017) showed that pantomime is ambiguous and context dependent. Adults were most likely to correctly interpret pantomimes that had a preferred form, with IO forms the easiest to interpret, particularly in a forced choice task. Most of the objects associated with IO were tools, but there were a few tools that elicit frequent BPO gestures from adults.

Van Nispen et al. (2017) argue that the regularity of form indicates some conventionalization in pantomime production. Although there are no standards for acceptable pantomime, it appears that objects afford certain default representations. The use of BPO among many adults to depict *scissors* is an excellent example of such a default. Research with signers and non-signers has shown semantic category effects: Tools (which includes all of the objects used in study reported here) were strongly likely to be depicted with handling (IO) forms (Hwang et al., 2017; Ortega & Özyürek, 2020). That default or preferred forms are more successful in a communicative task presents a strong argument for conventionalization of forms. Arbib's (2012) mirror system hypothesis provides a good mechanism for the preference of handling or IO forms. Pantomimes that replicate one's use of an object are likely to be readily interpreted by the receiver, as they activate the mirror neuron system. This explanation is weaker for objects whose default is BPO, though van Nispen et al. (2017) found that BPO forms did not differ in comprehension.

Accurate grasp and use of an object requires knowledge that goes beyond symbolic representation. Buxbaum, Kyle, and Menon (2005: 236) showed that skilled tool use requires more than a perceptual recognition of the affordance of an object, and further sometimes grasp and functional use differ, requiring specific knowledge. Indeed, England and Nicoladis (2018) showed an increase in BPO forms when adults were asked to pantomime objects described as having multiple functions. We speculate that although three-year-olds are familiar with most of the objects used in pantomime tasks, they may still need to develop knowledge of functional use of these objects, as well as the fine motor control for skilled handling. Development of this kind could readily take place between the ages of three and six years. By school age, most children have had enough exposure to the adult gesture use to conform to the defaults noted by van Nispen et al. (2017). Since these are hearing children it is reasonable to expect this process of noting iconic convention to take longer than it does with more frequently occurring symbols (for example words, or emblems).

The children in object-use studies, such as the one described in this chapter, may be developing familiarity with a communicative convention. Young children may prefer BPO because it is maximally informative: it provides information about form (shape of the hand) and function (the movement of the hand). Despite our use of a friendly puppet, Sammy's birthday is, to paraphrase Bronfenbrenner (1979: 19), a strange task in a strange place with strange people. Adults, without apparent reason, ask questions for which they clearly know the answer on the pretext that because Sammy is a sloth, Sammy doesn't know. One child told us (quietly, in case it might upset us?), "you know, Sammy isn't real." Perhaps in this strange situation, the default is to provide as much information about form and function as possible.

It is difficult to believe that children who functionally use speech, an arbitrary and symbolic form of reference, are forced to rely on subtle differences in iconicity in gesture to support their cognitive processes. Indeed, it is by no means agreed which mode of representation is "easier." Werner and Kaplan argue for BPO forms being easier due to symbolic distancing. Zlatev et al. argue that IO is more pantomimic, which leads to the prediction that IO should then predominate in children's use.

Given the logical options about which form is "easier" because it is concrete or more complex because arbitrary and therefore more symbolic, and given also the presence of both forms in three-year olds (and in two-year olds. Marentette et al., 2016), we propose that alternative explanations should be considered. These are iconic communicative gestures used in an unfamiliar task that assumes communicative intent and does not test receiver comprehension. The evidence here suggests that children do not show any association between the cue, the production of speech, and the form of gesture itself. It is clear that children are not producing "silent gesture." In addition, the task does not warrant much complexity. There is no requirement of repetition or sequencing of forms. Further exploration of the status of these gestures requires more detailed semiotic analysis.

Conclusions

As with much research with small children, more would be better. Despite having collected hundreds of gestured responses, with the number of conditions and variables, statistical analysis remains inconclusive. Further research could test specific hypotheses including whether the gestured responses examined here meet the criteria for primary iconicity. While it is true that the communicative context of 3-year-olds differs markedly from that of a first communicative exchange, it remains possible that their untutored use of gesture to describe form could be instructive. Although challenging with 3-year-olds, it would be ideal to create a task that requires successful communication in gesture. Sammy the Sloth accepted all responses. Further research could examine the ease of interpretation of children's IO and BPO forms.

In this chapter we demonstrate that children's use of body part as object and imagined object modes of representation does not fit definitions of pantomime that focus on the absence of speech or the use of non-manual articulators. Further the interpretation of these forms may be better explained by social and communicative factors rather than symbolic mastery. We argue they do not effectively serve the purpose of revealing children's symbolic development. This ontogenetic research suggests that the use of different modes of representation occurs only in children who are already deeply embedded in a communicative context.

Funding

This research was supported by funding from the Social Sciences and Humanities Research Council of Canada (IG 435–2018–004) to PM.

Acknowledgements

Thanks to the class of AUPSY 393 for collaborative design and piloting of the Sammy's Birthday task, and to Jaden de Waal and Jennifer Green for coding and data collection. Particular thanks to Elena Nicoladis for ongoing conversations about gesture and pantomime and to Michael Arbib for a great conversation on a long taxi ride. The comments of Johan Blomberg and Przemek Żywiczyński on an earlier draft were instrumental in the organization of this chapter. We remain deeply appreciative of the small window between delta and omicron waves that permitted in-person attendance at the stimulating Workshop "Perspectives on Pantomime" (Toruń, 18–19.11.2021).

References

Acredolo, L.P., & Goodwyn, S. (1988). Symbolic gesturing in normal infants. *Child Development*, 59(2), 450–466.

Arbib, M.A. (2012). *How the brain got language: The mirror system hypothesis.* Oxford University Press.

Bates, E., Benigni, L., Bretherton, I., Camaioni, L., & Volterra, V. (1979). *The emergence of symbols: Cognition and communication in infancy.* Academic Press.

Behne, T., Carpenter, M., & Tomasello, M. (2014). Young children create iconic gestures to inform others. *Developmental Psychology*, 50(8), 2049–2060.

Bellagamba, F., & Tomasello, M. (1999). Re-enacting intended acts: Comparing 12- and 18-month-olds. *Infant Behavior & Development*, 22(2), 277–282.

Bigham, S., & Bourchier-Sutton, A. (2007). The decontextualization of form and function in the development of pretence. *The British Journal of Developmental Psychology*, 25(3), 335–351.

Boyatzis, C.J., & Watson, M.W. (1993). Preschool children's symbolic representation of objects through gestures. *Child Development*, 64(3), 729–735.

Brentari, D., Coppola, M., Mazzoni, L., & Goldin-Meadow, S. (2012). When does a system become phonological? Handshape production in gesturers, signers, and homesigners. *Natural Language & Linguistic Theory*, 30(1), 1–31.

Brentari, D., Di Renzo, A., Keane, J., & Volterra, V. (2015). Cognitive, cultural, and linguistic sources of a handshape distinction expressing agentivity. *Topics in Cognitive Science*, 7(1), 95–123.

Bronfenbrenner, U. (1979). *The ecology of human development.* Cambridge, Mass.: Harvard University Press.

Chapter 8. Symbolic distancing in three-year-old children's object-use Pantomime   **213**

Brown, S., Mittermaier, E., Kher, T., & Arnold, P. (2019). How pantomime works: Implications for theories of language origin. *Frontiers in Communication*, 4, 9.

Buxbaum, L. J., Kyle, K. M., & Menon, R. (2005). On beyond mirror neurons: internal representations subserving imitation and recognition of skilled object-related actions in humans. *Cognitive Brain Research*, 25(1), 226–239.

Buxbaum, L. J., Shapiro, A. D., & Coslett, H. B. (2014). Critical brain regions for tool-related and imitative actions: a componential analysis. *Brain: A Journal of Neurology*, 137(pt 7), 1971–1985.

Capirci, O., Caselli, M. C., & Volterra, V. (2022). Interaction among modalities and within development. In *Gesture in language: Development across the lifespan* (pp. 113–133). De Gruyter Mouton.

Capirci, O., Cristilli, C., de Angelis, V., & Graziano, M. (2011). Learning to use gesture in narratives: Developmental trends in formal and semantic gesture competence. In G. Stam & M. Ishino (Eds.), *Integrating Gestures* (pp. 187–200). Benjamins.

Carlson, S. M., Davis, A. C., & Leach, J. G. (2005). Less Is more: Executive function and symbolic representation in preschool children." *Psychological Science*, 16(8), 609–616.

Caselli, M. C., Rinaldi, P., Stefanini, S., & Volterra, V. (2012). Early action and gesture "vocabulary" and its relation with word comprehension and production. *Child Development*, 83(2), 526–542.

DeLoache, J. S. (1991). Symbolic functioning in very young children: Understanding of pictures and models. *Child Development*, 62(4), 736–752.

DeLoache, J. S. (2004). Becoming symbol-minded. *Trends in Cognitive Sciences*, 8(2), 66–70.

Dingemanse, M., Blasi, D. E., Lupyan, G., Christiansen, M. H., & Monaghan, P. (2015). Arbitrariness, iconicity, and systematicity in language. *Trends in Cognitive Sciences*, 19(10), 603–615.

Edmiston, P., Perlman, M., & Lupyan, G. (2018). Repeated imitation makes human vocalizations more word-like. *Proceedings of the Royal Society B: Biological Sciences*, 285(1874).

Elder, J. L., & Pederson, D. R. (1978). Preschool children's use of objects in symbolic play. *Child Development*, 49(2), 500.

England, M., & Nicoladis, E. (2018). Functional fixedness and body-part-as-object production in pantomime. *Acta Psychologica*, 190, 174–187.

Goldin-Meadow, S., McNeill, D., & Singleton, J. (1996). Silence is liberating: Removing the handcuffs on grammatical expression in the manual modality. *Psychological Review*, 103(1), 34–55.

Goodglass, H., & Kaplan, E. (1963). Disturbance of gesture and pantomime in aphasia. *Brain: A Journal of Neurology*, 86, 703–720.

Goodwyn, S. W., & Acredolo, L. P. (1993). Symbolic gesture versus word: is there a modality advantage for onset of symbol use? *Child Development*, 64(3), 688–701.

Goodwyn, S. W., Acredolo, L. P., & Brown, C. A. (2000). Impact of symbolic gesturing on early language development. *Journal of Nonverbal Behavior*, 24(2), 81–103.

Gullberg, M. (1998). *Gesture as a communication strategy in second language discourse*. Lund University.

Hockett, C. F. (1958). *A course in modern linguistics*. MacMillan.

Hopkins, E. J., Smith, E. D., Weisberg, D. S., & Lillard, A. S. (2016). The development of substitute object pretense: The differential importance of form and function. *Journal of Cognition and*, 17(2), 197–220.

Hwang, S.-O., Tomita, N., Morgan, H., Ergin, R., İlkbaşaran, D., Seegers, S., Lepic, R., & Padden, C. (2017). Of the body and the hands: patterned iconicity for semantic categories. *Language and Cognition*, 9(4), 573–602.

Iverson, J. M., Capirci, O., Volterra, V., & Goldin-Meadow, S. (2008). Learning to talk in a gesture-rich world: Early communication in Italian vs. American children. *First Language*, 28(2), 164–181.

Jackowitz, E. R., & Watson, M. W. (1980). Development of object transformations in early pretend play. *Developmental Psychology*, 16(6), 543–549.

Johnston, J. C., Durieux-Smith, A., & Bloom, K. (2005). Teaching gestural signs to infants to advance child development: A review of the evidence. *First Language*, 25(2), 235–251.

Kaplan, E. F. (1968). Gestural representation of implement usage: An organismic-developmental study [PhD]. Clark University.

Kirk, E., Howlett, N., Pine, K. J., & Fletcher, B. C. (2013). To sign or not to sign? The impact of encouraging infants to gesture on infant language and maternal mind-mindedness. *Child Development*, 84(2), 574–590.

Klima, E., & Bellugi, U. (1979). *The signs of language*. Harvard.

Labuschagne, L. G., Cox, T.-J., Brown, K. & Scarf, D. (2017). Too cool? Symbolic but not iconic stimuli impair 4-year-old children's performance on the delay-of-gratification choice paradigm. *Behavioural Processes*, 135, 36–39.

Levy, E. & McNeill, D. (2015). *Narrative development in young children: Gesture, imagery, and cohesion*. Cambridge University Press.

Marentette, P., Furman, R., Suvanto, M. E., & Nicoladis, E. (2020). Pantomime (not silent gesture) in multimodal communication: Evidence from children's narratives. *Frontiers in Psychology*, 11(November), 575952.

Marentette, P., Pettenati, P., Bello, A., & Volterra, V. (2016). Gesture and symbolic representation in Italian and English-speaking Canadian 2-year-olds. *Child Development*, 87(3), 944–961.

McNeill, D. (1992). *Hand and mind: What gestures reveal about thought*. University of Chicago Press.

McNeill, D. (2012). *How language began: Gesture and speech in human evolution*. CUP.

McNeill, D. (2016). *Why we gesture: The surprising role of hand movements in communication*. Cambridge University Press.

Mineiro, A., Báez-Montero, I. C., Moita, M., Galhano-Rodrigues, I., & Castro-Caldas, A. (2021). Disentangling pantomime from early sign in a new sign language: Window into language evolution research. *Frontiers in Psychology*, 12(December), 1130.

Mitchell, R. W., & Clark, H. (2015). Experimenter's pantomimes influence children's use of body part as object and imaginary object pantomimes: A replication. *Journal of Cognition and Development*, 16(5), 703–718.

Mizuguchi, T., & Sugai, K. (2002). Object related knowledge and the production of gestures with imagined objects by preschool children. *Perceptual and Motor Skills*, 94, 71–79.

Moita, M., Abreu, A. M., & Mineiro, A. (2022). Tracking the evolution of iconic signs to understand the emergence of a phonological system. [Manuscript submitted for publication]. Instituto de Ciências da Saúde, Universidade Católica Portuguesa.

Müller, C. (2014). Gestural modes of representation as techniques of depiction. In C. Müller, A. Cienki, E. Fricke, S. H. Ladewig, D. McNeill, & J. Bressem (Eds.), *Body-Language-Communication: An International Handbook on Multimodality in Human Interaction* (Vol. 2, pp. 1687–1702). de Gruyter Mouton.

Namy, L. L. (2001). What's in a name when it isn't a word? 17-month-olds' mapping of nonverbal symbols to object categories. *Infancy*, 2(1), 73–86.

O'Reilly, A. W. (1995). Using representations: Comprehension and production of actions with imagined objects. *Child Development*, 66(4), 999–1010.

Ortega, G., & Özyürek, A. (2019). Systematic mappings between semantic categories and types of iconic representations in the manual modality: A normed database of silent gesture. *Behavior Research Methods*, 52(1), 51–67.

Ortega, G., & Özyürek, A. (2020). Types of iconicity and combinatorial strategies distinguish semantic categories in silent gesture across cultures. *Language and Cognition*, 12(1), 84–113.

Overton, W. F., & Jackson, J. P. (1973). The representation of imagined objects in action sequences: A developmental study. *Child Development*, 44(2), 309–314.

Padden, C. A., Meir, I., Hwang, S.-O., Lepic, R., Seegers, S., & Sampson, T. (2013). Patterned iconicity in sign language lexicons. *Gesture*, 13(3), 287–308.

Perniss, P., Thompson, R. L., & Vigliocco, G. (2010). Iconicity as a general property of language: Evidence from spoken and signed languages. *Frontiers in Psychology*, 1, 227.

Piaget, J. (1962). *Plays, dreams, and imitation in childhood*. Norton.

Schouwstra, M., Swart, H., & Thompson, B. (2019). Interpreting silent gesture: Cognitive biases and rational inference in emerging language systems. *Cognitive Science*, 43(7), 1–27.

Sonesson, G. (2007). From the meaning of embodiment to the embodiment of meaning: A study in phenomenological semiotics. In T. Ziemke, J. Zlatev, & R. M. Frank (Eds.), *Body, Language, and Mind*, Vol. 1. Embodiment. (pp. 85–128). De Gruyter Mouton.

Sonesson, G. (2010). From mimicry to mime by way of mimesis: Reflections on a general theory of iconicity. *Sign Systems Studies*, 38(1/4), 18–66.

Stokoe, W. C. (1960). Sign language structure: An outline of the visual communication systems of the American deaf. *Dept. of Anthropology and Linguistics*, University of Buffalo.

Striano, T., Tomasello, M., & Rochat, P. (2001). Social and object support for early symbolic play. *Developmental Science*, 4(4), 442–455.

Tomasello, M., Striano, T., & Rochat, P. (1999). Do young children use objects as symbols? *The British Journal of Developmental Psychology*, 17, 563–584.

Troseth, G. L., & DeLoache, J. S. (1998). The medium can obscure the message: Young children's understanding of video. *Child Development*, 69(4), 950–965.

Vallotton, C. D. (2011). Sentences and conversations before speech? Gestures of preverbal children reveal cognitive and social skills that do not wait for words. In G. Stam & M. Ishino (Eds.), *Integrating gestures: The interdisciplinary nature of gesture* (pp. 105–120). Benjamins.

Vallotton, C.D., & Ayoub, C.C. (2010). Symbols build communication and thought: The role of gestures and words in the development of engagement skills and social-emotional concepts during toddlerhood. *Social Development*, 19(3), 601–626.

van Nispen, K., van de Sandt-Koenderman, W.M.E., & Krahmer, E. (2017). Production and comprehension of pantomimes used to depict objects. *Frontiers in Psychology*, 8(July), 1095.

Wacewicz, S., & Żywiczyński, P. (2015). Language evolution: Why Hockett's design features are a non-starter. *Biosemiotics*, 8(1), 29–46.

Weidinger, N., Lindner, K., Hogrefe, K., Ziegler, W., & Goldenberg, G. (2017). Getting a grasp on children's representational capacities in pantomime of object use. *Journal of Cognition and Development*, 18(2), 246–269.

Werner, H., & Kaplan, B. (1963). *Symbol formation: An organismic-developmental approach to language and the expression of thought*. Wiley.

Zlatev, J., Żywiczyński, P., & Wacewicz, S. (2020). Pantomime as the original human-specific communicative system. *Journal of Language Evolution*, 5(2), 156–174.

Żywiczyński, P., Wacewicz, S., & Lister, C. (2021). Pantomimic fossils in modern human communication. *Philosophical Transactions of the Royal Society of London. Series B, Biological Sciences*, 376(1824), 20200204.

CHAPTER 9

Gestural mimesis as "as-if" action

Cornelia Müller
European University Viadrina Frankfurt (Oder)

It is argued that gestural mimesis involves "as-if" actions that explain the transition from practical and literal actions with the hands to communicative actions of the hands. Concerning the term and the concept "pantomime," it is suggested that it be primarily reserved for artistic practice and used for this type of communicative action only with great care. Given the fundamental role of mimesis to gestures (hand-gestures as well as full body gestures), it is proposed that gestures in general be conceived of as "mimetic expressive movements" – no matter whether they are used in the presence or absence of spoken or signed language. In order to underline the continuity between gestures created on the spot and conventionalized gestural forms, It is suggested to use the term miming or mimesis no matter whether gestures replace or accompany language. The chapter offers an introduction to the theoretical motivations and illustrates the empirical and methodological implications of this proposal. It *first* sketches three key aspects of an approach to gestures as *mimetic expressive movements, then* shows that mimesis grounds gestures with different communicative functions, illustrating its emergent productivity along the dynamics of different types of discourse and briefly touches upon dynamics in terms of historical change and *how* this affects the kinesics and the meaning of gestures. Finally, it is briefly indicated how conceiving of gestures as mimetic expressive movements affects the methodology for gesture analysis.

Keywords: gestural mimesis, gesture studies, as-if action, mimesis, hand-gestures, mimetic expressive movements

Introduction

In the field of gesture studies, a dimension of human gestures came to be recognized as more and more important that hitherto had been of minor scholarly interest: the close connection of gestures with language. At the time, gestures were predominantly conceived as one aspect of nonverbal communication, yet they were also discussed as evolutionary precursors of language (Kendon 2011, 2016).

https://doi.org/10.1075/ais.12.09mul
© 2024 John Benjamins Publishing Company

While investigations of facial expressions flourished (Ekman, 1993), co-speech gestures received very little attention in nonverbal communication research. Most likely, this was because of their close connection with speech. Here is where the pioneering work of Adam Kendon and David McNeill made a difference. Coming from different academic backgrounds they both highlighted that gestures and speech are, in fact, intimately intertwined. Kendon argued that speaking involves body movement and speech, and that gestures and speech are "two sides of the process of utterance" (Kendon, 1980). McNeill engaged in a scholarly debate with the then current psycholinguistic view, claiming that gestures are far from being NON-verbal, but form one psychological system with language (McNeill, 1985). More than two decades later, the study of this relation has become a widely researched subject, receiving interest from many different disciplines. The international journal GESTURE, and the founding of an International Society for Gesture Studies (ISGS) provide transdisciplinary fora for this research and the publication of a two-volume handbook in 2013 and 2014 documents the state of the art of research into the relation of body movement, language and communication (Müller et al., 2013, 2014). More recent developments in various disciplines have come to address language use as multimodal or even considered language itself as inherently multimodal (Müller, 2018; Vigliocco et al., 2014). The latest developments in multimodal language research include the establishment of a multimodal language department at the Max-Planck-Institute for Psycholinguistics in Nijmegen. Max-Planck Institutes are world-leading research institutions and the recent establishment of this department documents that the importance of understanding the multimodal nature of language has been internationally and across disciplines recognized to figure on the same level as genetic, developmental, neurobiological, and psychological aspects of language and communication (e.g., the topics of the other departments). Another testimony of this growing recognition is the funding of a large research priority program on "Visual Communication. Theoretical, Empirical, and Applied Perspectives (ViCom)" by the German Science Foundation (DFG).

So, roughly forty years after Kendon's and McNeill's important noticing of the intimate relation between gestures and speech, there appears to be a widely shared agreement on language use as being multimodal and of gestures and speech as closely related. However, controversies remain as to the very nature of semiotic and cognitive relations between gesture and language (Müller 2018) which result in different conceptions of their phylogenetic (see Arbib, Gärdenfors, Wacewicz & Żywiczyński, this volume) and ontogenetic relation (see Marentette, this volume). Scholars working in the McNeillian tradition favor a view that disconnects gestures from language in language evolution (McNeill 2013) but also in the emergence of signed languages (Goldin-Meadow & Brentari, 2017). For McNeill's

Chapter 9. Gestural mimesis as "as-if" action **219**

dynamic theory of gesture and speech the idea of two fundamentally different modes of expression is central, because he assumes that the non-linguistic (gesture) and the linguistic (vocal language) create a psychological dialectic in which the tension between the two expressive modes pushes thinking forward. Notably, McNeill's model includes only those gestures that are spontaneously created and idiosyncratic, (see also Arbib, 2012, and this volume) because only those types of gestures allow a direct access to thinking processes while speaking. More conventional gestures are excluded, because they have moved sides so to say and become more language-like:

> The focus of this book is on spontaneous and idiosyncratic gestures ... but it is useful to begin ... with the more language-like gestures that constitute sign-languages. These are signs organized into true linguistic codes. We benefit in this way from the sharp contrast that we can draw between the spontaneous and the socially regulated kinds of gesture. (McNeill, 1992: 36; emphasis added)

Now, the controversy becomes how the transition from spontaneously created gestures to conventionalized ones is to be explained. Do we assume a continuum or rather a categorial break between spontaneously created gestures and conventionalized ones which also brings in the potential development of gestures into linguistic signs within signed languages. In language origins, this is essentially the problem of improvised gesture changing into protolanguage (Arbib, 2012, this volume; Gärdenfors, this volume; Zlatev et al., this volume) In a joint paper, Singleton, Goldin Meadow and McNeill, argue for a cataclysmic break between gestures and more linguistic forms, as observed for example in evolving signs of home-signing children (Singleton, Goldin-Meadow & McNeill, 1995, in contrast to e.g., Mineiro & Moita, this volume).

Kendon, on the other hand, pointed out many years ago that some co-speech gestures may undergo processes of lexicalization and become "like words" (Kendon 1988, 2014) and thus become more "linguistic." Against the backdrop of this debate (cf., Müller, 2018), and based on many years of collaborative research on "a grammar of gesture," my own work suggests a three party distinction between singular, recurrent and emblematic gestures to reflect an emergent transition from spontaneously created singular gestures through hybrid recurrent gestures to fully stabilized emblematic gestures (Figure 1) (see also Arbib's notions of proto-sign and ur-pantomime and the problem of conventionalization and/or ritualization, this volume).

The continuum assumes that a transition from singular gestures to recurrent and emblematic gestures can actually be observed in the everyday usage of gestures along with speech (probably relevant to the study of emerging sign languages, see Mineiro et al., 2017; and Mineiro & Moita, this volume). So we may find

Figure 1. Variable degrees of stabilization in gestures

instances in which a grasping motion of index and thumb is used to depict how somebody picked up a strand of spaghetti and lifted it to his/her/their mouth in order to test whether it was cooked enough. Such a gesture emerges spontaneously in the moment of speaking; it is created on the spot, involves a creative abstraction from the actual action (Müller 2014, 2016) and is thus a case of a singular gesture. In other usage contexts, however, we very often encounter a hybrid version of this "picking-up-something-small gesture," here connected with a different meaning, namely as a gestural form of expressing the preciseness of an argument. Ethologist Desmond Morris proposed to call this gesture "precision grip" (Morris, 1977). Inspired by Kendon's work on gesture families (Kendon, 2004; chapters 12 & 13), we have argued that recurrent gestures are characterized by a stable kinesic core (index and thumb in a grasping configuration) with a stable meaning (preciseness of an argument) (Bressem & Müller, 2014a,b, Ladewig, 2014a,b; Müller, 2017). Other aspects of the kinesic form (the shape of the remaining fingers, the position of the gesture in the gesture space, the orientation of the hand and the movement of the hand) are flexible, rather than stabilized. Speakers use the precision grip with all kinds of orientations, with different movement patterns and also with different hand-shapes assuming local ad-hoc created meaning that may modify the meaningful core of "making a precise argument." Figure 2 shows how former US president Barack Obama uses a precision-grip gesture with vertical orientation, forward movement and in the upper center of the gesture space.

Recurrent gestures thus are hybrid gestures – partially stabilized and partially created on the spot. They are hybrid in kinesic form and hybrid in meaning, showing a transition phase between gestures created on the spot and gestures with stabilized forms and meanings, i.e., emblematic gestures. In emblematic gestures, we see a stage in which all aspects of kinesic form and their meaning are fully stabilized; they are like "gesture words" as Kendon called them many years back (Kendon, 1988). As an emblematic gesture, the precision grip is well-known as an expression of perfection, excellence and exquisite taste. In the emblematic precision-grip gesture, all kinesic elements are stabilized: position (next to the face), orientation (facing outwards in a vertical position), movement (small forward movement with accentuated stop and a post-stroke hold) and all the kinesic aspects of hand shape as well.

I suggest that the hybrid kinesic forms as well as hybrid gestural meanings that we observe in recurrent gestures indicate a phase of transition between gestures that are spontaneously created and fully stabilized, sometimes fully conventional-

Precision grip as recurrent gesture

Hand shape GRASPING: index & thumb as stable kinesic core, other fingers variable

Orientation: variable

Movement: variable

Location: variable

Precision grip as emblematic gesture

Hand shape GRASPING: index & thumb *and* spread fingers are stabilized

Orientation: vertical (stabilized)

Movement: accelerating movement forward and hold (stabilized)

Location: upper center (stabilized)

Figure 2. Recurrent and emblematic precision grip differ in degree of stabilized aspects of kinesic form and of meaning

ized, gestural forms. Rather than assuming a cataclysmic break between gestures that are *not* like language on the one side (iconic, metaphoric, cohesive, beats) and those that *are* language-like (pantomime, silent gestures) and signs within signed languages on the other side (Goldin-Meadow & Brentari, 2017; McNeill, 2000), I suggest moving beyond the idea of a cataclysmic break and to conceive instead of relations between not-stabilized and stabilized gestures as variable and dynamic, depending on the practices of use in a given communicative community. From such a perspective, gestures are distinguished according to their degrees of stabilization, with singular gestures that are created on the spot, recurrent gestures that show partial stabilization, and emblematic gestures that are fully stabilized in form and meaning. Importantly, the distinction is not categorical but gradual. Put differently, no rigid boundaries between the three types of gestures are assumed; their differences are gradual with the different types of gestures flowing into one another (in line with gradualistic scenarios in evolution studies, see Arbib, Mineiro & Moita, Zlatev et al., and Gärdenfors, this volume).

The view of gradual rather than categorical differences between singular and emblematic gestures parallels assumptions from researchers on signed languages that observe similar lexicalization processes in signed languages (see Wilcox, 2007).

Elsewhere, I have suggested that this gradual view alludes to conceive of gesture-sign relations as dynamic in two senses: (1) the historical (evolutionary) dynamics of *gesture change*, and (2) a dynamic relation between two *multimodal languages in contact*, for example, the German Sign Language (DGS), and spoken

German. This means that we observe singular, recurrent, and emblematic gestures in collaboration with both spoken as well as with signed languages.

Now, how does this debate relate to the question of gestural mimesis, pantomimic and silent gestures? The argument presented here is that all of these based on mimesis, i.e., that they all emerge from the communicative practice of miming as "as-if" action. What we view in gestures are processes of abstraction from manipulative and other practical bodily actions. We see a dynamic, gradual relation between them and not a cataclysmic break. We therefore assume that the characteristics observed in pantomimic and in silent gestures are gradual and not categorically different from more or less complex gesture sequences that speakers and signers use along with spoken and signed language. Concerning the term and the concept "pantomime," it is suggested that it be primarily reserved for artistic practice and to conceive of gestural mimesis as an as-if action – no matter whether gestures are used in the presence or absence of language (be it spoken or signed) and no matter whether singular, recurrent or emblematic gestures are concerned. The questions at stake are not so much the presence or absence of vocal or signed language, but a deep understanding of the characteristics of mimesis as a human faculty and a cultural product (see also Marentette, this volume). Many of the processes discussed in research on pantomimic gestures can be observed in gestures produced along with speech as well. We need to continue to study gestural mimesis further and seek a deeper understanding. The proposal made in this chapter shall be understood as a step in that direction.

It offers an overview of the theoretical motivations and of the empirical and methodological implications for this proposal. It *first* sketches some key aspects of an approach to gestures as *mimetic expressive movements, then* shows that this approach applies to gestures with different communicative functions (depictive and pragmatic gestures) and touches on *how* historical change affects the kinesics of gestures and their meanings, and, *finally*, it briefly indicates how conceiving of gestures as mimetic expressive movements affects the methodology for gesture analysis.

1. Gestures as mimetic expressive movements

There is wide agreement in gesture studies and beyond that mimesis plays a significant role in motivating gestures as well as signs (Müller, 2014, 2016). It thus seems worthwhile to further explore the mimetic processes that ground gestures in everyday practices. I believe that a consideration of gestural miming must take into account that gestures are body movements that unfold in time or – put differently that "gestures are temporal forms."

In the following, three essential/central characteristics of gestures as mimetic expressive movements are outlined: (1.1) Kendon's notion of gestures as unfolding in gesture phrases and the relation of gesture segmentation and gestural meaning; (1.2) Plessner's notion of expressive movements as movement images and how they are understood/their intersubjective character; (1.3) Aristotle's idea of mimesis as anthropological trait and, based on Aristotle's systematics of mimesis, a systematics of gestural mimesis.

1.1 Gesture phrases and the meaning of a gesture (Kendon)

Kendon's concept of gesture phrases involves a segmentation of gestures as movements in time that goes along with ascribing 'meaning' to only certain parts of the gestural movements. Kendon (1980, 2004) distinguishes three core phases of a gesture: preparation, stroke, and recovery, with preparation and stroke forming the meaningful part of the gesture, termed *gesture phrase* (Figure 3).

> The phase of the movement excursion closest to its apex is usually recognized as the phase when the 'expression' of the gesture, 'whatever it may' be, is accomplished. "It is the phase of the excursion in which the movement dynamics of 'effort' and 'shape' are manifested with greatest clarity (see Laban & Lawrence 1947; Bartinieff (sic!) & Lewis 1980). This phase is called the stroke.
> (Kendon 2004: 112)

In short, Kendon establishes the gesture phrase as the basic meaningful temporal form of a gestural movement (Kendon, 1972, 1980, 1983, 2004).

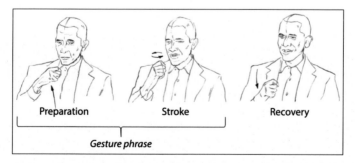

Figure 3. Kendon's Gesture Phrase forms the meaningful core of the gestural movement

This segmentation has been extremely important for contemporary research on gesture and quite a few alterations have been proposed (Bressem & Ladewig, 2011). What is important for the point presented in this chapter is that Kendon bases his account of the gesture stroke as the meaningful part of the gesture phrase on the expertise of an eminent German expressionist dancer, choreographer, inventor of a dance notation system still in use and founder of movement analysis, Rudolf Laban (1956). Kendon's connection of expression and meaning is more than a historical aside, it leads us to reconsider an academic discourse of Laban's contemporaries that offers interesting reflections, not only on how gestures become meaningful expressions, but also on how they are understood.

1.2 Expressive movements as movement images and how gestures are understood (Plessner)

Laban's expressionist reflections on dance and his explorations into the "natural" logic and principles of body movements were part of a remarkable intellectual reflection on "expressive movement" carried out in the late 19th and early decades of the 20th century. Those reflections overarched disciplinary discourses. We find sociological, anthropological, aesthetic, linguistic, semiotic and psychological reflections on the nature of human and animal body movements as "expressive movement" (German: *Ausdrucksbewegung*). Reaching an understanding of the human form of expressive movement was conceived as a vital question to understanding human nature in its anthropological, cultural, social, linguistic, cognitive facets. Prominent figures in this discourse were: Karl Bühler (Psychology and Linguistics), Wilhelm Wundt (Psychology), or Helmuth Plessner (Philosophical Anthropology) (c.f., Müller & Kappelhoff, 2018, Chapter 8). What these reflections have in common is – roughly speaking – an attempt to overcome the Cartesian body-mind dualism. "Expressive movement" offers an alternative explanation to the dualistic idea of bodily expression as an outer indication of a subject's inner states (Kappelhoff, 2004, 2018; Müller & Kappelhoff, 2018).

In Plessner's philosophical anthropology in particular, expressive movements are not expressions of inner states of an individual, but a form of behavior that synchronizes an organism with its environment. This synchronization is a coordination of movement rhythms and movement qualities; it is an affective attunement between different bodies. The affective quality is thus identical with the body movement; it *is* the movement. In Plessner's understanding, expressive movements unfold as wholenesses, as movement gestalts – or as movement images. He offers the example of a happily barking and jumping dog whose movement patterns unfold as a movement shape that extends over a certain time forming a movement image, a temporal form. For Plessner, expressive movements are not restricted to affective forms; "affectless" movement forms such as grasping, seeking, walking, flying or swimming are also conceived as "wholenesses" that form movement-images:

> These wholenesses belong to the organism through its relation to the environment, its morphology, its specific instincts as motor categories ... As a result, the movement shapes are pictorial, even stretched out over a certain duration of time, are co-present with the observer ... Grasping, fleeing, repelling, seeking, but also the 'affectless' forms such as walking, flying, swimming ... represent such movement-images. (Plessner 1982 [1925]: 78)

Notably, expressive movements are *not* conceived as symptoms of inner psychological processes, their quality and their 'meaning' is their temporal form. As such, expressive movements are immediately perceived and felt sensations, and they become movement-images only in the process of perception. Expressive movements are bodily expressions that are felt as sensations and hence are understood through the body. It is in this sense that expressive movements ground intersubjectivity in the bodily felt sensation of another body in motion. Figure 4 shows an example of a common form of gestural movement-image that only emerges in the perception of the viewers. It shows former German chancellor Angela Merkel performing a series of small arc-shaped gestures while giving a speech in the German Bundestag.

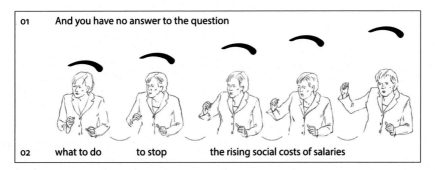

Figure 4. A series of gestured arcs?

In a response to interventions from the audience, Merkel makes a sequence of small arcs, each of which is positioned a little higher in the gesture space. The series of gestures accompanies the part of the following utterance highlighted in boldface: "and you have no answer to the question **what to do to stop the rising social costs of salaries**." (German: "Und Sie haben keine Antwort auf die Frage, was man denn tut, um die immer steigenden Lohnzusatzkosten zu vermeiden."). The outlining movement of the hands alone does, however not "make" the staircase – it only depicts a rising series of small arcs. The image of a staircase only emerges in the embodied perception of the audience – as a movement-image (Kappelhoff, 2019; Müller & Kappelhoff, 2018; Müller, 2019). Perceived in conjunction with the verbal utterance, it becomes clear that the series of gesturally sketched arcs describes in fact something like a rising staircase – forming a verbo-gestural metaphoric expression for the growth of social costs of salaries. The sketch of the gesture's movement path in Figure 5 below illustrates this process, in which only in the perception of the audience an ephemeral staircase emerges.

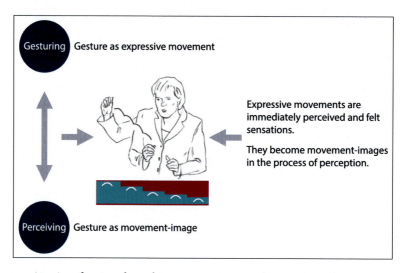

Figure 5. A series of gestured arcs becomes a movement-image

To conclude: The historical concept of "expressive movement" not only details which parts of the gestural movement figurations are meaningful, namely the gesture stroke (cf., the Kendonian gesture phrase: preparation and stroke), but also offers a theoretical frame as to how gestures are understood. Put differently, intersubjectivity is grounded in an intercorporeal understanding of expressive movement, in immediately perceived and felt sensations.

1.3 Mimesis as anthropological constant (Aristotle)

The third key aspect of miming as "as-if action" is a systematics of gestural mimesis that is inspired by the Aristotelian account of mimesis. According to Aristotle's treatment of mimesis in his poetics, mimesis is an ordinary human practice of imitation, an anthropological faculty (cf., Müller, 2016). In his proposal to distinguish different art forms, Aristotle introduces three general conditions of mimesis: means, objects and modes of mimesis. Mimetic means address the kind of articulator used, mimetic objects are the referents or actions referred to and the mimetic modes spell out how mimesis is achieved. Applied to gestural mimesis, this brings to our attention different bodily articulators that may be involved in gesturing as well as their interplays. It also underlines that gestural mimesis may actually refer to different kinds of "objects," such as actions, shapes, objects, events (see also Arbib, Ferretti, Gärdenfors, Zlatev et al., this volume). This distinction is reflected in different kinds of gestures. So, for example, people use depictive gestures to depict concrete and abstract actions, shapes, objects, events. In other contexts, people employ pragmatic gestures to perform communicative actions.

Figure 6 shows examples of depictive and pragmatic gestures. The examples all come from a German Late Night Show with former US President Barack Obama as guest (the interview was carried out in 2020 and is accessible on YouTube). The first two examples are performed within one utterance. The sequence begins with a pragmatic object of gestural mimesis, more specifically, a recurrent precision grip gesture. Obama uses many versions of the precision grip gesture in a fashion typical of political speakers. The one he is using in this example highlights the precise point he wants to make when responding to a question of how moving into the White House actually felt. He responded by giving a highly precise answer to a rather general question: said that his significant moment was *sleeping* in the White House for the first time, because, in fact, the moving itself was done by other people. The precision grip gesture is synchronized with the part of the utterance in boldface: "The first night **that you sleep in the White House.**" Here the action of as-if grasping something tiny is used to perform a communicative action, here a meta-communicative act, expressing the preciseness of the point he wants to make. And in fact, as he continues, he illustrates what sleeping in the White House felt like. He verbally and gesturally describes the mundane action of "brushing your teeth" as part of one's bedtime ritual. Here he performs a depictive gesture with a concrete object of gestural mimesis: a gestural enactment of brushing one's teeth.

At a later point in the interview, Obama makes a kind of boxing movement when he describes part of the story of America as a kind of "battle" between different political positions. This is an example of a gestural depiction of an abstract object, i.e., of gestural mimesis; a concrete kind of action comes to describe an abstract situation of conflict. Together, words and gestures form a verbo-gestural or more generally speaking a multimodal metaphoric expression. Note that gestures that are used to depict something abstract are quite similar to concrete depictives in that they often enact some practical action, describe the shape or become a model of an object or an event. The difference is that the gesturally depicted actions, objects or events are abstract ones.

The third characteristic of mimesis that Aristotle mentions are the modes of mimesis. Transferred to the realm of gesture, the modes of gestural mimesis serve to answer the question of HOW gestural mimesis is achieved (elsewhere I have used the term 'Modes of Representation', Müller, 2014, 1998). Figure 7 illustrates the four basic forms of gestural mimesis: (1) The hands act as-if performing an

Figure 6. Means, objects and modes of gestural mimesis

everyday action (acting as-if pulling a gear-shift), (2) The hands act as-if molding some shape (the round shape of a picture frame), (3) The hands act as-if drawing some shape or line (the oval shape of a frame), (4) The hands act as-if they were a model of some object, (flat hand represents a piece of paper for taking notes) (body-part as object, Lausberg et al., 2003) (see also Brown, Marentette, and Zlatev et al., this volume).

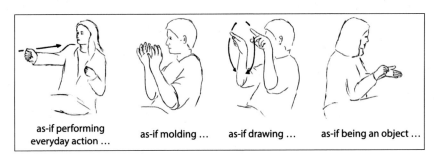

Figure 7. Modes of gestural mimesis (Müller, 1998, 2010, 2014, 2016)

When revisiting the Obama examples, it becomes clear that all three examples are based on the mimetic mode (1) "acting as-if performing an everyday action." In Obama's pragmatic precision grip gesture we see *acting as-if* holding a tiny object, in the concrete depictive, we see him *acting as-if* holding and moving a tooth brush in one's mouth, and in the abstract depictive Obama *acts as-if* boxing to depict a political battle.

It is in this sense that Gestures are conceived mimetic expressive movements that rest upon the human capacity for mimesis (Aristoteles) and in many cases they involve as-if actions.

2. How miming as as-if action grounds gestural meaning dynamically

Gestural mimesis is, however, not an isolated process – rather students of gesture must systematically take into consideration that gesturing is embedded in the flow of discourse. It is important to bear in mind that gesturing participates in communicative interaction and in this process gestures and speech form multimodal utterances that, strictly speaking, belong to all participants of a conversational social encounter. This dynamics of language use in which gesturing participates concerns both the micro-level of here and now multimodal interactions, and historical processes of language and gesture change on the level of a linguistic community.

This section illustrates how, in both these dynamic processes of language use, miming as as-if action plays a vital role in grounding gestural meaning in the intercorporeal experience of mimetic expressive movements. We are going to take a closer look at how concrete and abstract depictive gestures as well as pragmatic gestures are embedded in longer sequences of talk and focus on how miming as as-if action is used to ground gestural meaning dynamically along the flow of a conversation and also across time.

2.1 Miming as as-if action in a story-telling about a family event

This example comes from a naturalistic coffee table conversation. Two friends discuss Spanish politics. Since the conversation took place in the early nineties, the change from Franco's fascist regime to a democratic one was still very present. Luis' family had lived in exile in Venezuela during the Franco period and Luis now tells his German friend Paul a quite astonishing family story. A few days before fascist military walked into the Spanish parliament and tried to degrade the democratically elected government, a picture of the Spanish king Juan Carlos fell down from the wall, all by itself, while the family had dinner in the other room. Since Juan Carlos was a strong defender of the democratic change in Spain, his falling down from the wall was conceived as a kind of predestination of the coup d'etat. Figure 8 shows a transcript of the conversational exchange, italics mark the contributions of Paul, boldface indicates the co-articulation of gestures with speech.

Luis begins his story-telling with a word search and a gesture that fills in a speech pause. He has difficulties finding the appropriate term for the kind of picture his mother had, but his hands already "know" that the picture frame was round, his hands acting as-if molding some roundish vertically oriented object. What then follows is a side sequence in Luis' storytelling, motivated by Paul's laughing intervention "Haha of the king" which leads Luis not only to confirm this as a story about the king "Of the king, of the king of course," but to further specify where the royal picture was located: "She had it hanging on the wall there

Figure 8. Gestural mimesis as as-if actions in the course of a storytelling

in Venezuela." Paul however, still has difficulties understanding what kind of picture Luis is talking about: "But a painting or what?" which Luis confirms "That's it. More or less like a painting, but made out of wood." Paul responds with rising and falling "Mhm" intonation that Luis treats as a confirmation "Mh" and then continues his story and now delivers a verbo-gestural description of the picture: "And she had it with a round frame and a small crown on top of it." With his first gesture Luis acts as-if drawing an oval shape with his index fingers, this gesture is temporally coordinated with "round frame" and leaves an ephemeral object on which – with the next gesture – Luis acts as-if placing a small object on top. This happens in synchrony with saying "a small crown." Now, the protagonist of the story is clear: a wooden picture of the Spanish king with a royalistic frame. However, before moving on to the plot of the story Luis reminds Paul of the picture's location. This time he uses a verbo-gestural expression "there in the living-room," acting as-if his left vertically stretched hand was the picture that is placed high up and at the edge of his gesture space. With the stage so nicely set, and no further interventions from Paul, Luis comes to the plot of the story: "We were eating, and suddenly, all by itself, the picture fell down to the floor." He underlines this core event of his storytelling with another verbo-gestural expression that refers to the picture. This time he performs an energetic downward motion of the hand, acting as-if the flat hand was the picture that fell down. As a consequence, Paul expresses his understanding of the story with an exclamation "damn" and with describing the event as a "miracle," a reading that is immediately confirmed and reformulated by Luis: "Yes it was. Something like a miracle. A predestination."

What this example shows is a "thinking by hand" that is mimetic and that happens easily along with the flow of a conversation. We see a transfer from practical actions to gestures of the concrete through as-if actions. Luis employs all four mimetic modes in his storytelling; the ones he chooses react to the moment and needs of the conversation – clarifying the object at the stake, providing the background information that puts Paul, his interlocutor in place to understand the plot of the story. So, while all four gestures refer in some or the other way to the protagonist of the storytelling, each gesture highlights a different aspect of it, each gesture is based on a different kind of as-if action: as-if molding, as-if drawing, as-if performing an everyday action, as-if being an object (Figure 9).

Figure 9. Gestural mimesis as as-if action in the flow of a storytelling

The example nicely illustrates how ready we are in designing and understanding concrete depictive gestures in terms of the as-if actions they perform. But how about abstract depictives?

2.2 Miming as as-if action in an interview with barack obama

At one point in the interview during the Markus Lanz German late night show, former US president Barack Obama describes his vision of an inclusive idea of America (Figure 10). He does that in a comparably complex and dynamic multimodal performance that matches the complex dynamics we have just seen in the storytelling. Moreover, although Obama speaks about abstract political ideas, he uses gestural mimesis as as-if actions in a way that is very similar to what we have seen in Luis and Paul's naturalistic coffee-table conversation.

The sequence begins with a loose palm-up-open hand, presenting his introduction to his interlocutor as-if it would lie on his open hands: "And you know, part of the (0.8 pause) the story of America." This acting as-if presenting gesture is followed by an acting as-if boxing movement that describes the story of America as being in a kind of "battle." As he goes on, Obama uses further abstract depictive gestures to illustrate contrasting positions clashing in this battle. He begins with an account of those people "who want to include more people" and when speaking of including more people, he moves his bent arms and hands together and shapes a big circle almost as-if "embracing" as much space as possible. With this movement, the abstract action of including people is gesturally depicted and this depiction is based on a mimetic as-if action: he acts as-if he would embrace something or someone. This inclusive gesture is followed by the outlining of a sphere – that he uses as a gestural depiction of the abstract concept of ‚this idea' and it is done with the as-if drawing mode of gestural mimesis. After that he returns to a smaller version of the embracing gesture specifying this idea as the inclusive notion of "we the people."

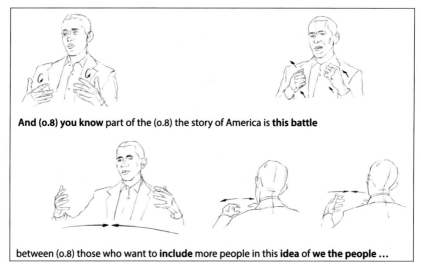

Figure 10. Gestural mimesis as as-if actions emerging in the flow of an interview

The example shows how commonplace abstract objects of gestural miming are and that mimetic as-if actions are highly productive in co-speech gestures no matter whether abstract or concrete. It illustrates that mimetic as-if actions are dynamically employed also when talking about abstract objects and actions speakers. Figure 11 offers an overview of the mimetic modes Obama uses in this sequence. He employs three versions of the mimetic mode: acting as-if performing an everyday action and one version of the acting as-if drawing some ephemeral contour. This is thinking by hand about politics based on doing mimesis, it is miming as as-if action in the flow of an interview.

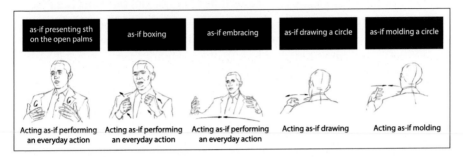

Figure 11. Mimetic modes as as-if actions grounding meaning in situ

As a last point in this section, miming as as-if actions and historical processes of stabilization are considered.

2.3 Miming as as-if action and historical processes of stabilization

In an historical perspective, the reconstruction of gestural mimesis is a kind of gesture etymology. Of course, in retrospect we can only assume plausible explanations. All the more the study of singular, recurrent and emblematic gestures in contemporary context may help to shed light on those transformative processes.

The precision grip gesture is a very nice example to study these processes, since it continues to be used in all three stages: from not stabilized through hybrid and fully stabilized forms. At the same time, we can observe the precision grip as an immensely widespread action of the hand, one of the first coordinated grasping movements in child development and essential whenever we pick up or hold something small: a pin, a rice corn, a pencil, or a piece of paper.

Miming as as-if action plays a role in all stages, while acting as-if holding a piece of paper is an evident singular depictive gesture, the precision necessarily involved in this manual action becomes a communicative action in the recurrent pragmatic gesture.

As mentioned in the introduction, it was the ethologist Desmond Morris who suggested this "etymology" as well as the term precision grip (Morris, 1977). Notably, the precision ring is known as a gesture of public orators since Quinitilian's rhetoric (Kendon, 2004; Müller, 1998a, 2014). Quintilian describes many different contexts of rhetorical use of this gesture and, interestingly points out that Roman and Greek orators used a different hand-shape to perform the ring gesture. Quintilian warns his Roman students of rhetoric to make the ring with index and thumb and not – as the Greeks do – with middle-finger and thumb. This shows that, more than two thousand years ago, people used stabilized gestures with cultural differences marked by differences in kinesic form. The process we observe is here mimesis as as-if action: grasping with precision is being transposed to advancing arguments with precision. However, the cultural difference between the two gestures is marked by a change in kinesic form that, notably, does not affect the rhetorical meaning of the pragmatic gesture.

Since the precision-grip is used as a recurrent gesture and as an emblem, it is a very interesting case to study how gestural mimesis plays out in the dynamics of historical processes of stabilization. It offers a glimpse on how those processes of transition may affect the kinesics and the meaning of a gestural movement selectively. Rather than assuming a rigid boundary between singular gestures and conventional ones, the hybrid forms that we observe in recurrent gestures speak for a successive process of stabilization, a process that appears to involve an emergent decomposition of forms and meanings (Müller, 2017, for a discussion of the diversity of recurrency see Harrison, Ladewig & Bressem, 2021).

As we have already mentioned, the precision grip as a rhetorical gesture is a case of a hybrid form: while the hand shape shows *a stable core* – the finger-thumb grasp – all other kinetic aspects are *variable.* This is different for the ring gesture as an expression of excellence and perfection (Figure 2). In this gesture, *all kinesic aspects are stabilized.* Hand shape, finger and thumb form a ring, the movement is accentuated and then held in a post-stroke hold. The orientation is palm vertical, away from the body, the position in the gesture space is center / upper periphery. A change of any one of those aspects would include a loss of the meaning of excellence and perfection. The Ring-gesture as an expression of perfection and excellence is a "classical" example of an emblematic gesture, a gesture word, a fully lexicalized gestural form.

Looking at singular, recurrent and emblematic gestures with a shared form thus allows us to study processes of stabilization in gestures, it enables us to study how mimesis as as-if action grounds their meaning and how processes of stabilization lead to the emergence of hybrid and fully stabilized gestural forms and meanings. Allowing the idea of a continuum between these gestural forms thus opens up a pathway to study the role of gestural mimesis as as-if action in the development of more language-like gestural forms.

3. Miming as as-if action in the context of gesture analysis

Reflections on gestural mimesis always have methodological consequences. If we are convinced that gestures are grounded in as-if actions, then this dimension of gestures deserves a systematic place in gesture analysis. In the Methods for Gesture Analysis (Bressem, Ladewig & Müller, 2013; Müller, 2010; in press) that I have developed with my team over the past decades, reconstructing as-if actions that speaker-gesturers appear to re-enact when performing a certain gesture was and continues to be the primary access to account for the meaning of a gesture – if possible without having listened to the speech beforehand. Many times gesture analysis is strongly tainted by co-expressive words – we tend to see in the gesture what we hear somebody say – yet in doing this we often miss important aspects of the specific mimetic meaning of a gesture – let alone the specifics of kinesic forms or the qualities of movement execution, all of which contribute to the multifaceted meaning of a given gesture. It is noteworthy, that attributing such an important role to a systematic account of gestural mimesis includes pragmatic gestures as much as concrete and abstract depictives; it also includes metaphoric gestures (most of the time they are abstract depictives). In short, including the analysis of potential mimetic as-if actions that are gesturally enacted is essential not only to McNeill's iconics, but to all other types of gestures as well.

This approach to gesture analysis is part of a Toolbox of Methods for Gesture Analysis that offers flexible methodological pathways, depending on one's specific research question and depending on the particular framework adopted (Figure 12) (Müller, in press).

We distinguish macro- and micro-levels of gesture analysis. The first step in any methodological process is to decide on which of the macro-levels one's investigation is located: does the study address gesture dynamics (along a multimodal discourse event or along an interaction or historical changes of gestures in cultural communities) or does it target a comparative investigation (for example, comparing gestures with signs or comparing gestures across contexts, cultures or species)? Several macro-levels may be touched in one study. So, in the present chapter, I have mostly touched upon dynamic processes both along multimodal discourse events and across time; only very briefly, a comparative aspect was included, the cultural difference between Greek and Roman performances of the rhetorical precision grip gesture.

In fact, micro-analyses are a pre-requisite for the study of macro-levels of gesture usages. Micro-analysis always requires the determination of the temporal unit of analysis, where the gesture or the gesture sequences begin and where they end. The temporal placement of gestures in relation to speech but also in relation to other body movements or the communicative actions of other co-participants, or

> **MACRO-LEVELS OF GESTURE ANALYSIS**
>
> **STUDIES OF GESTURE DYNAMICS**
> - Unfolding of gestures along a multimodal discourse event or interaction
> - Historical changes of gestures in cultural communities
>
> **COMPARATIVE GESTURE STUDIES**
> - Comparing gestures and signs
> - Comparing gestures across context, cultures, species,
>
> **MICRO-LEVELS OF GESTURE ANALYSIS**
> - Analyzing a single gesture in a given context (a metaphoric gesture, a specific pragmatic gestures,
> - Analyzing shorter and longer sequences of gestures (repetitions, scenarios, complex sequences)
> - Analyzing interactive constructions of gesture (sequences)
>
> **GUIDELINES FOR MICRO-LEVEL ANALYSES**
>
> **CARRY OUT ANALYSIS OF GESTURE FORMS**
> - Determine temporal unit of analysis
> - Decide which aspect of form analysis is relevant tor a given micro-analysis
>   - Movement analysis:
>   kinesic form, qualities of expressive movement, motion events (...)
>   - Hands as as-if action:
>   acting as if performing an everyday action, as-if molding, as-if drawing, as-if representing sth.
>
> **CHOOSE TYPE OF CONTEXT ANALYSIS**
> - Cognitive Linguistics, Conversation Analysis, Discourse Dynamics, Metaphor Studies, Studies, Pragmatics (...)

Figure 12. A toolbox of methods for gesture analysis

the placement within a montage sequence of a televised political speech is essential to their meaning in context. So any analysis begins with the establishment of the relevant *temporal unit of analysis*.

In a second step, the analyst decides which aspect of form analysis is relevant for a given micro-analysis: the analysis of the gestural movement as movement, i.e., the kinesics of gestural forms, their movement qualities or their expression of motion events, and/or is the gestural mimesis, i.e., the reconstruction of a ges-

Chapter 9. Gestural mimesis as "as-if" action 237

ture as an as-if action what is at stake in a given research design. Which of those aspects are necessary, depends on one's specific research question and on the framework one has chosen. Gesture analysis has become a topic of interest in many different schools of thought and is conducted within many different academic fields. This results in different potential frameworks for gesture analysis most vital in how they conceive of "context." Since a gestural form only acquires its local, situated meaning only within a specific context-of-use, as Adam Kendon used to put it, the notion of context is essential to what is considered as the meaning of gesture. Cognitive linguistics, conversation analysts, people studying metaphor or pragmatics will most likely have different accounts of what they conceive of as context for a given gesture performance. So, reflecting upon one's concept of context is very important – because it will determine the outcome of one's assumption of what a gesture means in a specific context-of-use.

Summary and conclusion

In the introduction the question of how to conceive of pantomime has been put into relation with an enduring debate in the field of gesture studies. It has been argued that while there is widely shared agreement on the intimate relationship between gesture and spoken language – some nowadays speak of language as being multimodal – controversial positions co-exist concerning the developmental, evolutionary, historical relationship between gesture and language. Here, the issue at stake is the question of a continuity or discontinuity between spontaneously created and conventionalized gestures, the latter ones being seen as more language-like. The position advanced in this paper suggests an emergent transition from spontaneous (singular) through hybrid (recurrent) to fully stabilized (emblematic) gestures. It suggests that all three stages of this transition can be observed in co-speech gesturing, and that not only are gestures in all three stages based on mimesis, but mimesis can be seen as grounding depictive as well as pragmatic gestures. In a nutshell, the argument is advanced that gestures generally speaking are *mimetic expressive movements.*

In the first section, the theoretical framework that motivates the idea of gestures as mimetic expressive movements was outlined: (1) Drawing on Kendon's work on "gesture phrases and gestural meaning it was shown that meaning of a gesture is connected with its unfolding in time"; (2) With recourse to Helmuth Plessner (Philosophical Anthropology), the notion of expressive movement as a temporal form was introduced. Expressive movement was described as a gestalt showing a specific temporal contour that only becomes a movement image in an immediate process of perception and felt sensation of a perceiver. (3) Drawing on the Aristotelian approach to mimesis as an anthropological trait, a systematic of gestural mimesis (means, objects, modes) was presented and it was shown that pragmatic as well as concrete and abstract depictive gestures are based on as-if actions.

In section two, it was illustrated how miming grounds concrete, abstract and pragmatic gestures dynamically, both along the micro scale of a communicative encounter and along the macro scale of historical change within a cultural community. Exemplary analyses of gesture use in different discourse contexts (a naturalistic conversation and a tv-interview) were presented. It was described how miming as as-if action grounds gestural meaning in the dynamics of language use, no matter whether people speak about very concrete or rather abstract issues, or whether they perform communicative actions by using pragmatic gestures. Last but not least, the section took up the point of an emergent transition from spontaneous through hybrid to fully stabilized gestures, pointing out how historical processes of stabilization affect kinesic form while at the same time maintaining the kinesic core that constitutes the mimetic as-if action.

The last section has offered a glance into the toolbox of methods for gesture analyses, on which the analyses presented in this talk are based. In doing this, it was indicated that miming as as-if action offers a powerful perspective to steer methods for gesture analysis.

In a nutshell, this chapter has provided *theoretical, empirical* and *methodological* arguments for gestural mimesis as as-if action and for a continuum from practical actions to as-if actions. It suggests that thinking and acting by hand is anchored in the embodied practice of miming as as-if action and advances an understanding of gestures as *mimetic expressive movements*.

Concerning the question of pantomime and pantomimic gestures, it is suggested to reserve the term primarily for the artistic practice and approach gestural mimesis as an as-if action that grounds gestures more generally speaking. Using the term pantomimic gestures always insinuates that there is a categorial difference between gestures used in the absence of speech or sign. At least, as far as gestural mimesis is concerned this is not the case. Differences are gradual, not categorical. Notably, the differences between singular, recurrent and emblematic gestures do not affect their shared embodied ground in the experiences of human bodies in interaction with one another and with their ecological habitat. Like in linguistic change, kinesic forms may "bleach" or be reduced as they are used and re-used within a cultural community or over the course of conversational encounter, a dance class or a tv-interview. The fact that, for many historical gestural forms, we no longer know the experiential grounds of a given gesture does not rule out that argument. It is enough to look at kinesic homologies that exist between gestures that look similar but have very different embodied grounds, such as the "horn gesture" for example – known in Southern Italy, in Heavy Metal contexts, or as a symbol for the University of Texas in Austin, to see that a series of gestures may look alike while not necessarily grounded in the same kind of mimetic as-if action. In the same way that the cultural contexts of Southern Italians or of UT students and employees are not shared universally, historical roots of gestures may disappear with the disappearance of their cultural ecology.

Conceiving of gestures as *mimetic expressive movements* opens up a path not only for a better understanding of how humans use the embodied knowledge of their hands as well as their full bodies for communication but also indicates how gestures are understood, how intersubjectivity emerges in this process.

References

Arbib, M.A., (2012). *How the brain got language: The mirror system hypothesis* 16. Oxford University Press.

Bressem, J., & Ladewig, S. H. (2011). Rethinking gesture phases: Articulatory features of gestural movement? *Semiotica*, 184(1/4), 53–91.

Bressem, Jana, Silva H. Ladewig & Cornelia Müller (2013). Linguistic Annotation System for Gestures (LASG). In C. Müller, A. Cienki, E. Fricke, S. H. Ladewig, D. McNeill & S. Teßendorf (Eds.) *Body – language – communication: An international handbook on multimodality in human interaction. (Handbooks of Linguistics and Communication Science 38.1.)*, 1098–1124. Berlin/ Boston: De Gruyter Mouton.

Bressem, J., & Müller, C. (2014a). The family of Away gestures: Negation, refusal, and negative assessment. In C. Müller, A. Cienki, E. Fricke, S. H. Ladewig, D. McNeill, & J. Bressem (Eds.), *Body – language – communication: An international handbook on multimodality in human interaction* (Vol. 2, pp. 1592–1604). De Gruyter Mouton.

Bressem, J., & Müller, C. (2014b). A repertoire of German recurrent gestures with pragmatic functions. In C. Müller, A. Cienki, E. Fricke, S. H. Ladewig, D. McNeill, & J. Bressem (Eds.), *Body – language – communication: An international handbook on multimodality in human interaction* (Vol. 2, pp. 1575–1591). De Gruyter Mouton.

Ekman, Paul (1993). Facial expression and emotion. *American Psychologist*, 384–392.

Goldin-Meadow, S., & Brentari, D. (2017). Gesture, sign, and language: the coming of age of sign language and gesture studies. *Behav. Brain Sci.*, 40, 1–17.

Harrison, S, Ladewig, S. H. & Bressem, J. (Eds). (2021) Recurrent Gestures. Special Issue. *Gesture* 20/2.

Kappelhoff, H. (2004). Matrix der Gefühle. Das Kino, das Melodrama und das Theater der Empfindsamkeit (13774895). *Vorwerk 8*.

Kappelhoff, H. (2018). Kognition und Reflexion. *Zur Theorie filmischen Denkens*. Walter de Gruyter.

Kendon, A. (2004). *Gesture: Visible action as utterance (1. Aufl.)*. Cambridge University Press.

Laban, von R. (1956). *Principles of Dance and Movement Notation*. Macdonald & Evans.

Laban, R., & Lawrence, F. C. (1947). *Effort: Economy in body movement*. MacDonald and Evans.

Kendon, A. (1972). Some relationships between body motion and speech. In A. Seigman, & B. Pope (Eds.), *Studies in dyadic communication* (pp. 177–216). Pergamon Press.

Kendon, A. (1980). Gesture and speech: Two aspects of the process of utterance. In M. R. Key, (Ed.), *Nonverbal Communication and Language* (pp. 207–227). Mouton.

Kendon, A. (1983) Gesture and speech: How they interact. In Wiemann & R. Harrison (Eds.). *Nonverbal Interaction* (Sage Annual Reviews of Communication, Volume 11, pp. 13–46). Sage Publications.

Kendon, A. (1988). How gestures can become like words. In F. Poyatos (Ed.), *Crosscultural Perspectives in Nonverbal Communication* (pp. 131–141). Hogrefe.

Kendon, Adam (2011). Vocalisation, speech, gesture, and the language origins debate: an essay review on recent contributions. *Gesture*, 11(3), 349–370.

Kendon, A. (2014). Semiotic diversity in utterance production and the concept of 'language'. *Philos. Trans. R. Soc. B Biol Sci.* 369:20130293.

Kendon, Adam (2016). Reflections on the 'Gesture First' hypothesis of language origins. *Psychonomic Bulletin and Review.*

Ladewig, Silva H. (2014a). Recurrent gestures. In C. Müller, A. Cienki, E. Fricke, S. H. Ladewig, D. McNeill & Jana Bressem (Eds.,), *Body – language – communication: An international handbook on multimodality in human interaction* (pp. 1558–1575). De Gruyter Mouton.

Ladewig, S. H. (2014b). The cyclic gesture. In C. Müller, A. Cienki, E. Fricke, S. H. Ladewig, D. McNeill, & J. Bressem (Eds.), *Body – language – communication. An international handbook on multimodality in human interaction* (pp. 1605–1618). De Gruyter Mouton

Lausberg, H., Cruz, R. F., Kita, S., Zaidel, E., und Ptito, A. (2003). Pantomime to visual presentation of objects. Left hand dyspraxia in patients with complete callosotomy. *Brain*, 126, 343–360.

McNeill, D. (1985). So you think gestures are nonverbal? *Psychol. Rev.* 92, 350–371.

McNeill, D. (1992). *Hand and mind. What gestures reveal about thought.* University of Chicago Press.

McNeill, D. (2000). Language and Gesture. In D. McNeil (Hrsg.), *Introduction* (S. 1–10). Cambridge University Press.

McNeill, D. (2013). The co-evolution of gesture and speech, and downstream consequences. In C. Müller, A. Cienki, E. Fricke, S. H. Ladewig, D. McNeill & Jana Bressem (Eds.,), *Body – language – communication: An international handbook on multimodality in human interaction* (pp. 480–512). De Gruyter Mouton.

Mineiro, A., Carmo, P., Caroça, C., Moita, M., Carvalho, S., Paço, J., & Zaky, A. (2017). Emerging linguistic features of sao tome and principe sign language. *Sign Language & Linguistics*, 20(1), 109–128.

Morris, D. (1977) *Manwatching. A field guide to human behavior.* New York: Abrams.

Müller, C. (1998). *Redebegleitende Gesten: Kulturgeschichte—Theorie—Sprachvergleich.* Berlin Verlag Arno Spitz.

Müller, C. (1998a) *Redebegleitende Gesten. Kulturgeschichte – Theorie – Sprachvergleich.* Berlin Verlag Arno Spitz GmbH

Müller, C. (2010). Wie Gesten bedeuten. Eine kognitiv-linguistische und sequenzanalytische Perspektive. In Irene Mittelberg (Ed.), *Sprache und Gestik. Sonderheft der Zeitschrift Sprache und Literatur*, 41(1): 37–68.

Müller, C., Cienki, A., Fricke, E., Ladewig, S. H., McNeill, D. & Teßendorf, S. (Eds.) (2013) *Body – language – communication. An international handbook on multimodality in human interaction (Handbooks of linguistics and communication science 38.1.)* Berlin/Boston: De Gruyter Mouton.

Müller, C., Cienki, A., Fricke, E., Ladewig, S. H., McNeill, D., & Bressem, J. (eds.) (2014) *Body – language – communication. An international handbook on multimodality in human interaction (Handbooks of linguistics and communication science 38.2.)* De Gruyter Mouton

Müller, C. (2017). How recurrent gestures mean: Conventionalized contexts-of-use and embodied motivation. *Gesture*, 16(2), 277–304.

Müller, C., & Kappelhoff, H. (2018). Cinematic Metaphor. *Experience – Affectivity – Temporality*. De Gruyter Mouton.

Müller, C. (2014). Gestural Modes of Representation as techniques of depiction. Müller, C., Cienki, A., Fricke, E., Ladewig, S. H., McNeill, D., & Bressem, J. (eds.) (2014) *Body – language – communication. An international handbook on multimodality in human interaction (Handbooks of linguistics and communication science 38.2.)* De Gruyter Mouton.

Müller, C. (2016). From mimesis to meaning: A systematics of gestural mimesis for concrete and abstract referential gestures. In J. Zlatev, G. Sonesson, & P. Konderak (Eds.), *Meaning, mind and communication: Explorations in cognitive semiotics*. Peter Lang. 211–226.

Müller, C. (2018). Gesture and Sign: Cataclysmic Break or Dynamic Relations? *Frontiers in Psychology*, 10 September 2018.)

Müller, C. (2019). Metaphorizing as Embodied Interactivity: What Gesturing and Film Viewing Can Tell Us About an Ecological View on Metaphor. *Metaphor and Symbol*, 34(1): 61–79.

Müller, C. (in press). A Toolbox of Methods for Gesture Analysis. In Cienki, A. (ed.) *Handbook of Gesture Studies*. Cambridge University Press.

Plessner, H. (1982). *Ausdruck und menschliche Natur*. G. Dux, O. Marquard & E. Ströker (Eds.). 10 Vol. 7, *Helmuth Plessner. Gesammelte Schriften*. Suhrkamp. Original edition 1957.

Singleton, J. L., Goldin-Meadow, S., & McNeill, D. (1995). The cataclysmic break between gesticulation and sign: evidence against an evolutionary continuum of manual communication. In K. Emmorey & J. Reilly (Eds.), *Language, Gesture, and Space* (pp. 287–311). Erlbaum Associates.

Vigliocco, G., Perniss, P., Thompson, R. & Vinson, D. (Eds.) (2014). Language as a multimodal phenomenon: Implications for language learning, processing, and evolution. Philosophical *Transactions of the Royal Society B* 369(1651).

Wilcox, S. (2007) Routes from gesture to language. In E. Pizzuto, P. Pietrandrea & S. Raffaele (Eds.), *Verbal and signed languages: Comparing structures, constructs and methodologies*. Berlin: Mouton de Gruyter, 107–131

Index

A

affordances, 16, 19, 29–30, 32–35, 46, 204
alignment of interests, 27, 101, 105–6, 111
allocentric, 69–71, 121, 139, 140–6, 148–149, 154, 190, 207,
ancestors, 44, 50, 89–90, 95, 125, 150
apraxia, 181, 195, 209
Aristotle, 80, 84, 119, 121, 223, 226, 227
arts, 107, 121, 139–145, 147–155
as-if action, 189–190, 206, 217, 222, 226–239

B

biocultural evolution, 16–17, 19–20, 23, 26, 28, 45
bodily mimesis, 89–90, 100–1, 104, 106–8, 110, 125–6, 129, 135, 159–161, 180, 193
body movement, 42, 102–3, 124, 127, 179, 222, 224, 235
body part as object (BPO), 25, 33, 126, 143–144, 189–191, 195–8, 201–211 *See under* egocentric
bootstrapping, 103–4, 160, 182
Boyd, 87, 107, 124, 140, 151
brain, 16–19, 22–3, 38–40, 43–7, 80–1, 84–6, 88–9, 181–2, 195
Buxbaum, 209, 210

C

children, 72–3, 92, 126, 150–1, 188–191, 193–211, 219
chimpanzee (*Pan*), 17, 24, 60–1, 65, 102, 150
cognition, 17, 41, 46, 58–64, 67, 70–3, 86, 159, 163, 182
  causal~, 46, 58–60, 62, 64, 67, 70–1, 73
  event~, 46, 58, 60, 62–3, 70–3
cognitive: adaptations, 104, 161

~development, 191–2, 194, 209
~map, 48–49
~processes, 63, 69, 120, 211
~science (cognitive studies), 79, 116
~semiotics, 115–6, 129, 134, 191, 205
communication: animal~, 18, 44, 64–65, 111
  bodily-visual~ (bodily mimetic, visual), 90, 100, 102, 106–7, 110–11
  evolution of~, 27, 66, 68, 100–1, 105, 111
  human~, 45, 58–9, 72–3, 78–80, 86–7, 89–90, 92–4, 124, 147, 159
  system (of~), 18, 20, 27, 32, 37, 39, 65, 72, 100–1, 105, 148, 159, 162
communicative convention, 72, 159, 188, 210
conventionalisation of pantomime, 101, 104, 108, 110–111
cooperation, 44, 68, 86–7, 108–110, 141
Corballis, 23, 44, 48, 80, 85, 91, 92, 93, 159, 179, 182
co-speech gesture (cospeech gesture, **cosign gesture**), 16, 29, **33–34, 38**, 142, 179, 191, 198–9, 202–3, 205, 218–9, 232, 237,
cultural evolution (**biocultural evolution**), 16, **18–29**, 35, 39–40, 44, 46, 49, 147–8

D

dance, 105–107, 124, 139–141, 144, 148, 151–4, 224
deaf children, 162, 179
demonstration, 20, 30–32, 58–72, 108–9, 148

development: cognitive ~, 191–4, 209
  ~of communication, 208
  ~of language (language development), 43, 102, 161, 181, 198
  ~of symbolic (**reference**), **192**, 208
Donald, 19, 63, 90, 103, 104, 115, 124, 125
drawing, 33–34, 41, 145–8

E

egocentric pantomime, 69, 139, 142–4, 148–151, 154, 190
emblematic gesture (emblem), 193, 219–222, 233–4, 238
embodying, 126–7, 149
Emmorey, 160, 181
enacting, 67, 126, 130, 134, 164, 192
event cognition, 58–63, 70–73
event representation, 59–62, 182
event sequence, 119–120, 123, 127–9
evolution of language (language evolution), 26, 30, 45, 49, 87, 90, 102–3, 110, 160–2, 174, 192, 218

F

Fay, 24, 89, 103, 127

G

gestural mimesis, 222–3, 226–238
gesture studies (**ISGS**), 174, 217–18, 222, 236–7
Goldin-Meadow, 24, 174, 191, 218, 219, 221
grammar (**of gesture**), 16–18, 35–6, 40, 50, 83–4, 94–5, **219**
great apes, 17, 19–20, 24–5, 103

H

Hutto, 81, 82, 108

I

iconicity (*primary, secondary*), 102–4, **106**, 121, 123, 125–6, 135, 142, 148, 159, 165, 171–2, 180, 189, 192–5, 198, 205, 207–9

imitation, 17–21, 24, 30, 33, 44, 101, 147–151, 160, 182, 195, 209, 226

interaction, 18, 29, 44, 61, 87, 95, 128, 229, 235, 238

imagined object (IO), 33, 201, 207, 211 *See under* allocentric

K

Kaplan, 116, 188, 189, 190, 192, 193, 194–7, 205, 207–9, 211

Kendon, 23, 150, 179, 217, 218–220, 223–4, 226, 233, 237

L

language origin, 17, 23, 35, 43, 78–83, 87, 89, 92, 101–3, 108, 140, 142, 144, 150–1

language-ready brain, 17–18, 22, 38–9, 43–4, 46, 50, 160, 182

last common ancestor (LCA), 17–20, 44, 46–9

Leslie, 46, 61, 69, 81

linguistics: cognitive~, 236–7
general~, 70, 116
generative~, 36
sign language~, 193

M

manual gesture, 23, 37, 160–1, 182, 191, 195, 198, 206

McNeill, 23, 91, 92, 142, 179, 191–2, 194–5, 198, 205, 218, 219, 221, 235

memory, 20, 32, 48–9, 67, 90, 181

mimesis, 25–6, 28, 30, 33, 90, 104, 107–8, 140, 159–161, 206, 217, 222–3, 226–238

mimesis theory, 125, 179

Mirror System Hypothesis (MSH), 16–26, 36, 39, 40, 44, 160, 164, 182, 210

modes of representation, 188, 204–5, 207, 219, 227–8

music, 115, 117, 121, 141, 148, 152–4

N

narration, 68, 115–6, 119–124, 140

narrative (complex, simple), 115, 123–4, 129–133, 135

narrativity (primary, secondary), 115, 120–3, 135

navigation, 43–5, 48–50

newborn language, 159, 162

O

orofacial gestures, 29, 37

Ozyürek, 191

P

pantomimic fossil, 44, 106

pedagogy, 19, 22, 28, 29–30, 33–5, 50, 103

Perniss, 141, 161, 171, 194

persuasion, 45, 86–90, 94

platform of trust, 27, 45, 94

pointing, 26, 30–3, 35, 38, 193, 238

praxis (praxic action), 25, 29, 101, 109, 147–8

protolanguage, 18–24, 27–9, 32–9, 43, 50, 71, 91–3, 129, 133, 219

protosign, 20–50, 72, 101, 108, 111, 162, 166, 171, 174, 177–182

protospeech, 20–3

R

referent, 65, 102–5, 171, 177, 192–4

representation: mental~, 24, 59, 60, 63, 78–80
mode of~, 46, 79, 189, 196, 204–9
pictorial~, 28, 42

representational gesture, 146–7, 193, 198, 201, 209

ritualisation, 17–18, 21, 26–33, 108, 148, 153

Russon, 19, 20, 25, 67

S

Sandler, 23, 29, 160, 161, 162, 171, 173, 173, 178, 181

sign function, 22, 66

sign language (**emerging sign language**), 17, 23, 29, 43, 72, **103**, 160–4, 171–3, 177–9

signalling theory, 101, 105, 109–111

silent gesture, 191, 211, 221–2

Stokoe, 23, 91, 172, 194

storytelling, 46, 79–87, 93, 116, 140, 161, 229–231

Sonesson, 103, 116, 119, 192, 194, 207

symbol, 22, 141, 147, 192–198

symbolic distance (symbolic distancing), 188–197, 207–9

T

teaching, 25, 31–2, 59, 65, 68–71

theatre, 28, 124, 140, 144, 148, 151–2, 154

Theory of Mind (ToM), 33, 46, 61, 66, 81

Tomasello, 18, 23, 61, 65, 66, 67, 79, 91, 101–3, 124, 139, 161, 179, 188, 195

transparency, 90–1

V

visual art, 140–1, 144–9,

W

Werner, 116, 189, 192–7, 205, 207–9, 211

whole-body (gesture, pantomime), 42, 102, 116, 124, 142, 150, 161–2, 168, 171, 205

word order, 174–7, 180